All the Right Enemies

All the Right Enemies

The Life and Murder
of Carlo Tresca
by Dorothy Gallagher

Rutgers University Press, New Brunswick and London

Library of Congress Cataloging-in-Publication Data
Gallagher, Dorothy.
    All the right enemies.
    Includes index.
    1. Tresca, Carlo, 1879–1943.   2. Anarchists—
United States—Biography.   I. Title.
HX844.T73G34   1988   335'.83'0924   [B]   87-32360
ISBN 0-8135-1310-3

British Cataloging-in-Publication information available.

Permission to quote material from their collections has been granted by the following archives and individuals:

Aldino Felicani Interview, Roger Baldwin Interview, Oral History Research Office, Columbia University in the City of New York

Alice Inglis Papers, The Department of Rare Books and Special Collections, The University of Michigan Library

August Bellanca Papers, Amalgamated Clothing Workers of America Collection, Labor-Management Documentation Center, Cornell University

David Dubinsky Papers, Luigi Antonini Papers, ILGWU Archives, New York

Elizabeth Gurley Flynn Papers, State Historical Society of Wisconsin

Elizabeth Gurley Flynn Papers, Emma Goldman Papers, John N. Beffel Papers, Tamiment Institute Library, New York University

Emma Goldman Papers, Tresca Memorial Committee Records, Vito Marcantonio Papers, Rare Books and Manuscripts Division, The New York Public Library, Astor, Lenox, and Tilden Foundations

Estate of Elizabeth Gurley Flynn

Estate of Emma Goldman

Estate of Vito Marcantonio

Immigration History Research Center, University of Minnesota

IWW Papers, John N. Beffel Papers, and Mary Heaton Vorse Papers, The Archives of Labor and Urban Affairs, Wayne State University

Margaret Sanger Papers, The Sophia Smith Collection, Smith College

For Ben

Contents

Part Two

Illustrations appear between pages 136 and 137

Acknowledgments

FIRST things first: if I had not heard Elizabeth Ewen's stories about Carlo Tresca I might have remained forever ignorant of him. On that same occasion Peter Biskind also felt the glow of inspiration but gracefully relinquished his claim to me.

I am deeply grateful to Carlo Tresca's children, Beatrice Rapport and Peter Martin, for entrusting me with their memories; to Harrison and Burnham De Silver for their recollections of their mother, Margaret De Silver, and the years she spent with Tresca; to Jane Bobba, who talked to me about her mother, Bina Flynn Bobba, and her aunt, Elizabeth Gurley Flynn.

Sam and Esther Dolgoff, Tresca's friends, were immeasurably helpful in placing Tresca in an anarchist context, telling anecdotes that made him vivid, and adding warnings not to try to unravel the intra-anarchist feuds. For interviews, correspondence, and other forms of assistance I thank Federico Arcos, the late John Ballato, Isaiah Berlin, David Chavchavadze, Lester Coleman, Robert D'Attilio, David Eisendrath, Jack Frager, Frances Frenaye, Len Giovannitti, Anna Hamburger, Bernard Harkavy, Mary Hunter, Irving Ignatin, Valerio Isca, Peter Colt Josephs, Jerre Mangione, Vanni Montana, Albert Parini, John Burnett Payne, Roma Reiger, Bob Rossi, Edward Scheidt, Sidney Solomon, Sylvia Thompson, Diana Trilling, Gus Tyler, the late Vera Buch Weisbord, and Ella Wolfe.

Joseph Genco, Jacob Grumet, and Eleazar Lipsky, formerly of the FBI, the New York Police Department, and the New York district attorney's office, respectively, discussed the investigation of the Tresca case with me. Lt. Remo Franceschini spoke to me about Carmine Galante.

I was fortunate to have interviewed Roger Baldwin, James T. Farrell, and Dwight Macdonald. Each contributed substantial recollections of Tresca and spoke of him with pleasure. I am sorry that my gratitude must be posthumous.

Rosalyn Fraad Baxandall first showed me copies of Elizabeth Gurley Flynn's poems to Tresca; Helen Camp exchanged information with me from her research on Flynn; Philip Cannistraro discussed his work on the life of Generoso Pope. Alexander Stille helped with translation; Helene Pleasants read an early draft much to the benefit of the final copy. Richard Emery, then of the New York Civil Liberties Union, persuaded the New York Police Department to open its files of the Tresca investigation to me.

David Porter's early enthusiastic response to the manuscript was very welcome. Paul Avrich's interest has been important to me. Paul Berman and Philip Pochoda offered helpful comments. Nunzio Pernicone, a scholar of the Italian-American anarchist movement and of Tresca, kept me from foolish mistakes of fact.

I am happily indebted to Edward Said who was instrumental in bringing the manuscript to attention, and to John Patrick Diggins whose comments as a referee were heartening indeed. My agent, Andrew Wylie, persisted beyond the reasonable bounds of obligation. Vivian Mazur helped me to gather photographs. Everyone at Rutgers University Press has been welcoming to the manuscript and patient with my delays.

My parents, Bella and Isidor Rosen, were my first models of the committed political life, and they have been unfailingly generous with love and support. I have been fortunate in the friendship of Elsa Rush and Norman Rush which has spanned years, distance, and difficulties and has been, in every way, enabling. My husband, Ben Sonnenberg, lived this project with me. That he doesn't regret it is only a small measure of his valor.

Preface

HOMAGE *to the Imperishable Memory of Carlo Tresca.* When Carlo Tresca's comrades compiled the book of tributes so titled, they would not have believed that his name would fade with their own generation. That was in 1943, not very long ago in historical time for a man whose praises were sung publicly by writers, philosophers, labor leaders, and even some politicians, and whose murder was the political scandal of the day.

I first heard Carlo Tresca's name on an evening some thirty-five years after his death. On that occasion it was linked with two other names which I did already know: Elizabeth Gurley Flynn and Carmine Galante. Of this strange trio—an anarchist, a Communist party leader, and a gangster—only Galante was still alive, and he only for another year.

I heard enough about Tresca that evening to want to know more. Here and there in the following weeks I found admiring references to "the anarchist Carlo Tresca," but only in passing, as if the reader were expected to know of Tresca's career and legend and understand his significance.

I soon began to get a sense of the man. During his life, from 1879 to 1943, Carlo Tresca seemed to have set himself personally against all the varieties of tyranny that the era spawned. And if that seems a large order, opposition apparently came as naturally to him as his exuberance, his ability to charm, his love of sensual pleasures, his gift for friendship, his predilection for quarrels and conspiracies. To thousands of Italian immigrants Tresca was a hero; to the FBI he was "notorious"; to a number of American intellectuals and labor leaders he was a counsel; to American and

Italian fascists, a serious adversary; to the Communist party of the 1930s, a renegade and Trotskyite; to rival anarchists, a spy and traitor; to his friends a joy; to women, overpoweringly attractive; to the man who killed him, little more than a contract. And he is an obscure figure today, unremarked except by a few scholars of radical history.

Well, he was an anarchist and must take the consequences of a lost cause. The anarchist view has been overwhelmed by communism as the dominant expression of the Left. The battle joined by Marx and Bakunin in the First International is long over, and the uprisings of this century—the revolts that swept Europe after World War I and the revolution that erupted in Spain in 1936 and in which Tresca and other anarchists placed their hopes—have all failed.

But I have not undertaken to argue the merits of anarchism as a system of political thought, only to tell the story of Carlo Tresca. He was an anarchist. Or, as his friend the poet Arturo Giovannitti wrote after Tresca's murder, "He liked to call himself an Anarchist, and if that term connotes a man who was absolutely free, then he was an Anarchist; but from the point of view of pure doctrine he was all things to all men and in his endless intellectual vagabondage he never really sought any definite anchorage or moorings."

This book is divided in two parts. In the first I focus mainly on Tresca, but frequently shift to the events and people that formed the context of his life. The events span the years from his birth in the Abruzzi in 1879, through his emigration in 1904, to his murder in 1943. Of those who were significant in his life, I pay particular attention to Elizabeth Gurley Flynn, who was Tresca's companion for many years and whose life came to form a political counterpoint to his; and to Emma Goldman, Bill Haywood, Angelica Balabanoff, Mary Heaton Vorse, John Reed, Nicola Sacco, Bartolomeo Vanzetti, Vittorio Vidali, Norman Thomas, Max Eastman, and John Dos Passos. When Tresca's words have been reported to me second- or thirdhand, or have seemed to me apocryphal, I have reproduced them without quotation marks.

The second part deals with Tresca's assassination and carries events to the near present. Properly speaking, it has no place in a book about Tresca's life. But the manner of his death is so firmly connected with the manner of his life—as Max Eastman wrote, "He would have been surprised himself and also a little injured in his pride if he had died in bed"—and his death so cries out for elaboration that I have taken justification from Alexander Herzen, who wrote: "It may happen that a clear explanation is what matters most to a man. The reestablishment of the truth may be dearer to him than revenge."

Carlo Tresca placed himself not only in tyranny's path but in the path of the tyrant: not only fascism but Mussolini affronted him, and the pro-fascist newspaper editor Generoso Pope; and the Comintern agent Vittorio Vidali; and the mafioso Vito Genovese.

Max Eastman called his friend Carlo Tresca "a fortress. He stood so firm in this time of dissolving characters and standards. Firm in his courage both physical and moral. Firm in his love for the oppressed. He was the last of the great revolutionists who fought implacably with love instead of hate in their hearts." This is a good epitaph, but there is another I prefer, the words of Carlo Tresca's anarchist comrade Aldino Felicani: "Tresca was the type who faced the music."

All the Right Enemies

*In easy times history is a more or less
ornamental art, but in times of danger . . . we
need to know what kind of firm ground other
men . . . have found to stand on.*

—John Dos Passos, The Theme Is Freedom

*Bakunin grew younger; he was in his element:
he loved not only the uproar of the revolt and the
noise of the club, the market-place and the
barricade; he loved the preparatory agitation,
the excited and at the same time restrained life
spent among conspiracies, consultations, sleepless
nights, conferences, agreements.*

—Alexander Herzen, My Past and Thoughts

Prologue: January 11, 1943
The Long-Expected Enemy

THE moon made a late appearance on the night of January 11, 1943. With the street lamps dimmed and gas and rubber rationing keeping most private cars off the streets, the area just west of Union Square was dark and seemed deserted.

At about half past nine that night two men emerged from a six-story building on the southwest corner of Fifteenth Street and Fifth Avenue. Arm in arm they crossed Fifteenth Street to the northwest corner of the avenue. There they paused for a moment under a lamppost. Very quietly a third man stepped out from the darkness behind them. He moved quickly and was scarcely more than two feet away when he fired the gun in his hand. The two waiting men wheeled toward the sound. The larger of the two took an instinctive step toward the shooter, who fired at him once, twice, again. The shooter ran off into the darkness. In a minute or two the few passersby congregate, a double-decker Fifth Avenue bus passes, the police arrive and summon an ambulance from Saint Vincent's Hospital. Meanwhile, Carlo Tresca lies in the street. A newspaper photograph will show that his feet are touching the curbstone, his hat has fallen off, his beard is pointing straight up. Blood from the wound in his head shows as a dark stain.

January 11, 1943, was a Monday. At this time, a little more than a year after the United States' entry into the war, it is apparent that Mussolini's reign is coming to an end. The first news of internal resistance is being heard from Italy—strikes, clandestine newspapers, purges within the Fascist party. Italian troops have been defeated at El Alamein. Allied bombs are dropping on Genoa, Naples, and Turin. Soon the elite Italian Expeditionary Corps will be virtually destroyed by Soviet troops. The invasion of Sicily is six months away.

The fate of Italy was very much on Carlo Tresca's mind the day he died, as it had been since Mussolini seized power more than twenty years earlier. For Tresca, and for anti-Fascists of varying political shades, the consuming question was which of the contending forces would take control in Italy after Mussolini's fall. With Roosevelt and Churchill concerned primarily to take Italy out of the war as soon as possible and Stalin pressing hard for a second front, veteran anti-Fascists had good reason to fear that the Allies would make a deal with Fascists in Italy (as they had already made one with Darlan), and, in exchange for the ouster of Mussolini and support for an Allied invasion, the Fascist power structure would remain intact.

At home, there were more than enough clues to support this fear. The Office of War Information was urging a united front of the entire political spectrum of Italians in the United States—including those former fascists who had turned against Mussolini only on December 7, 1941, and the Communists who had seen the error of isolationism with the June 22, 1941, German invasion of the Soviet Union.

Carlo Tresca was the most premature of "premature" anti-Fascists. His newspaper, *Il Martello,* had been a propaganda tool against Mussolini since 1920, and he had used more violent methods against Mussolini's sympathizers on the streets of New York for almost as long. As for the Communists, he had made uneasy common cause with them for many years, but the Moscow trials and the Spanish Civil War had turned him into an implacable enemy of Stalin. The very words *united front* recalled to him the tragedy of Spain. At the time of his death a bitter political fight was brewing, one that would encompass lifelong passions.

January 11 began for Tresca in the apartment he shared with Margaret De Silver, at 130 West Twelfth Street. At about noon, presumably from his apartment, he telephoned Dr. Umberto Gualtieri to discuss a meeting with the Office of War Information scheduled for January 14. The purpose of the meeting was to plan the organization of the Italian-American Victory Council. "There is no question about it," Gualtieri later told newspaper reporters, "the OWI insisted on the inclusion of communists and also newly reformed fascists. Tresca was absolutely against it and planned with me, at midday of the day he was killed, to walk out of the OWI meeting that Thursday with those who might follow him, if the OWI carried out its insistence."

Not long after his conversation with Gualtieri, Tresca, together with Margaret De Silver and her son Harrison, went to John's, a longtime favorite restaurant, to meet John Dos Passos for lunch. Tresca was under doctor's orders to lose weight, but he ate a hearty meal of spaghetti, veal scallopine, wine, cheese, and coffee. The owner of the restaurant, John Pope, found him in a good mood. Luigi Antonini, head of the International Ladies' Garment Workers Local 89, stopped at the table to say hello. Dos Passos later recalled the lunchtime conversation:

> Carlo Tresca was the old time Italian anarchist whose information I had found so accurate at the time of the Spanish Civil War. We had been friends for years and had been associated together in various enterprises to try to find homes for the thousands of anti-communist Spaniards who had been driven out of Spain by Franco's victory. . . . From the moment it became obvious that Italy would soon be knocked out of the war, Carlo would describe the moves the communists were making in Italian anti-fascist organizations in this country and in Europe to get control of the government that would take over Italy after Mussolini's inevitable collapse. He was doing all he could to work against them. It was war without quarter for great stakes and he knew it. One day in January 1943 I had lunch with him in New York before taking the train out to the Cape. He talked about the pulling and hauling in Italian organizations in New York. Whomever Washington backed would rule the peninsula. The fight was getting hotter he told me with glee.
>
> Carlo Tresca was murdered that night.

Lunch lasted several hours, and it was late afternoon before Tresca arrived at his office. *Il Martello,* which had had a number of homes since 1919, was now housed at 96 Fifth Avenue at the corner of Fifteenth Street. The building, which no longer exists, was a six-story, shabby commercial building. The newspaper occupied the southwest corner of the third floor, a space at the very end of a high, dimly lit hallway. There was a reception room, bare and lit by a single bulb. A visitor entering the reception room would find a glass panel in one wall. Behind it might be a half-dozen men, whom Tresca called "my boys." A visitor would give his name, the name would be phoned into Tresca in an interior office, and only when Tresca pressed a buzzer would the visitor be allowed entry.

A number of visitors arrived to see Tresca that afternoon. Eugene Del Vecchio, from Tresca's native town of Sulmona, came to ask his help in finding a job. Tresca spoke to him and told him to return the next morning when he would be able to tell him something specific. A friend, Frank Cancelleri, spent about half an hour in Tresca's offices. John DeLeo arrived at about half past six in the evening to deliver a check for six hundred dollars, a contribution to the *Martello* from Local 155 of the Knitgood Workers Union. DeLeo remained for about an hour, chatting with Myrtle Vacirca, the bookkeeper.

The third-floor office of the *Martello* was the center of a small group of anarchists who acknowledged Tresca as a leader. By 1943, however, the great representatives of the anarchist movement were dead, and the movement itself, vigorous during the nineteenth and into the twentieth centuries, had suffered devastating defeats in the course of the Bolshevik revolution and the Spanish Civil War.

The anarchist ideal of a society of free individuals, freely associating in all social and economic activities, uncoerced by ruling authority, finds ancestral voices as ancient as Zeno and the Stoics; in the mid-nineteenth century it found a modern voice in Pierre-Joseph Proudhon. "To be governed," Proudhon wrote, "is to be watched over, inspected, spied on . . . controlled . . . ordered about by men who have neither the right nor the knowledge nor the virtue. . . . It is to be, on the pretext of the general interest, taxed, drilled, held to ransom, exploited . . . then at the least resistance, at the first word of complaint, to be repressed . . . bullied, beaten, disarmed. . . . That's government, that's its justice, that's its morality!"

Proudhon called himself an anarchist in 1840, the first man to willingly appropriate the term. Thirty years later, in the First International, Michael Bakunin differed violently with Karl Marx. In the schism that developed between the followers of Proudhon and Bakunin on the one hand, and the followers of Marx on the other, the modern anarchist movement was born. In 1868 Bakunin would say, "I detest communism because it is the negation of liberty. . . . communism concentrates and absorbs all the powers of society into the state."

A movement that refused to subordinate the liberty of the individual to any higher principle could not be a unanimous movement, and anarchists were by no means agreed on the paths to revolution or on the design of future society. Terrorism and passive resistance existed at the movement's extremes, while anarcho-syndicalism occupied its center.

In the United States a native anarchist tradition was formed of individualist and commutarian strains, manifesting itself in the early part of the nineteenth century in utopian colonies, in advocacy of small independent industries, free banking, and free trade. In 1883, in response to severe depression and social unrest, the International Working People's Association was formed, known also as the Black, or Anarchist, International. It was antagonistic to the state, to ballot box reform, and determined on confrontation between labor and capital.

There were about seven thousand anarchists in the United States in 1886, the same year in which police killed six strikers and wounded many more during a strike at Chicago's McCormick Harvester Company. At a protest meeting called by the anarchists, and held at Haymarket Square, a bomb was thrown. This act, for which four innocent anarchists were later executed, exploded anarchism into national consciousness. Two further events—Alexander Berkman's attempted assassination of Henry Frick in 1892, and Leon Czolgosz's assassination of Pres. William McKinley in 1901—increased public fear and government repression of anarchists, leading to the Anarchist Exclusion Act of 1903.

Carlo Tresca arrived in the United States in 1904. He was a socialist, not yet an anarchist. But although socialism then dominated the Left in the United States, Tresca would move inexorably toward anarchist ideas, specifically toward anarcho-syndicalism, with its tenet of the organization of workers to confront and demolish the state. In time, particularly after Emma Goldman and Alexander Berkman were deported in 1919, the name Carlo Tresca became synonymous with anarchism in the minds of Americans.

In the *Martello* office on the afternoon of January 11, 1943, an engraver named Renato Vidal, who also slept in the office, was trying to avoid Tresca. They had had some sort of quarrel, and Vidal remained in his room. But, "When I was in my room," Vidal later told police "Carlo came in and gave me a dollar. He said, 'Go eat something.' This was about half-past six."

Sometime during that afternoon or early evening, Tresca received a telephone call from Sidney Solomon, a comrade who had planned to come to the office to see him that day. When the two men had met a week or so earlier, Tresca had said: "Sidney [pronouncing the name Sideney] we've got something of tremendous importance. I can't say yet. I'm not ready. But it's coming in. It's about the collaboration of the Communists and Fascists in Italy. It's going to be a tremendous thing." Solomon was to have come to the *Martello* office on the 11th to discuss the information, but he called to say his wife was very ill and he could not leave her.

It was Tresca's custom to leave his office about seven in the evening, but on January 11 a meeting was planned for 8:30. Five men were expected. At approximately eight o'clock Tresca told his assistant, Louis Ciccone, to go home. Tresca was then alone in his office for more than half an hour until Guiseppe Calabi arrived.

Guiseppe Calabi, a lawyer and a Jew, had fled Italy in 1939, soon after Mussolini had enacted Italy's anti-Semitic laws. In New York he joined the Mazzini Society, organized about that time by exiled Italian intellectuals. Calabi had not met Tresca until a Mazzini Society meeting at the end of December 1942. At that meeting Calabi was designated, along with Tresca and four others, to serve on a committee scheduled to have its first meeting on the night of January 11. He had received formal notification of the time and place by mail a few days earlier.

Calabi was a little late for the meeting. He got off the subway at the Fourteenth Street stop on Sixth Avenue, walked a block up to Fifteenth Street, and turned east, walking down the south side of the street until he reached the Fifteenth Street entrance to 96 Fifth Avenue. The street was very dark and, as far as he could tell, completely deserted.

Calabi entered the building at about quarter of nine. He climbed the stairs to the second floor, where he met the building's superintendent, who directed him to the *Martello* office one floor above. There he found Tresca alone, sitting at his desk. Tresca greeted him cordially, speaking to him in Italian and using the familiar form. While they waited for the other members of the committee to arrive, he showed Calabi around the office, pointing out his library, some photographs, and discussing the possibility of using some extra rooms as a club.

By nine o'clock, when no one else had arrived for the meeting, Tresca became irritated. They could advise me, he said angrily to Calabi. They could telephone. Half an hour later when no one had telephoned or arrived, Tresca said there was no point in waiting any longer. He turned out the lights of his office and the two men left, taking the staircase. On the second floor Tresca spoke a few words to the superintendent; as he opened the door leading to Fifteenth Street, he remarked to Calabi that he had not had dinner and was hungry and suggested that they go to a nearby bar for sandwiches and beer.

The bar was located diagonally across Fifth Avenue. Walking arm in arm, Tresca and Calabi crossed Fifteenth Street, stopping, before crossing Fifth Avenue, at the northwest corner of Fifth Avenue, just beneath a dimmed-out street lamp.

Mentz Von Erpecom and Otto Namtvedt, both employees of the Norwegian consulate, were walking east toward Fifth Avenue after finishing dinner at the Casa Johnny. "It was very dark," Namtvedt told the police. "I saw shooting blue lights under the lamppost on the corner of Fifth Avenue. Then I heard the shots." One shot followed by three more. The two Norwegians ducked into a doorway. Von Erpecom peered out. He saw a man run from the north to the south side of Fifteenth Street and get into a car waiting at the curb, just east of the avenue. The running figure moved like an athlete with long steps. The car, already in motion as the man entered the streetside door, sped west. Von Erpecom had served in the Automobile Corps of the Norwegian army and was confident about the car. "I judge by the sound of the motor," he said. "I am absolutely sure it was a Ford. As to the year, I think it was a '38 or '39. It was a dark Ford sedan. Two or four doors, I don't know."

A few other people were in the vicinity. Roscoe Platts, a teacher at a nearby vocational school, heard the shots and saw the group of three men under the lamppost. He saw a man run and disappear into the darkness. Samuel Sherman, who owned a clothing shop at 100 Fifth Avenue, also heard the shots and saw the car speed west. He called the police.

***

Standing with Tresca under the streetlight, holding his arm, Calabi heard the first shot. "I heard a shot, very near. But what astonished me—the first shot was not so strong as the two shots that came after." He turned his head to the left at the sound. Tresca turned to the right. Tresca started toward the shooter. Then the second and third shots hit him. In the second before Calabi bent to look at Tresca on the ground, he saw a man, "about 35 years old, five feet, five inches no more. He came up to my nose. He had the hat really drawn down near his ears and it was possible to see only the lower part of his face; it was very pale, very regular, no characteristic sign . . . rather slender . . . dark the cloth, dark the hat. He turned immediately and stepped quickly through Fifteenth Street and reached the other side of Fifteenth Street and disappeared because it was completely dark, because the street light lit only 30 feet no more. . . . He was two feet away when he fired, north of us. I believe he stepped so soft I didn't notice the step of this man. . . . He was going very fast, not running . . . very quick, a young man."

A photograph of the body taken from directly above shows bloodstains on Tresca's forehead and a large dark stain spattering the street and curb. Another photograph shows that beyond the light of the flashbulb the street is very dark. A policeman is now standing in a doorway next to a barbershop pole. An ambulance from Saint Vincent's is parked near the body.

At Saint Vincent's Hospital Tresca was pronounced dead on arrival, and his body was moved to the Tenth Precinct. The autopsy shows that he was hit by two bullets, both deadly. The first entered his left side from the back and tore through his left lung; the second hit the right side of his face as he swung, passing through his brain and lodging at the base of his skull. Powder burns were found on his skin, indicating how near to him his killer stood.

At the time of his death Tresca was a few months from his sixty-fourth birthday. During the previous year he had suffered several episodes of severe nasal hemorrhaging and recurrent attacks of flu. Two of his brothers had died in 1942 and he was deeply grieved. "I get the idea of being a wanderer without a purpose or aim," he wrote to his son-in-law that December. "Will try to get on my feet," he added. "I must. It is too much work to do."

Tresca was growing older, his losses were mounting, but the fundamental passion that had nourished him all his life remained.

In a sense, as his friend James T. Farrell remarked, Tresca was larger than the life he now lived: the day of the revolutionary anarchist movement was over. And for a number of years, to Tresca's growing bitterness, he himself had been the target of virulent attacks by another anarchist group. Yet, as he wrote, he had work to do. Thousands of Italian-Americans loved him and revered him as the old antifascist and revolutionary who had led so many of their battles. Writers, intellectuals, labor leaders, and even politicians sought his views, acknowledging his shrewd political sanity in a world mad with war and ideology. On January 16, the day of his funeral, six thousand mourners filed past his open coffin; ninety cars, including ten of press and police, made up the funeral cortege; five hundred people stood in silence around the spot, now piled high with red carnations, where he had fallen.

When he was killed, Carlo Tresca was in the middle of yet another fight; Dos Passos recalled his glee at the prospect.

Part One

Chapter 1
My Native Place

"SULMONA, my native place, is a small town stretched out in a beautiful valley in Abruzzi and has all the shortcomings of provincial towns."

That is the extent of the physical description Tresca allows to his birthplace, though others have said much more. Ovid praised its lush fertility and the streams that ran full even in midsummer; Ignazio Silone wrote of the "tender green light" bathing the "fields, the trees, the little villages at the foot of the mountain" on the Sulmona plain. Mount Morrone, a spur of the Maiella, rising two thousand feet above Sulmona, was once home to the hermit monk Fra Pietro, who broke his solitude in 1294 to be ordained Pope Celestine V, only to abdicate and return to his hermitage in what Dante scorned as "the great refusal."

Of life in the villages of the limestone Apennines, Silone wrote, "This region, which because of the harshness of the passes that lead into it, and the taciturn nature of its inhabitants, has always been difficult for new beliefs to penetrate. . . . Christianity took hold and became, for the Abruzzesi, the most accessible form of escape and release from a human condition that was very hard and close to desperation." Even in the middle of the twentieth century, travelers in the mountains have found the Abruzzi a remote and difficult province, more akin to the Mezzogiorno than central Italy.

But the valleys of the Abruzzi have a softer aspect. When Carlo was born on March 9, 1879, Sulmona, ninety miles east of Rome, was a city of about thirteen thousand inhabitants. The town had been destroyed several times by earthquakes over the centuries, but evidence of the thirteenth century was seen in an ancient aqueduct. The streets were cobbled; there was a Renaissance fountain, houses dating from the fourteenth century, and large open squares that on market days filled with peasants and their donkey carts. There was a section of very poor houses for peasants and of better houses for the artisans who made hats and violin strings. The Trescas were housed very well indeed.

Though it is no longer a private house and a bakery occupies the first floor, the Palazzo Tresca still stands on a side street in the center of town, a thick-walled building of squared stones, three stories high, and designed around a large central courtyard. Eight children—Carlo, the sixth—were born there to Filippo and Filomena Tresca, wealthy, prominent citizens of the town. Filomena was a daughter of the Faciani family, proprietors of a famous music school; Filippo, the son of a large landowner, had inherited his father's estates and was also a man of great political influence in the town, a "master vote getter," as his son recalls him. Every man, Carlo wrote, raised his hat to "Don Filippo to whom anybody could go for a favor, and all need to go to him when in distress."

In addition to their lands, which were farmed, the Trescas also owned two businesses in town—a carting firm and a stationer's shop, both of which were managed by Filomena. Filippo had little interest in the family business, or even in his lands, which were managed by his mother. He, himself, was primarily occupied with town politics, conducted in the coffee houses.

Carlo was not close to his father. Filippo was strictly authoritarian with his children, and Carlo writes that as a boy he longed for his father's approval. Still, by all accounts, his own included, he was the family favorite. He was called *lo scapestrato*—the unbridled, the unrestrainable one. He was an exuberant, disobedient, bold, and boastful boy. Years later he recalled his mother's loving plaint: "Carlùccio! What a bad, smart boy. I do not know if I love him so much because he is so bad or because he is so smart."

Carlo was often truant from school, and when he was absent he could be found at the local courthouse, memorizing the speeches and dramatic gestures of the lawyers to mimic them later at home.

His ambition was to be a great lawyer, and it was intended that he should study law.

Sulmona's prosperity was founded on agriculture, primarily the export of unfinished wine to France. But in the late 1880s a commercial rupture occurred between France and Italy, curtailing the export of wine and olive oil and causing an agricultural depression. In addition, the small industries began to suffer from the importation of cheap factory goods.

The Trescas were soon affected by this economic downturn. They might have been able to hold on to their lands until better days if Filippo had not seen it as his obligation to cosign bank notes for his friends. The friends could not repay, and the Tresca estates became forfeit. The family's last hope of salvation lay in an inheritance from Filomena's rich bachelor brother. When this brother died, however, it was discovered that he had invested his fortune in religious relics. They were worthless. Carlo was "furiously mad"; he had counted on the inheritance to see him through school. Toward the middle of the 1890s, the family home itself was claimed by a creditor.

Carlo was then about fifteen. He was humiliated by his helplessness, by his mother's tears, and was enraged and resentful at his own losses. He had known a life of privilege and domestic comfort; now the big house, once filled with noise and activity, grew empty and cold. The garden fell into ruin, the white horse and carriage, and even the wine barrels, had to be sold. More than anything he missed the gaiety of the harvest season when the peasants had brought the produce from the estates into the central courtyard, pressed the grapes and olives, drunk the wine, sung and told stories. His powerful father shrank into depression.

The other Tresca children managed as best they could. Luisa, the eldest, somehow gathered a dowry and married before the last of the money disappeared. Ettore, Carlo's senior by about eight years, was already at medical school at the University of Naples, and Filomena squeezed enough money from the remains of the estate to enable him to finish. Mario, the second son, did not require education; he was extremely nearsighted and apparently content to wrap packages in the carting firm, although that business too was foundering as the railway came into greater use. Anita married a sculptor and, in time, emigrated with him to the United States, where he became a carver of tombstones. Beatrice, something of an uncloistered nun, remained at home to help Filomena and died there while still very young. Lelio and Arnaldo, the two youngest boys, were still children.

There was no money to send Carlo to university. Filomena was a religious woman. She decided to turn her intelligent, ambitious son into a priest. Carlo thought she had gone mad. He came by anticlericalism through his father and his uncle Paolo, and he believed passionately in Free Thought. But he loved his mother, and since he could not think of anything else to do, for a few months he pretended to attend classes at the seminary. He despised the seminarians: "embryo priests," he called them. He hated their meekness, their obedience, the pious expressions they wore. As they walked in strict formation on their daily outings, Carlo led a group of his friends to attack them with sticks and stones. He was already thinking in political terms, seeing himself as a champion of free thought.

Italy was still in its infancy as a unified country when Carlo was born. His father's cousin, Paolo, had fought with Garibaldi and told his stories often to the boy all too ready to dream of battles and wars for freedom. Liberty, change, free thought, fight—these words were in the air. At sixteen Carlo made plans to run away and join the legions of Garibaldi's son to fight with the Greeks against the Turks. With his innate sense of drama, he promised his sweetheart, Alessandrina, to return to her or, if not, to die in battle with her name on his lips. Their romance was secret; Alessandrina's father, the Baron Sardi, happened to be Filippo's principal rival in local politics. Their situation was, Carlo thought, something like that of the Montagues and the Capulets. In any case the leave-taking was aborted when Filomena discovered her son's plan and prevented his departure.

The financial difficulties of the Trescas were symptomatic of Italy's plight. The agricultural depression of the late 1880s set off a train of events: in Sicily, a peasant rebellion led to emigration to the industrial cities, where uprisings followed as industry was unable to absorb the influx. All through the 1890s scattered uprisings occurred. Sardinia was starving. Italian children were sent to work in French factories. In 1898 Rome was in a state of siege for several days. In Milan, eighty people were killed in street fighting. Italians streamed into the river of European emigration to America.

In 1892 the Italian Socialist party met for the first time; a socialist review, *Critica Sociale,* was founded, at Rome University; Antonio Labriolo lectured on Marxist thought; Garibaldi's influences remained strong. "Socialism," wrote Benedetto Croce, "conquered all, or almost all, the flower of the younger generation."

Carlo's way to socialism had been paved by stories of the Risorgimento, by his hatred of the clergy, and by the felt injustice that had led to his own disappointed hopes. And at that moment, toward the end of the 1890s, several militant leaders of the Railroad Workers Union were sent to Sulmona, where it was hoped they would be too isolated to make trouble. The unionists opened a club and sponsored political lectures. At first, Carlo admitted, he found the lectures boring, the dense Marxist theory dull and lifeless. But he continued to go to the club. There was little else to do in town apart from playing cards and carousing. In addition the railroad workers had a certain glamour. they were traveled men who had seen the world beyond his valley. In a short time, the talk of class struggle and the coming revolution seized Carlo's imagination. He began to read. He became Sulmona's first and, for a time, only recruit to the Socialist party. His new allegiance was fortified by the union men, who made much of him, and by his father, whom it infuriated. "Damn you and your socialism!" Filippo shouted as Carlo's applications for civil service jobs were rejected again and again. "You are ruined!"

In 1899, at the age of twenty, Carlo Tresca was on the path of his life. He was a very attractive young man. He was six-feet tall, slim, with blue eyes, and brown hair. He had all the assurance of his class and the buoyancy of his nature. What he had feared—a dreary life shuffling papers in some government office—had been averted. Longing for action, he decided to organize the peasants.

The more experienced union organizers had failed at this task. They had distributed circulars to peasants who could barely read, waited outside churches on Sundays to make speeches to people who only wanted to go home. Tresca knew his peasants. They had taken him on their knees when he was small, sung to him, told him stories. He now went to them in their cantinas, where they greeted him as Don Carlo. Please, his peasants would say, have a drink. After much drinking in many cantinas the peasants elected a Socialist delegate from each district. It mattered little to Tresca whether the motivating factor was the persuasiveness of his arguments or the deference to his family. The result was that when the government decided to dissolve both the Republican and Socialist parties, Tresca's call brought out almost a thousand peasants to a protest demonstration.

Life was heady to him now. On May Day, 1900, only a few weeks before King Umberto would be assassinated by Gaetano Bresci, an emigrant anarchist from Paterson, New Jersey, thousands of peasants poured into the town square. Red flags waved. Tresca made his maiden speech. What did he say? He never could remember. But he remembered the roar of applause, saw the sea of hands waving at him, and thought: My people are christening me. I am a man now, a man of command and action. The moment remained with him the rest of his life.

Tresca was now secretary of the Railroad Workers Union and was earning a small salary, which went some way toward reconciling Filippo to his way of life. He also began to write articles for *Il Germe,* the local Socialist newspaper. His first article, a defense of the prostitute "forced to sell her kisses," seemed to him "the best prose ever written in the language of Dante." He conceived an ambition to be editor of *Il Germe* and proposed himself when the current editor was forced to resign because of his ferocious attacks on the clergy.

Tresca's journalistic voice emerged whole with *Il Germe.* It was based on a simple premise: no class, no individual, no institution was immune from attack. In one issue, the new editor promised that the following issue would contain an attack on the vicar. Filomena pleaded with her son, but the vicar was duly accused of sexual misconduct, behavior for which Carlo would castigate the clergy again and again.

The prominent citizens and institutions of Sulmona did not submit passively to the assaults of *Il Germe.* Tresca was briefly arrested, and then released, during a street demonstration, but he rapidly exhausted the indulgence of the city's powerful. When he accused the captain of police of gambling, the captain sued for libel and

Tresca went to jail for two months. It was not a fearsome experience. Friends sent all his meals to the jail, and he ate with such relish that when he was released his clothes no longer fit. Back at home with his family he found that his time in jail had made a difference in their perception of him. After dinner, with the family gathered at the table, Filippo offered him a cigar, the first Carlo was allowed to smoke in his father's presence.

Shortly after his release from jail, Tresca published some documents about the torture of prisoners. In Rome, Enrico Ferri, a leader of the left wing of the Socialist party who was known as a brilliant lawyer and criminologist, reprinted the material from the *Germe* in the national Socialist paper, *Avanti*. Ferri wanted to discuss the matter further. He wired Tresca: "Come to Rome at once." It was Carlo's first trip away from home. Ferri, he recalled, seemed like a god to him. Ferri made a speech mentioning Tresca's name, and Carlo could barely restrain himself. Here I am! he wanted to shout to the audience. *I* am Tresca!

In 1904 Tresca was once again charged with libel. He was confident of an acquittal because he was now defended by lawyers sent by the Socialist party from Rome and Naples. While waiting for the verdict he cheerfully went to a nearby café to have a drink. He was called back to hear a verdict of guilty and a sentence of a year in jail, six months of it to be spent in solitary confinement. Carlo could have appealed the sentence, but he chose not to. His brother Ettore was already in New York. Hundreds of Sulmonese had emigrated to the United States, and the *Germe* had followed them to their new settlements in New York, Philadelphia, and New England. America exerted a tremendous pull, and Carlo had always intended to leave Sulmona one day. On July 7, 1904, promising Filomena that he would keep her rosary with him always, Carlo, accompanied by his father, set out for the train station. On a day far in the future, when both men were dead, the principal street of Sulmona would be renamed the Piazza Carlo Tresca and a bronze head of Tresca would stand in a public garden.

At the moment, however, he was a fugitive from justice. He saw his father's white handkerchief grow small in the distance. He would never again see his mother or his father, his sisters Luisa and Beatrice, or Lelio and Arnaldo, the two youngest boys. But he now had a wife, who in less than a year would follow him.

After a stop in Milan to attend a convention of the Railroad Workers Union, Tresca crossed the border into Switzerland; in Lausanne he made contact with the community of Italian Socialists. Among them at that time was Benito Mussolini, who had fled Italy two years earlier, probably to avoid the draft. For two years Mussolini had lived by a series of menial jobs (for which he had little stomach), by begging, and by stealing food, reportedly by using threats of physical harm. At least once he was arrested as a vagabond. At the same time he wrote for the local Socialist newspaper and made public speeches for which he gained some reputation.

Shortly before Tresca's arrival, Mussolini had made one of his characteristic speeches: challenging a Reverend Tagliatela to a debate, he placed his watch on the podium and announced that if God existed, He had five minutes to strike him dead. Among the people who knew Mussolini well during this time was Angelica Balabanoff, the Russian socialist (who later became the first secretary of the Comintern, and still later broke with the Bolsheviks, eventually coming to New York). When Balabanoff wrote about Mussolini in her memoir, she described a loud-mouthed derelict whose ideas were formed less from conviction that from a desire for notice and who displayed symptoms of hysteria. Errico Malatesta, too, noted that Mussolini did not discriminate among ideas, but adopted those that suited his immediate purpose.

Tresca, on being told about this man, was curious to meet him. After several days Mussolini appeared. As Tresca recalled, the two spent a night in argument and Carlo, who was five years the elder, took a paternalistic tone to what seemed to him only youthful impetuosity. For his part, Mussolini found Tresca of too legalistic and reformist a turn of mind. When they parted it was he who condescended: "Well, Tresca," he said, "I am sure that in America you will become a true revolutionary comrade." A few months later, when the Swiss tried to expel Mussolini, Tresca responded from the United States by raising some money for his defense. In gratitude Mussolini sent him a pamphlet of the debate with Reverend Tagliatela, inscribed, "To my dear Comrade Carlo Tresca, with best wishes and greetings."

Leaving Lausanne, Tresca made his way to Le Havre, where he had barely enough money to book passage on the SS *Tourraine*. Some ten days later, in an August dawn, the immigrant-packed

Tourraine sailed past the Statue of Liberty, carrying in steerage at least one confused and heartsick passenger.

Ettore Tresca had set up his medical practice on Bayard Street, near Mulberry Park on the Lower East Side. Ettore was eager to show his brother the sights. One night they went to a Chinese theater, but the guttural language and the cries of the audience were hideous to Carlo's ears. On another evening Ettore took him to a German saloon near the Bowery, where the drunkenness of the patrons and the elaborate dresses and jewels of the women repelled him. Ettore took him to a prize fight. He thought the faces of the audience like those of beasts, screaming for blood. In bewilderment he turned to Ettore: Where are the Christians in America? He took a walk by himself through the Lower East Side where merchants stood outside their shops crying for business. Everywhere there was talk of money. He went home thinking of money: If I had money . . . I *must* make money. One night on the Third Avenue el, on his way to dinner in Harlem, Carlo missed his stop and found himself at the end of the line. At the gates of Woodlawn Cemetery he uttered the Italian immigrant's cry: *Mannagia America!* Damn America!

At the end of 1904, Tresca left New York for Philadelphia to edit *Il Proletario,* the organ of the Italian Socialist Federation. The first issue of *Il Proletario* under Tresca's editorship appeared in January 1905. Under Garibaldi's motto, *Il socialismo e il sole dell' avvenire,* the paper carried a report of a strike in Utah, with a warning to readers not to accept job offers in that state; a translation of Robert Ingersoll's "Why I Am an Atheist"; and a column on health contributed by Ettore Tresca. It also carried an attack on the editor of a socialist paper in Newark who had apparently accused Carlo of some sort of swindle. This was only the first of many personal feuds carried on in the pages of Tresca's papers.

By his own account, Tresca had as yet no sense of the American labor movement. "I was still living in Italy, both with my heart and mind. . . . I launched a vigorous attack on whatever fledgling exploiters there were among the Italian workers." These included priests and the *prominenti* of the Italian colonies; the criminal gangs, the *camorra,* often in league with the *prominenti;* and the *padrone* system of contract labor which mercilessly exploited illiterate workers until in 1907 it was finally outlawed as peonage.

Acting as contractor the padrone negotiated with the employer to supply workers at a set price, whom he then undertook to maintain. A supply of unemployed immigrants was gathered up and taken to the construction site, where the padrone set their hours of work and their wages, housed and fed them, and took his profits from their work.

Tresca answered an advertisement from an Italian agency asking for three hundred workers at good pay. At the employment agency he was charged five dollars for being hired and seven dollars for his railroad fare. The men were taken "like a herd of cattle," he wrote, to build tracks for the Lackawanna Railroad. He lasted five days, returning to New York "a sick man, physically and morally" disgusted by "the revolting spectacle of men living promiscuously in a railroad car in great numbers . . . the terrible odor of their bodies . . . their sexual perversion, their supreme obedience to every command . . . did produce in me a sense of hopelessness. I felt as if I'd been submerged in the depths of the sea of human degradation." In the camp, workers were frequently robbed. They were charged large amounts for room, board, commissions, and traveling expenses. When the job was finished they returned to the cities with nothing to show for their labor, and were sent out again by the contractor to a new job.

These details appeared in *Il Proletario*, along with reports of the system of organized prostitution, often run by agents of the prominenti, who placed marriage advertisements in Italian newspapers to attract young girls to American cities. And it was a rare issue of the paper that had nothing to say about venal, sexually active priests.

In March 1905, Tresca experienced what may have been his first disillusionment with the Socialist party. At the Stetson Hat Company in Philadelphia, six hundred unorganized Italian workers went out on strike to protest a tyrannical superintendent, while the AFL members remained on the job. *Il Proletario* took up the cause of the strikers, only to learn that some of the most enthusiastic strikers, some of them Socialists, were in league with the superintendent to break the strike.

In 1906 the Italian consul in Philadelphia charged Tresca with libel; he was sentenced to three months in prison and resigned as editor of *Il Proletario* then. No doubt there were already differ-

ences between him and the Italian Socialist Federation on the im-
moderation of his editorial voice. On his release from prison,
Tresca entered into a partnership with a Giovanni Di Silvestro to
publish a new newspaper, *La Voce del Popolo.* The partnership did
not last long, and Tresca resigned to launch his first independent
paper, *La Plebe.* "The newspaper," he wrote, "was christened by a
series of criminal proceedings against me and consequent arrests
and releases on bail." A Rev. Carmi Falconi told the Bureau of Investigation many years later that Carlo Tresca had threatened him
with personal violence and with the destruction of his church at
Charleroi, in the period around 1906. Tresca, he said, was a ter-
rorist, not a socialist.

Tresca now began to visit the mining camps of western Pennsylvania. He toured a camp at Iselin where a young miner had invited
him to speak. "Silhouettes of men and machines mingled together,
great furnaces and rivers of melting lead, towering smoke stacks."
Of the seven workers who served as his guides, four had lost hands
in accidents. As he stood with them looking at the bare wooden
shacks, in one of which he had slept the previous night, in the
same bed with a miner and his four children, "We heard the bell of
an ambulance . . . more human flesh ground by the machinery of
capitalist production. You did not need to read Karl Marx after
this to be convinced that society as it stood must be changed."

On October 24, 1908, the Italian ambassador in Washington
had occasion to write to the postmaster general:

> Carlo Tresca is an anarchist or the like, condemned in Italy and the
> United States . . . he publishes a newspaper under the name of "La Plebe,"
> intended for propaganda of every kind of bad and dangerous ideas against
> constituted authorities, social order etc. He has asked for the privilege of
> the second class mailing matter which would, of course, increase the cir-
> culation of his newspaper. It is an internal matter and I must not interfere
> in the position of your department. However, as "La Plebe" is written in
> Italian and published to be spread among Italians I venture to point out to
> you the fact and the danger.

The Pittsburgh Post Office regularly began to deny second class
mailing privileges for individual issues of *La Plebe.*

Chapter 2
Family Life

HELGA Guerra arrived in Sulmona sometime in 1903. She had been invited by the Baronessa Sardi as a suitable friend for her daughter Alessandrina. Helga was an intelligent, spirited young woman of striking blonde looks. She came of a family of high social position, and in this she took pride, telling often about her grandmother having been introduced to Napoleon at a ball. But for all her good fortune in looks and intelligence, Helga Guerra faced a bleak future: as the youngest of six children, and a girl, she was expected to remain unmarried and stay home to care for her parents in their old age.

For the moment in Sulmona, however, Helga was free of parental supervision. One warm day Carlo arrived at the Palazzo Sardi to visit Alessandrina; he found her sitting in the courtyard with the blonde girl from the north and began a romance that, Helga would later tell their daughter, "went like wildfire."

On the face of it, the match was not a suitable one for Helga. Had she reflected she might have considered that Carlo had neither money nor any profession likely to earn him any. He was also a proclaimed enemy of the class values she cherished. But apparently none of this weighed with her. Her suitor was immensely attractive and intelligent; his politics even gave him an outlaw's glamor. What, after all, had Helga to oppose to him but a life of spinsterhood?

Helga told her parents nothing, and she married Carlo Tresca on April 8, 1904. In the months remaining before Carlo's abrupt

departure, the couple lived with the Trescas. Their marriage ceremony had been a civil one; at Filomena's urging they repeated it in
church (in a secret ceremony, so as not to damage Carlo's reputation). Afterward Helga informed her parents of the accomplished
fact, but she left Italy without bringing her husband to meet them
or going to see them herself. It was a profound breach that did not
heal for many years.

Carlo met Helga's ship in New York on May 11, 1905. A year
later their daughter was born in Philadelphia. She was named
Beatrice, for Carlo's sister who had died not long before the child's
birth.

The Trescas lived at 1103 Ellsworth Street, in one of a row of
narrow two-story brick houses with two small rooms on each floor.
Years later Helga took Beatrice to see the house. She pointed to
two marble steps leading to the front door. "See!" she said bitterly,
"*these* are the steps I had to scrub."

During her year in Italy with the impoverished Trescas, Helga
had sewn shirts to help earn money. In America her life did not
improve. She had no family, no friends, no money beyond the six
dollars a week Carlo earned. In addition she was often alone with
the baby and the housework. At best Carlo left her to travel to distant meetings; at worst, he was in jail. The adventure of forbidden
marriage and emigration must have palled very quickly.

As far as Beatrice knows, Helga was out of touch with her parents for at least four years after her marriage. But at the end of
1907 or early in 1908 she wrote to them. More than half a century
later Beatrice, sorting through her mother's papers, found the
crumbling reply to Helga's letter: "My dear Helga," Vincenzo
Guerra wrote in formal Italian, "You made your bed so do not
complain to us."

The complaint that prompted Helga to swallow pride and write
home was not a matter of poverty or loneliness. Its source is located in the records of the Philadelphia courts. On February 20,
1908, a grand jury handed down a true bill indicting "Carl" Tresca
on charges of assault, battery, rape, and adultery. The charges
were brought by one Antonio Di Antonio, who, like the Trescas,
was a resident of Ellsworth Street. They were made on behalf of
Marietta Di Antonio, described as "a woman child under the age
of sixteen years," perhaps the daughter of Antonio.

J. Joseph Murphy represented Tresca. He presented a strong case for his client, arguing that the original charge was statutory rape, which was inconsistent with the indictment for forcible rape. He intended the court to infer that Marietta had been a willing partner and that the rape charge was a fiction to salvage honor. A year later, in April 1909, when Tresca's case came to court, he pled guilty only to the charge of adultery; on this charge alone he was sentenced to nine months in the county jail.

Tresca's lawyer continued his advocacy while his client was in jail. He filed a long brief pleading for reduction of sentence on the basis of his client's character and work. Murphy's document summarizes, in the best possible light, the story of Tresca's activities during his first four years in the United States. From the brief we learn that Tresca has moved his family from Philadelphia to 712 Webster Street in Pittsburgh, where, his lawyer noted, "He was among the first to call attention to the fact that the Italian authorities unable themselves to cope with and stamp out the Black Hand in their own country, have encouraged the emigration of these criminals to America," where they have "made the life of every successful and respectable Italian in this country precarious." Week after week, Murphy wrote, his client made an effort to stamp out the Black Hand in the United States. For the most part he fought alone, but on a few occasions he was able to enlist the assistance of the police. One such occasion was the arrival in the United States of a former member of the Italian Chamber of Deputies, Polazole by name, "exposed and rendered infamous in his own country as leader of the Black Hand." When Tresca heard of the arrival of this criminal he "immediately got out an extra edition of the paper . . . giving an account of numberless crimes which Polazole had been connected with, and copies of this edition he distributed free at an immense mass meeting held in New York at which Polazole was scheduled to speak." As Polazole spoke at meetings in Philadelphia, Pittsburgh, and other cities, Tresca followed in order to expose him. Subsequently, the police commissioner of New York, acting on Tresca's information, "turned the case over to Detective Petrosino, who was but recently assassinated at Palermo, and died martyr to the cause for which Tresca has also been fighting. Petrosino and Tresca thereafter worked hand in hand until sufficient evidence was secured against Polazole to secure his deportation."

For his efforts, Tresca earned the hatred of this organization of criminals and "on the 6th of January of this present year (1909) a hired assassin made a deliberate attempt to take the life of Tresca in broad daylight on the principal street of the Italian Colony of the City of Pittsburgh."

After this recitation of Tresca's activities against criminals and his partnership with the police, Murphy noted his client's attacks on the padrone system, by then outlawed, "whereby the ignorant immigrant sells his labor for years to come, securing therefore a mere pittance, while his more enlightened countryman secures the bulk of the wages earned by him." Tresca also exposed a scheme of blackmail carried on by local Italian consuls to sell Italian immigrants exemptions from compulsory military service in Italy. For a fee of one hundred to two hundred dollars an immigrant might buy a certificate stating that he was physically unfit for military service and thus avoid deportation to Italy. "This fraud has often been exposed by Tresca [with] irrefutable proofs."

It was true, Murphy admitted, that these proofs were ruled inadmissible in court, but only on a technicality, and in fact the consul Tresca had exposed was recalled. As for the criminal libel charge for which his client had been sentenced to six months in jail (and of which he had served only twenty days in the Uniontown, Pennsylvania, jail), this charge too was based on a technicality; more important was that Tresca had exposed a priest who seduced his young housekeeper. "Thus it will be seen that the publications for which the laws of this country have compelled Tresca to do penance, are such as every Italian resident of America is entitled to know."

More than seventy years later many elements of Murphy's brief can be confirmed. For instance, in August 1908, while Tresca was free on one thousand dollars bail on the Di Antonio charge and after he had moved *La Plebe* from Philadelphia to Pittsburgh, an inspector from the Department of Immigration called at the newspaper office. He found Helga by herself. On being questioned she told him her husband was traveling through New England collecting subscriptions for the paper, but would be home later in the week. She was sure of this because he was due to appear as a defendant in Uniontown, in Fayette County, to face a libel charge. On being further pressed, Helga told the inspector that a Catholic priest had brought the charge in connection with a photograph printed in *La Plebe* showing him in a compromising posture with a young woman.

The inspector demanded to know whether *La Plebe* was an anarchistic paper. No, Helga told him, it is a socialist paper. Why, then, the inspector wondered in his report, was the entire staff of the paper present and vocal at a recent lecture given by Emma Goldman? He noted that the paper had a subscription list containing three thousand names; also, the local Italian consul had informed him that Carlo Tresca was a thoroughly bad man and that the better class of Italians in the city believed that *La Plebe* advocated anarchy.

The man referred to as "Polazole" in Murphy's brief was in fact Raffaele Palizzolo, a former deputy from Palermo and an acknowledged mafioso who had stood trial for murder in Sicily. Palizzolo arrived in New York on June 8, 1908, planning a tour of Sicilian immigrant communities to raise money to finance another campaign for Parliament. He was met, on arrival, by the Italian consul and thousands of Sicilians; the Italian-language press greeted him warmly. Palizzolo himself claimed to be on a mission from the Italian government to conduct an educational campaign against the Black Hand.

New York police commissioner Bingham gave him an official welcome. "I am certain," Bingham told the press, "that the Honorable Mr. Palizzolo will be able to offer valuable help to the New York police in their fight against the Black Hand." But Bingham was disabused of this notion by Detective Joseph Petrosino, head of the police Department's "Italian squad." Petrosino (who would be murdered on March 12, 1909, in Palermo as he investigated connections between the Black Hand and the Mafia) broke up several of Palizzolo's lectures. Although not formally deported, Palizzolo was persuaded to leave the country sooner than he had intended. He sailed for Italy on August 8, 1908. Neither official records nor Petrosino's biography mentions Carlo Tresca's name in connection with the campaign against Palizzolo. But there was such a campaign, and Tresca was active against the Black Hand. In any case if such a collaboration had existed between police and an anarchist, public knowledge of it would have embarrassed both sides.

Murphy's brief also referred to an attempt on his client's life.

Such an attempt certainly occurred on a crowded Pittsburgh street in midday of January 6, 1909. A razor-wielding assailant approached Tresca from behind with the clear intention of cutting his throat. The blade, deflected as Tresca ducked his head at the crucial moment, cut through his cheek and jawbone. Twenty-six stitches were taken to close the wound by an apparently incompetent doctor. Infection set in and Ettore came down from New York to care for his brother. The assailant, a man named Giordano, was immediately captured. He was released on bail, fled, was brought back from his refuge in a mining camp in West Virginia to stand trial, and was acquitted by the jury. According to Murphy, the judge "scored" the jury severely for this verdict in the face of overwhelming evidence, but Giordano went free.

Tresca maintained that the attack on him was a collaborative effort by representatives of the church, the Italian government, and the Black Hand. He said that a man named Zappia, head of a gang of blackmailers, was hired to warn him that if he did not leave town he would be killed. The attack by Giordano was made a month after the warning.

Carlo's version may be accurate, but in later years Helga offered another story. She told her daughter about an afternoon in 1908 when she and Carlo were out for a stroll. They were accompanied by a young girl who lived nearby. Carlo walked between the two women, one on each arm. With her hand tucked in her husband's elbow, Helga could feel the pressure transmitted as he squeezed the hand of their young neighbor, presumably Marietta Di Antonio. Helga always insisted to Beatrice, and also to Carlo's sister Anita, that Giordano was either related to or hired by the Di Antonios when the course of legal justice proved slow.

Carlo recovered slowly from the infection caused by the knife wound. When Ettore judged him well, he gave him the news that their father had died.

Beatrice recalls very little of events before 1910. By that time she was four years old, a pretty, grave little girl with gray eyes and brown hair. She was now living in New Kensington, a small town not far from Pittsburgh where the local postmaster had offered second class mailing privileges to the second of Carlo's newspapers, *L'Avvenire*, which he began in 1909.

New Kensington was an area subject to frequent flash floods.

Beatrice remembers sitting at the top of the cellar stairs, watching the water rise step by step. After a while men in hip boots arrived to turn off the gas in the cellar. Carlo must have been away from home.

She called her father *Babo,* or Papa. He often went away to the mining camps of western Pennsylvania, and on one occasion he took Beatrice with him. On the train from New Kensington the conductor had some question about their tickets. Carlo's English was unreliable. He lifted Beatrice to stand on the seat, and she was conscious of the passengers' amusement as she translated for her father.

That night they slept at a miner's house. Like all mining camps in that area, it was a desolate place of wooden shacks built in straight lines along one or two dirt streets. Up on a rise was the church; a few hundred feet off, the mine. Each shack sheltered a family of anywhere from four to ten children and as many boarders as there was floor space for mattresses.

Carlo and Beatrice, as honored guests, were offered a bed. Beatrice had a tantrum. There were no sheets! She refused to sleep on soiled mattress ticking! Her father then spoke to her more sharply than he ever had. Go to bed, he said. You are to accept this hospitality graciously. Remember that just so a fat, spoiled little girl can sleep in a bed, the people who live in this house must sleep on the kitchen floor.

Helga ran the newspaper when Carlo was away from home. Beatrice was trained from early childhood to keep quiet while her mother worked. One day as Beatrice sat at the table watching her mother read copy, the heavy glass globe on the gas mantle fell and hit the child on the head. All she thought of was that her blood was spattering the proofs.

Chapter 3
The Bull of Lawrence

I N the fall of 1910 an article appeared in *L'Avvenire* reporting that a priest, unnamed, in Butler, Pennsylvania, had fathered a child by one of his parishioners. *L'Avvenire* often referred to the clergy as "pigs in cassocks," "rabid dogs," "black pigs," or "carrion," and *Risveglio*, the Catholic newspaper, responded with not much Christian forbearance. In this case, the Reverend Marinaro, who was a priest in Butler, decided to take the article personally. Although the article was unsigned, the priest sued the editor of *L'Avvenire* for libel.

Priest baiting was only one of Carlo Tresca's activities at this time. Six years after his emigration he was a well-known agitator among Italian workers in Pennsylvania as well as Ohio, New England, and Illinois. In the fall of 1910 he was making speeches to steel workers at McKees Rocks, Pennsylvania. At the Westmoreland mines he documented his accusations that officials of the United Mine Workers were in league with the coal operators. He held meetings in New Castle and Youngstown, Morgan and Freeport. In October he attended a "grand libertarian soiree" in New York. "Now Carlo Tresca is calling together the band of free men," *L'Avvenire* announced, and "all us hatters . . . hold Tresca as a comrade and a guide in the struggles . . . against priests, padroni and camorra." *L'Avvenire* also congratulated the parents of newborns who shunned baptism and pledged to raise their children to be champions of "free thought."

In the fall of 1910 Tresca's activities were somewhat curtailed by the effort to raise money and prepare for his libel trial. The trial opened on October 20. Broadly, his defense was that he was not the author of the offending article, and witnesses were called to confirm this. When Tresca himself was called to testify, the prosecuting attorney objected that since Tresca did not believe in God, he could not be sworn to tell the truth. The judge sustained the objection. The jury was sent out to deliberate and returned a few minutes later with a verdict of guilty as charged. The verdict was appealed, and a new trial was granted in which Tresca was permitted to testify on his own behalf, and in June he was once again found guilty. He was sentenced to a fine of three hundred dollars and nine months in the Allegheny County Jail. As a result he was still in jail when, on January 12, 1912, the Industrial Workers of the World was called to lead the landmark strike of textile workers in Lawrence, Massachusetts.

There is no indication that Tresca had contact with the IWW before the Lawrence strike, although the IWW had led a strike at McKees Rocks in 1909, and Tresca also knew Arturo Giovannitti, a poet from the Molise who was associated with the IWW. It is certain, however, that he was in sympathy with the goals and tactics of the Wobblies and that the IWW represented to him a way to connect with the broad American labor movement.

Tresca had already distanced himself from the Socialist party, with its program of ballot box politics. He had involved himself with the unskilled, unorganized Italian workers, and when he spoke at the "grand libertarian soiree" in New York he had extolled the "new principle of syndicalism which aims to unite all wage earners." The IWW principle of direct action, intended to build the "One Big Union" to "take possession of the earth and the machinery of production" and thus, with the general strike, to create "a new society within the shell of the old," held immense appeal.

Syndicalism, however, was not an idea embraced by all anarchists. The Italian anarchist leader Errico Malatesta believed that the notion was "pure utopia. Either the worker dying of hunger after three days on strike will return to the factory hanging his head . . . or else he will try to gain possession of the fruits of his production by open force. Who will he find facing him to stop him? Soldiers, policemen, perhaps the bourgeois themselves and then the question will have to be resolved by bullets and bombs . . . victory will go to the strongest."

In only a few years the IWW would be destroyed by forces stronger than itself, and by its own internal quarrels as well. But at that moment, in 1912, the Wobblies had emerged strong from seven years of activity in the West; when they sang, "In our hands is placed a power greater than their hoarded gold/Greater than the might of armies magnified a thousand fold," Tresca felt, he later wrote, that he could break the prison bars with his bare hands, so eager was he to get to Lawrence.

In 1912 Lawrence was an exemplary industrial city. It called itself "the worsted center of the world" and was home to about thirty-five thousand immigrants who were the hands of the brick woolen mills that were lined up along the banks of the Merrimack River—Italians, Poles, Lithuanians, Greeks, Syrians, Portuguese, Russians and more, all drawn to Lawrence by recruiting posters placed in their villages by agents of the American Woolen Company. The posters pictured a happy worker, bags of gold at his feet, books in his hand, standing beside a pretty vine-covered house which he certainly owned. The arriving immigrant found a different reality: foul wooden four-story tenements jammed into back alleys; rents so high that four or five people slept in each room; vermin and disease; salaries so meager that even with entire families, children as well, working in the mills for an average work week of fifty-six hours, there was not enough money for the bare necessities of life. In "the worsted center of the world" woolen cloth was far beyond the means of its producers.

Before the strike broke out the Massachusetts legislature was presented with certain facts: the average mill worker's life was twenty-two years shorter than that of the average manufacturer; the average wage was nine dollars a week for male workers and much less for women and children; pneumonia and tuberculosis killed children by the thousands. The legislature took modest action, passing a law reducing working hours for women and children from fifty-six to fifty-four hours a week. The law went into effect on January 1, 1912. On January 11, the first payday that followed, Polish women working the looms in the cotton mills opened their pay envelopes to find, as they expected, that wages had been cut by thirty-two cents in accord with the shortened work week.

Thirty-two cents was three loaves of bread. A cry of "Short pay! Short pay!" rang out. The women stopped their looms and ran from the mills. The next day the Italian workers, blowing fuses and breaking machinery in their anger, joined the strike. By evening the strike was ten thousand strong; the next day, twenty thousand. By January 15, Lawrence's mills were dark.

There were fewer than three thousand unionized workers in Lawrence at the time; of those, only three hundred were IWW. Nevertheless the small IWW local took charge and wired for organizers. Joe Ettor arrived on January 13 along with the poet Arturo Giovannitti. A week later Elizabeth Gurley Flynn and Bill Haywood arrived.

Joe Ettor was the primary organizer. Strike committees of the different nationality groups were formed; relief committees organized donations of food and set up soup kitchens; a list of demands was drawn up that included a 15 percent wage increase, double pay for overtime, elimination of the bonus system for speeded-up production, no retribution against strikers. The moving picket line was invented in Lawrence when town ordinances forbade the massing of strikers. Strikers paraded through the streets of Lawrence daily, singing the "Internationale" and the "Marseillaise." In a tactic borrowed from European strikes, Elizabeth Gurley Flynn gathered up the malnourished, threadbare children and sent them out of the violent city to the care of sympathetic families in New York.

Late in January, in one of the confrontations between strikers, state militia, and police, Anna Lo Pizzo, a striker, was killed, probably by a policeman's stray bullet. A week later both Joe Ettor and Arturo Giovannitti were arrested for her murder, charged as accessories before the fact on the grounds that their speeches had incited the violence that led to the shooting.

But the intention to deprive the strike of its leaders failed, as Elizabeth Gurley Flynn and Bill Haywood took over. The Lawrence strike was drawing wide and favorable publicity. The Lawrence children, skinny and shabby, marched up Fifth Avenue, exciting enormous sympathy and drawing famous journalists to Lawrence. Lincoln Steffens and William Allen White made the journey, as did Mary Heaton Vorse, reporting for *Harper's*. The House Rules Committee in Washington began hearings on conditions in Lawrence. In March the strike was settled to the satisfaction of the strikers and the IWW. Ettor and Giovannitti were not released, however, but remained in jail awaiting trial. Because Bill Haywood had left Lawrence, fearing arrest under an indictment for conspiracy, Giovannitti suggested that Carlo Tresca be called to the city to organize the workers for the defense. He came at once, "like a Mohammedan to Mecca." When the train conductor called out the Lawrence station, "my heart began to palpitate like the engine of a great electric generator."

On May 1, 1912, Tresca descended from the train in Lawrence and entered into the mainstream of American radicalism. That same day Elizabeth Gurley Flynn saw him for the first time, "a very important event for me then," she would write, "and one destined to have far-reaching consequences in my life." In the days that followed she observed that he was "very resourceful, a good strategist . . . an eloquent and dynamic speaker . . . a powerful agitator."

Tresca was quite sophisticated about techniques of agitation, which were "different from organization work which is methodical, slow and quiet. Agitation is done in the open . . . with the intelligent and full use of individual and mass emotions stirred up by deeds and words, capable of creating strong passions of hatred, sympathy, love and anger." He spoke little English as yet. Flynn noted that when he was presented with a problem, his response was "I fix." So he became known as an agitator and a fixer and also, as a newspaper called him, as "The Bull of Lawrence."

As Tresca saw it, there were two aspects to his job at Lawrence. He must find witnesses who would counter the prosecution testimony that Ettor and Giovannitti had incited violence and also persuade prosecution witnesses to change their testimony. In addition, the threat of another strike must hang over the city should Ettor and Giovannitti be convicted. To this end the workers, who had returned to their jobs, had to remain mobilized: "I had to find . . . some emotional motive that would induce thousands of workers into the streets." In defiance of a police ban, Tresca led ten thousand workers to the Lawrence Common, where he demanded an oath. "You must swear," he cried, "to fight every day, every minute of your lives, without truce or repose, for the liberation of Ettor and Giovannitti." Ten thousand Italians answered, "*Giuriamo!*" We swear!

For Anna Lo Pizzo, buried months earlier, he organized a funeral march, and two weeks later, a second. When he felt that yet a third funeral march might push passion toward indifference, he hired a train to carry workers to Boston, where Bill Haywood was waiting. The round-trip tickets were printed with red IWW initials, with Tresca's signature on the back of each.

Tresca had not yet met Bill Haywood. When the train arrived in Boston and he saw the workers "frantic with joy" at the sight of Haywood, Tresca's admiration for the man was mixed with jealousy. But Haywood placed an arm around his shoulders, and Tresca was content, at least for the moment, to be a protégé.

The agitation and the demonstrations continued throughout the summer. Haywood returned to Lawrence, although he, Tresca, and Flynn were under constant threat of arrest. Each night they slept in the houses of workers, changing houses constantly, and protected by a bodyguard of young Italian workers. During the day they moved around the city. Mary Heaton Vorse watched one day as Tresca was seized by the police; at once a line of workers formed a flying tackle to push him through police lines to safety.

Serious as circumstances were, gaiety was not precluded. One night Vorse, Haywood, Tresca, and Flynn went to dinner at Rosa Candello's house. Police and hoodlums were prowling the streets looking for them, but the guests brought spaghetti and wine, Rosa cooked, and everyone had a good time. Flynn missed her son. She convinced her mother to bring two-year-old Buster up from New York.

On September 30, eight months after their arrest, the trial of Ettor and Giovannitti opened in Salem, Massachusetts. The mills in Lawrence were dead that day in a warning strike, and sympathetic strikes took place in industrial towns as far away as Ohio. In preparing for the trial, Tresca had worked with Fred Moore, one of the defense lawyers (whom, eight years later, he would ask to defend Sacco and Vanzetti), and he had rehearsed defense witnesses and probably suborned testimony as well. He persuaded one prosecution witness not to testify in exchange for ending a boycott on his saloon. Since the testimony of the strikers themselves would be suspect, he found a respectable Italian doctor to recall speeches Ettor and Giovannitti probably never made. Late in November, Ettor and Giovannitti were found not guilty of murder; they returned to Lawrence for a final demonstration of twenty thousand workers organized by Tresca.

Tresca had been away from home for seven months when the Lawrence events ended. He may have returned for brief visits during that time, although Beatrice thinks not. But toward the end of November all the principles were preparing to leave the city: Bill Haywood on a lecture tour for the *International Socialist Review;* Joe Ettor to New York where three thousand Wobblies would carry him in triumph down Fifth Avenue. Elizabeth Gurley Flynn, too, was going home to New York. Tresca was going back to New Kensington, but this could not have been a happy prospect.

During the summer and fall of 1912 Carlo and Elizabeth had fallen in love. The progress of their affair can be followed in the edition of D'Annunzio's *The Maidens of the Rocks,* which Carlo presented to Elizabeth, inscribing it first, "For Fellow Worker E. G. Flynn." Later he added another inscription: "Sometimes this book will capture your heart for love. Remember at this times your best love." And, on November 24, as the day when they would separate approached, he added, "Enter into the garden of my heart Elisabetta."

For her part, either at Lawrence or a little later, Elizabeth gave him a tiny paper edition of *Sonnets from the Portuguese* in which she underlined certain passages: "was caught up into love and taught the whole of life in a new rhythm. . . . Before thy saving kiss! My own, my own / Who camest to me when the world was gone."

Carlo spent Christmas with Helga and Beatrice in New Kensington. The misery in the house must have been palpable. Just before the new year, Carlo received a telegram from Vincent St. John asking him to take charge of a textile strike in Little Falls, New York. When that strike was over, St. John wired, "You are wanted in New York Hotel Workers on Strike."

In his memoir Tresca put the best face on his move to New York. For the first and only time he refers to the fact that he had a family: "duty to his family . . . the urgent appeal of persons whom he loves or is loved by, all other considerations that are in his life important and imperative are set aside by any good fighter. . . . Even if I wanted to, it would have been impossible for me to overcome the desire to be in the tumultuous streets of New York."

Even had he wanted to, but he did not want to, and he never again returned home.

Helga took Beatrice to Philadelphia, and then to New York, where she got a job in an Italian delicatessen on Fortieth Street and Third Avenue. She took a furnished room for herself and Beatrice across the street. In May 1913 she filed a petition for divorce on the grounds of desertion and nonsupport. Carlo filed a countersuit the following year for divorce and for custody of Beatrice on the grounds that Helga was unfit to care for the child because she was living with a man not her husband. It was a foolish move in the circumstances; while it was true that Helga had formed an alliance with a waiter, Tullio Belotti, she proceeded to file a second divorce suit charging adultery, naming Elizabeth Gurley Flynn as corespondent. She also charged Carlo with brutality.

Helga sent Beatrice out of the city. There was too much unpleasantness. Carlo came to see the child sometimes, but visits always resulted in a fight with Helga, usually about money. He was supposed to pay four dollars a week in child support, but he often did not, or could not. For a year Beatrice lived on Long Island with a French-Swiss couple. When she returned to the city in 1916 the three-year legal battle between her mother and father was settled. Helga had been refused a divorce on a technicality; Carlo had lost his suit for custody and divorce. They remained legally married until 1942.

Beatrice lived with Helga and Tullio Belotti in an apartment on West Forty-third Street, Carlo with Elizabeth and her family at 511 East 134th Street in the Bronx. On occasion Helga dressed Beatrice in her best clothes and sent her uptown to visit her father. Beatrice enjoyed these visits. The Flynn household was always festive and full of people—Elizabeth, her sisters Kathie and Bina, her brother Tom, her parents Thomas and Annie Gurley, and Buster, Elizabeth's son, who was four years younger than Beatrice. There were also visitors like Emma Goldman and Alexander Berkman to make a fuss over her.

Many years later Carlo remarked to Beatrice that he never understood her mother. Had Helga been patient he would have returned. She was, after all, his wife and he had not married anyone else.

Chapter 4
Elizabeth Gurley Flynn

Elizabeth Gurley Flynn, born in 1890 in New Hampshire, was the oldest of Thomas and Annie Gurley Flynn's four children. Her father was an itinerant civil engineer and a socialist, her mother a professional tailor and a feminist. By 1900 Annie Gurley, tired of dragging her family around the country after her husband, took the children to New York and settled with them in the South Bronx, where her husband came and went as his work took him. For twenty-seven years the Flynns lived at 511 East 134th Street, in a sunny cold water flat overlooking the Harlem River.

In an early school photograph taken just after the turn of the century, Elizabeth is shown to be a plump and prim serious child. But by the age of seventeen, when Alfred Stieglitz photographed her, seriousness had been transformed into tender gravity, and she is ethereally slender. By that time she was an accomplished public speaker. At the debating society of her grammar school, she had practiced the techniques she heard at the Sunday night socialist forums to which her parents took her. She had read *Looking Backward, The News from Nowhere,* and Kropotkin's pamphlets. At the Harlem Socialist club in 1906 she delivered her first public speech: "What Socialism Will Do for Women." She was soon being asked to speak in Newark, Philadelphia, and Boston. In August 1907, a reporter for the *Philadelphia Bulletin* noted that "she has an odd manner of making what might be called short-hand gestures, pothooks, curves, dots and dashes written in the air." The *New York World* found her "gifted with a quick brain and a facile oratory . . . the divine fire of a cause gleams like a beacon-light." She was something to see as well as hear, an oddity among soapbox speakers, who were usually men with foreign accents, if they spoke English at all. In 1906 Elizabeth stood on a soapbox in Rutgers Square, her long black hair tied back, wearing a white shirtwaist and a red tie, with a placard behind her: "Socialism in Our Time. Labor is Entitled to EVERYTHING it Produces. Workers of the World Unite."

Flynn left school to join the IWW in 1906 and began traveling for them, making speeches on behalf of Bill Haywood, who was imprisoned on a murder charge in Idaho, and getting her first taste of a strike in Bridgeport, Connecticut. "An East Side Joan of Arc," Theodore Dreiser called her in *Broadway Magazine* in September 1906, "she is only a girl, just turned sixteen, as sweet a sixteen as ever bloomed, with a sensitive flower-like face. . . . She has been reared in the shadow of the red flag of the proletariat."

The Joan of Arc tag stuck to Elizabeth during her youth; everyone responded to its implications of impassioned cause, innocence, promise of martyrdom, and inviolability of spirit and body. "Gurley is as safe with us as if she was in God's pocket," said the Wobblies she traveled with. When the anarchist Hippolyte Havel got drunk one night and proposed something earthy, Alexander Berkman kicked him under the table. What the hell's the matter with you Sasha, Havel protested, I'm not doing anything! David Belasco wanted to make her into an actress. She was indignant. I don't want to be an actress, she told him. I'm in the labor movement and I speak my own piece.

In 1907 Flynn attended the IWW convention in Chicago where she met Jack Archibald Jones, a miner from Minnesota. He asked her to come to the Iron Range to speak; she went, in the dead of winter, speaking in meeting halls in Hibbing and Biwabik, to miners huddled around red-hot stoves. Then she married Jack Jones. "Elizabeth fell in love with the west and the miners," Vincent St. John said. "She married the first one she met."

The marriage took place in January 1908. Annie Gurley had strong objections: Elizabeth was too young, and Annie Gurley knew very well how a woman's life was transformed by marriage and children. And by summer 1908, Elizabeth was pregnant. The baby, a boy, was born in the back room of a Chicago boardinghouse. He lived long enough to be named John Vincent for the IWW's general organizer, Vincent St. John, before he died that same night. Things did not go well between Elizabeth and Jack Jones after that, and by the next summer she was glad to leave for a speaking tour of the West Coast. She and Jones were apart until the fall when, wearing an outfit that included a large sombrero and a red neckerchief, she joined him in Missoula, Montana, for an IWW free speech fight. She was pregnant again when she left him to go to Spokane, Washington, for another free speech fight. And although she was arrested three times in Spokane and spent nights in a filthy jail, Jones did not come down from Missoula to see her.

Temperamentally Elizabeth and Jack Jones were badly matched. "He drove me nearly crazy in Chicago" with a complicated system of wheels and charts Jones was trying to work out; "I was high spirited and headstrong," Elizabeth wrote. Jones was also jealous of his wife. He was particularly jealous of her relationship with the IWW lawyer Fred Moore, who was with her in Spokane. Eventually Jones came to Spokane and proposed that Elizabeth should come to Butte and settle down to domestic life with him there.

She said no. She was nineteen years old and flush with her own power. She was convinced that Jones was not equal to her. "I don't love him anymore," she told her father a few months later. "Besides, he *bores* me."

But Elizabeth was going to have a baby. She took the train East and went home to her family, where, on May 19, 1910, she gave birth to a boy she named Fred. The family called him Buster. He was Buster Flynn, never Jones, and he was raised by Flynn women, as much Annie Gurley's and Kathie's child as Elizabeth's.

For the next two years Flynn lived the life of an IWW "jaw-smith." She traveled on her own to hostile areas of the country, arriving at her destination late at night. In a strange small town she would make her way to the house of a Wobbly, knock on the door, and announce, "I'm Gurley. St. John sent me." Later when she thought back on those days, she felt there had never again been anything like the ease of comradeship she found in those early years of the IWW.

Chapter 5
Carlo and Elizabeth

"CARLO Tresca moved his paper to New York City," Elizabeth Gurley Flynn recalled in her memoir. "He was then a tall, slender handsome man in his mid-thirties and I was deeply in love with him." Flynn was then twenty-two, as lovely as Tresca was handsome, as gifted a rabble-rouser as he, as profoundly political a being. For the next twelve years people spoke of Carlo and Gurley, Gurley and Carlo; one name was seldom heard without the other.

It was early in 1913 when Tresca moved to New York, a time radicals would look back on as "a brief paradise," or so Max Eastman recalled it. No one, Eastman wrote, could yet conceive of the world war so near at hand, of Bolshevism and fascism which would shortly follow that "protected little historic moment. . . . We were children reared in a kindergarten." Or, as Lillian Symes wrote, there were few intelligent Americans under the age of forty "who did not profess some form of heterodoxy. To be a socialist, a syndicalist, an anarchist, a feminist . . . was merely to be in tune."

More than one thousand socialists held political office in 1911. Emma Goldman was the most popular lecturer in the country. Eugene Debs polled almost a million votes in the 1912 election. It seemed more than possible that the insurgency in the air would become the solid shape of the future. Tresca plunged directly into New York life. He found an office for *L'Avvenire* in Italian Harlem. The hotel workers' strike was in progress and Gurley was already involved.

At Bryant Hall, where the socialist Jacob Panken urged the strikers to register their grievances at the ballot box, Tresca stood up on a chair. What is this? he called. A strike or a course of lectures? Follow me! The strikers followed him out to Broadway, blocking traffic and smashing windows at the McAlpin and Knickerbocker hotels. "Striking Waiters Storm the Hotels," the *New York Times* reported on January 24, 1913. "Carlo Tresca, agitator for the Industrial Workers of the World was in charge of the demonstration." The next day two strikebreakers were beaten and a dozen strikers, "including Carlo Tresca," arrested. "Many Italians . . . led by Carlo Tresca . . . ran from Bryant Hall to aid . . . the rioters. . . . Earlier in the afternoon 1,000 strikers paraded up Fifth Avenue led by a woman said to be Miss Elizabeth Gurley Flynn."

"Kill the cops! Kill the cops!" someone shouted, the *New York World* reported. "The police thought the voice was Tresca's so swinging their clubs they charged that part of the mob where he stood with Miss Flynn. Both Tresca and Miss Flynn were struck. The girl . . . across the right hand which nearly paralyzed her arm. . . . Tresca got a severe clubbing."

"I am with the downtrodden every time," Flynn told a reporter who asked her to account for her success in holding together a strike of four thousand Italians, Greeks, and Germans. "And I am able to show these people a way out of the difficulties. Is it any wonder they stick to me?"

Tresca was arrested, taken to the police station, and searched for weapons. In his torn vest pocket, the police found the copy of *Sonnets from the Portuguese* tenderly inscribed by Flynn. The papers began to call them the trade union lovers. A month later the trade union lovers were in Paterson, New Jersey.

The Paterson strike promised to be another Lawrence. Twenty-five thousand silk workers closed the mills on February 25, 1913, in protest against low pay, long hours, and a technological speedup. The AFL's United Textile Workers insisted that the speedup was technological progress and refused to lead the strike. "Instead," wrote John Fitch in the June 7, 1913, issue of *Survey* magazine, "came Haywood, Elizabeth Flynn, Quinlan and Tresca—empty-handed, with neither money nor credit nor with the prestige of a 2,000,000 membership, but willing to work and go to jail."

The IWW poured all its resources into the strike. Sixty years later a woman who had been a seventeen-year-old silk worker at the time remembered: "Haywood! That voice. He filled the whole hall with his voice. And Gurley Flynn. She was beautiful. Tresca, so good-looking, so nice. We were all in love with him. Beautiful people. They were so wonderful. They gave us hope. They just made us feel as if we were going to change the world." The women were on the picket lines every day; they were charged by mounted police and beaten, but they listened to their leaders and went back to the line again and again.

Paterson's proximity to New York brought out the cultural radicals. Max Eastman came to a Sunday meeting at the nearby town of Haledon, where he heard Haywood, Flynn, and Tresca speak to strikers picnicking in the fields. Of Tresca's speech, which "took possession of all outdoors as an organ does a church," Eastman understood only a few words: "Occhio per occhio, dente per dente, sangue per sangue!"

John Reed went to Paterson to report the strike for the *Masses*. He was arrested and pushed into a cell with a tall Italian who, with difficulty, was trying to explain class war to a Negro prisoner. That night the strikers in the jail took up a chant:

> Do you like Miss Flynn?
> Yes, Yes, Yes, Yes!
> Do you like Carlo Tresca?
> Yes, Yes, Yes, Yes!
> Do you like Mayor McBride?
> No! No! No! No!

The Paterson strike was slowly starved out. It lasted through the winter with only the barest trickle of money coming in to support the workers. Men walked the picket lines with paper bags on their feet in place of shoes. Flynn visited the homes of women who had nothing to feed their children. The Socialist party, which could have poured money into Paterson, was instead heady with the election victories of 1912. The party had decided that the IWW was not a fitting ally. The IWW scorned electoral politics; it advocated direct action, which included sabotage and violence—not a program to enhance Socialist electoral changes. The party expelled Bill Haywood in 1912.

Accusations of sabotage and violence were made against the IWW throughout the years of its existence. In fact, for all the rhetorical violence, there was little documented violence by workers. Apart from self-defense against the police, the most violent thing a worker could do, Bill Haywood told strikers, was to fold his arms: "We have a new kind of violence, the havoc we play with money by laying down our tools." "I don't say violence should *not* be used," Flynn wrote, but "in the Paterson strike, for the first four months, there wasn't a single scab in the mills. . . . Now where any violence should be used against non-existent scabs passes my understanding. Mass action is far more up-to-date. . . . Mass action means that the workers withdraw their labor power . . . cut off the means of life, the breath of life of the employers. . . . That doesn't mean that violence shouldn't be used in self-defense. Strikers don't need to be told that . . . men and women who go out as strike agitators should only advocate violence when they are absolutely certain that it is going to do some good other than to spill the blood of the innocent workers on the streets of the cities."

With the Paterson strike in deep trouble, the idea of the pageant was conceived. Mabel Dodge, who liked to gather "dangerous characters" in her salon, among whom she was proudest of Haywood, later claimed credit for the idea. Flynn disliked Dodge so much that she refused to remember whether Dodge had any hand in it. "Yes," she wrote to a friend many years later, "I remember that horrible rich woman, Mrs. Dodge. She patronized all of the poor folks in Paterson insufferably. Was crazy about Jack Reed and other celebrities." As it turned out, Flynn had few good words to say about the pageant either.

The pageant was held on the night of June 7, 1913. Early in the day, twelve hundred strikers, who had been rehearsed by John Reed, ferried over from Paterson and marched up Fifth Avenue, Tresca and Flynn with them. As night fell, red electric lights spelling out the letters IWW blazed out over Madison Square Garden.

The Garden was filled to its capacity of fifteen thousand when the pageant began. But most of the expensive tickets, those that were to be sold for $1.50 to make some profit for the strike, had not found buyers; tickets not given away were sold for fifty cents. The pageant had cost an enormous amount to stage; Madison Square Garden had been expensive to rent. At one point it seemed

that the whole project would have to be abandoned until the New
York silk workers advanced six hundred dollars to see it through.
Still, the organizers thought that the spectacle itself, and the pub-
licity it generated, would stimulate donations for the strike.

According to all accounts the Paterson pageant was a magnificent spectacle. A painted backdrop of a silk mill, two hundred feet
wide, stretched across the stage. Its windows showed bright in
early morning dusk. The workers began to gather at the entrance,
old men, young children, women, walking slowly and sadly into
the mill. The work whistle blew. The whirring sound of the looms
began. Then, suddenly, the looms died. The workers rushed from
the mills, shouting and dancing. The notes of the "Marseillaise"
were heard. The strike had begun.

The pageant was a reenactment of the Paterson strike: picket
lines formed, police clubbed and arrested workers, a striker was
killed by gunshot, his funeral procession was accompanied by the
"Death March." Tresca appeared, to reenact his "Blood for blood"
speech. Mass meetings were held. Flynn led a May Day parade. At
last the strikers met to legislate the strike's outcome, and once
more listened to the words of Tresca, Flynn, and Haywood.

The audience was thrilled, moved to tears and cheers. But,
Flynn said a year later, "I consider that the pageant marked the
climax in the Paterson strike and started the decline in the Paterson
strike." She enumerated the reasons: the workers had been dis-
tracted for weeks, and while they rehearsed for the pageant, the
first scabs got into the Paterson mills. Then, "This thing that had
been heralded as the salvation of the strike, this thing that was
going to bring thousands of dollars to the strike—$150 came to
Paterson. . . . Bread was the need of the hour, and bread was not
forthcoming."

The Paterson mill owners offered the hungry workers a shop-
by-shop settlement, and with no money and with proclamations in
the local Socialist paper that "industrial action had failed," the
strike was broken. By July 29, those strikers who had not been
blacklisted were back in the mills under the same conditions in
which they had left them. "Humiliation," mourned Dominic Mignone, a Paterson worker, sixty years later. "We lost our fight. . . .
Broken hearted, broken hearted because we lost our goal. Our
goal was to win the strike, see, to have one union throughout the

world, but we lost. . . . The strike had no money . . . the union didn't pay the rent . . . winter time was approaching. . . . So we lost, just hard luck, that's all, hard luck."

When she spoke of the strike a year later, Flynn referred to the "dilettante element who figured so prominently, but would have abandoned [the pageant] at the last moment had not the silk workers advanced $600 to pull it through."

Soon after the pageant John Reed and Mabel Dodge left for Europe to officially begin their famous love affair. Bill Haywood, who was ill, also went to Europe and then to Provincetown for a rest. Carlo and Elizabeth remained in New York, both under indictment on charges arising from the strike. The IWW had lost the prestige in Paterson that it had won at Lawrence.

Chapter 6
Before the War

O N a winter night during 1914, a number of people gathered at
Mary Heaton Vorse's little pink brick house in Greenwich Village. It was an unusually cold winter: "The snow never stopped
falling," Vorse recalled. "The breadlines by the Vienna bakery on
Broadway near Grace Church grew longer nightly. The city was
full of shelterless men."

In the city that winter more than a quarter of a million people
were without jobs, and the IWW was leading the unemployed in
marches on the churches to demand shelter there. According to
the Bureau of Investigation, which now began to keep track of
Carlo Tresca's activities, "demonstrations were staged throughout New York city by the subject and his companions." At the
meeting in Union Square, Tresca exhorted the jobless. He later remembered his words: he told them that men have become like
sheep in organized society. They have lost even their will to survive. If you were not sheep, he said, if you were wolves, you would
not be begging for charity. You would go to the places where food
and clothing were stored and take what you need!

In response to language like this, the *New York Times* demanded
that offenses against property and law and order be met by "a few
determined police . . . with heavy clubs," which was the police response to meetings of the unemployed at Union Square and at
Rutgers Square. The group of people gathering at Mary Heaton
Vorse's house had come to organize a defense committee for those
arrested in the demonstrations.

Even apart from their purpose, they were an extraordinary

gathering: Elizabeth Gurley Flynn, Carlo Tresca and Bill Haywood, Emma Goldman and Alexander Berkman, Frances Perkins and John Collier, Ben Gitlow and Juliet Stuart Poyntz among them. There were already disagreements. Mary Vorse recalled that Flynn and Haywood were unhappy about the presence of some young anarchists, and Ben Gitlow wrote that Flynn "sharply" criticized Emma Goldman for disregarding IWW decisions. But in a few years events would sweep them apart, ideologies would harden, and even agreements such as those reached that night would become unthinkable.

Toward the middle of April many of the unemployed left the city to look for work in other parts of the country and Carlo and Elizabeth took a boat trip down the inland waterway to Tampa, where the cigar workers had invited them to speak. They both needed to rest. Elizabeth had suffered with bronchitis all winter; Carlo had had chronic stomach problems since being struck in the stomach by a policeman during the hotel workers' strike a year earlier. The trip did them good. They returned to New York early in May, just after the massacre of miners in Ludlow, Colorado.

The strike at the Rockefeller-controlled subsidiary of the Colorado Fuel and Iron Company had lasted for more than a year. John D. Rockefeller was determined to make the issue of union organization a principle. "We would rather," he said before the House Mines Committee on April 6, 1914, "that the unfortunate conditions should continue and that we should lose all the millions invested, than that American workmen should be deprived of their right, under the Constitution, to work for whom they please. That is the great principle at stake."

The miners, evicted from their company-owned houses, had set up a tent colony. On April 20, 1914, the state militia set fire to the encampment. Women and children died in their sleep, and the death toll rose to forty-seven in the next few days. The front page of *L'Avvenire* carried an illustration of a rifle, with the caption: "Italian miners of Colorado. Remember! This is the only and best citizenship you can carry in defense of your life and liberty."

Among the miners killed was a friend of Tresca's, Carlo Costa. His body contained twenty bullets when it was found, and his wife and three sons died in their tent. On May 1, Tresca spoke at a demonstration in Union Square. Tears came to his eyes, he wrote, and his voice trembled when he talked of Carlo Costa. "Name the murderer!" he demanded of his listeners. "Rockefeller!" angry voices answered, and calls for *vendetta* rang out.

At the end of May, Tresca was one of the organizers of a demonstration near the Rockefeller estate at Tarrytown. Refused a permit, he spoke anyway and was arrested. On the second day of the demonstration the meeting was broken up forcibly by police, and a young anarchist, Arthur Caron, was badly clubbed. Later in June, at another meeting, Caron was stoned as he stood on the platform. Three weeks later, on July 4, Tresca read in the papers that a bomb had exploded in a Harlem tenement, killing Caron and two other men as they were in the process of assembling it. When reporters questioned Tresca, he told them that he had known Caron well, that Caron had told him that he wanted to kill Rockefeller. He may or may not have added, as was reported, that he believed Caron to be justified in what he was planning.

The issue of Caron proved divisive. Bill Haywood and Joe Ettor quickly announced that Caron had no connection with the IWW. On July 5, on *L'Avvenire* letterhead, Flynn wrote to Mary Vorse who had gone to Provincetown for the summer: "It is all very terrible and everybody is busy here repudiating the poor boys although no connection was actually established between them and the bomb or dynamite. Even if they were responsible, the terrible treatment Caron received at the hands of the police, plus his personal suffering is responsible for his psychology."

Flynn went on to speculate about a possible agent provocateur, but this was disingenuous. Tresca knew Caron had been responsible for the bomb, and he made no excuses for him. Elizabeth was concerned that if a connection could be made between Carlo and Caron, Carlo might be deported. She wanted to get him out of the city. "Carlo is suffering very much lately with stomach trouble," she continued, "and I am so anxious to get him away for a change . . . you know he is *hot headed* and requires ballast just now. He is almost a nervous wreck over this tragedy. He knew them all, whereas I don't remember one."

Tresca refused to leave New York. The anarchists wanted to organize a memorial demonstration for Caron, and the IWW was refusing to participate. Tresca, who had never formally joined the IWW, now saw his position as a connecting link between the anarchists and the IWW, and he felt it was crucial for him to resolve this difference.

A meeting was held at Mary Vorse's house, with Tresca arguing that the IWW and the anarchists had acted together in organizing the unemployment demonstrations of the previous winter. Now another dimension had been added to the alliance, but this was no reason to break solidarity, Tresca said.

The room was filled with Wobblies. John Reed and Lincoln Steffens were present, but the argument was between Tresca and Haywood. There exists only Tresca's version of the event, but it foretells the split between them that would occur two years later. Haywood argued that the IWW could not afford to countenance the propaganda of the deed, the individual acts of violence which were a tenet of anarchist thought. Confident that his influence would prevail, he asked for a vote. According to Tresca, the vote went against Haywood: "We'll do as Carlo says."

"A dead silence followed," Tresca wrote later. "Bill was pale. The lines on his face deepened. . . . For the first time in our relationship I was no longer his lieutenant but his equal. Then in a voice I'll never forget, he said, 'It's settled boys.'"

Caron's memorial demonstration was held in Union Square. Flynn wrote to Mary Vorse,

> I felt it would be a disgrace for all of us to remain silent after Ettor's repudiation of Caron . . . I wanted to strike the keynote that Caron had not been proven guilty of anything and possibly was not the responsible person. . . . But Saturday made me decide never to speak with the anarchists again. They insisted on speaking one after the other until we were completely exhausted [in the hot sun] . . . shouting "We believe in dynamite" until instead of a dignified memorial meeting it became hysterical proclamations of personal opinions . . . they had such a unique opportunity to fix the full responsibility on society as it is and give an inspiring and sympathetic presentation of their principles. . . . Of course all arrangements made are by Berkman . . . the rest of the anarchist boys and girls are expected to hustle and keep quiet.

Tresca and Berkman had worked closely together, but Flynn's letter said nothing of Carlo's role. Only again that "Carlo is suffering very much from stomach trouble and I am hoping he will be ready to go to Provincetown by August 1st. . . . I am going to Philadelphia for a week. . . . I must earn a few dollars to help Carlo out, otherwise I'm afraid he'll never be free to go. He is having such a hard struggle and so many people have enlisted as regular retainers [at *L'Avvenire*] that he is bled systematically."

Whatever political differences existed between Carlo and Elizabeth, she had no heart to make anything of them for a long time to
come. For Haywood, however, it seems that a gauntlet had been
thrown down.

In 1915 Tresca moved the office of *L'Avvenire* from East Harlem
to Lafayette Street in downtown Little Italy. In March he attended
Emma Goldman's Red Revel, a celebration of the tenth anniversary of *Mother Earth,* where those "of red revolutionary blood"
were invited to celebrate an evening's holiday from the war in
Europe and the capitulation to it of European radicals.

Also during that year Tresca was active in the defense of Joe
Hill; he attended a demonstration on behalf of Margaret Sanger
who was on trial; he called for a general strike in protest against
the war in Europe. At a Philadelphia meeting where he spoke
against the war, thousands of Italian immigrants, charging that
the IWW and the Socialist party were attempting to prevent patriotic reservists from returning to Italy to fight, demonstrated
against him; some of the seven hundred reservists who sailed for
Italy on the S.S. *Ancoma* in July 1915 complained to authorities
that Tresca had tried to bribe them with twenty dollar bills to remain. On April 3, 1915, Tresca told a reporter from the *Morning
World* that two men who had been convicted of placing a bomb in
Saint Patrick's Cathedral were innocent. "If these defendants are
guilty I want to see them convicted. I believe in violence," he said,
"but only in violence when it advances the cause of labor."

Flynn went on a cross-country tour for the IWW in April 1915,
stopping in Salt Lake City to see Joe Hill in a jail there. In September she and Tresca were in Paterson, where police evicted them
forcibly from town. They were also refused entrance to Bayonne
when they arrived in that city to take part in a strike at the Standard Oil plant. In November, through her rich and influential
friends J. Sargeant and Edith Cram, a meeting was arranged between Flynn and Pres. Woodrow Wilson. Flynn urged Wilson to
intervene in the Joe Hill case. Before Hill was executed by firing
squad eight days later, he wrote the poem "The Rebel Girl," inspired by her visit. He wired her, "And now Goodby, Gurley dear,
I have lived like a rebel and I shall die like a rebel."

Chapter 7
Mesabi

IN late winter of 1916, Tresca and Flynn went on the road for the IWW, Tresca to California and Flynn on an eight-state tour of the Midwest. In the cities where she stopped Flynn said, again and again, "Let those who own the country, who are howling and profiting by preparedness, fight to defend their property. . . . It is better to be a traitor to your country than a traitor to your class."

In April she was back on the Mesabi Iron Range, the scene of her romance with Jack Jones eight years earlier. She had kept a romantic feeling for the fierceness of that glacier-carved landscape, its "wild desolate beauty." In later years she would locate at Mesabi much of the glory and sorrow of her youth.

Flynn toured the Range towns that April. The miners were Montenegrins, Bulgarians, Croatians, Finns, and Italians, many of them imported as strikebreakers nine years earlier to break the hold of the Western Federation of Miners. Although war orders poured into the Oliver Mining Company, miners still worked in the wet and cold, on a piecework system, and under a hiring system controlled by foremen who sold the most desirable locations— for money, beer, sexual favors from wives and daughters. Wages had not risen. The miners, paid once a month, were entirely dependent on the company that owned their houses and the railroads. Flynn urged them to organize.

On June 4, two months after she left the Range, a strike broke out in the town of Aurora. The men complained of short measure: a miner had filled eighty cars with ore, but was paid only for sixty.

The strike spread to sixteen thousand miners over the breadth of the Range, and the Oliver Mining Company responded by hiring private police to work with the local sheriffs. The miners called them "plug-uglies." They were men recruited from the slums of Chicago and Minneapolis. "They were pretty husky guys, every one of them was over six foot tall, fat and ugly looking," a miner named George Andreytchin later testified. "I mean they were men who would not spare a human life when they were given orders. . . . They tried to intimidate us by stopping our meetings, our parades. . . . Then later they shot one man. . . . I knew that man well; he was a member of the IWW, and he had a wife and two children. His name was John Alar."

It was mid-June when Alar was shot. Tresca had arrived on the Range with Sam Scarlett, Joseph Schmidt, and James Gilday, the other IWW organizers, shortly before the shooting. He at once wrote to Haywood asking for reinforcements. On June 24, Haywood replied that he was sending Frank Little out from Chicago that night. On June 26, three thousand miners followed Alar's coffin to the cemetery. When no priest could be found to perform the burial service, Tresca spoke over the grave. There were reporters present who could not understand Italian. But then Tresca raised his hand and, in English, he said, "Fellow workers, swear with me: I solemnly swear that if any Oliver gunman shoots or wounds any miner, we will take an eye for an eye, a tooth for a tooth, blood for blood."

From the day of Alar's funeral until July 3, Tresca was apparently able to move around the Range freely. The mood was ugly, the Range swarmed with gunmen, but the strike continued without incident. On the morning of July 3, he left the town of Hibbing, accompanied by a local lawyer, a driver, and two other men and headed for Grand Rapids, Minnesota, where the miner George Andreytchin was in jail. Andreytchin had turned out to be a valuable organizer, and Tresca hoped to negotiate his release by threatening disorder among the strikers. He was unsuccessful, however, and as he and his companions left town they were followed by five cars filled with armed deputies. At the mining town of Mishaevaka, a column of armed plug-uglies lined each side of the road, waiting for them. Calls of Damned foreigner! Agitator! rang out. It's a lynching party said the lawyer. Confrontation,

Tresca knew, was sometimes an effective tactic. He got out of the car and walked slowly down the road between the lines of gunmen, somehow reaching the end of the town without incident.

Back in Hibbing he learned that in the town of Biwabik, a deputy sheriff and an innocent bystander had been killed and that a miner, Philip Masonovich, his family and boarders, had been taken to jail. The day had promised trouble from the beginning. At three o'clock that morning Tresca was wakened by shouts outside his hotel. Searchlights played into the windows. Together with Frank Little, James Gilday, Sam Scarlett, and four strikers, Tresca was handcuffed, taken to the railroad station, and put aboard a railroad car for Duluth. All the organizers were charged with being accessories to the murders in Biwabik.

Flynn's arrival on the Range was announced by the *Duluth Labor World:* "Elizabeth Gurley Flynn, the most feared woman in the whole of the Corporation world, is now in the Hibbing district." She and Joe Ettor, sent by Haywood to take charge of the now leaderless strike, arrived in mid-July. On July 24 she wrote to Mary Vorse:

> [I] am surprised you didn't know what a terrific struggle Carlo and I are now in. . . . Carlo, Joe Schmidt and nine others are in jail here in Duluth since July 3, charged with first degree murder. It is terribly serious. They are concentrating the fight on Carlo—as the brains of the crowd etc. Mary dear, there never was a time when we needed our writer friends to get busy more than right now. . . .
>
> There are 16,000 iron ore miners on strike. . . . Conditions are frightful. . . . The Range is covered with gunmen (plug uglies) armed with clubs and Winchesters. There are 3,000 here now, paid by the companies and deputized by the Sheriff. . . . Carlo and the boys are in over a case in Biwabik, Minn. where four deputies entered a striker's home without a warrant and attempted to arrest him. His wife objected and they clubbed her into insensibility. The husband and three boarders (Montenegrins) jumped to her defense and in the fracas a deputy, Myron, and a strikers' sympathizer sitting on a pop wagon outside the door were killed. No guns were in the crowd but the deputies, and an eleven year old son testified that he saw the mine guard Nick Dillon (ex-bouncer for a disorderly house) fire directly at the man on the wagon. The boarders were all shot and lay in jail wounded for days. The woman had to be taken to the hospital. The [IWW] speakers were at once arrested, charged with murder, on the theory that the speeches incited to violence. It is like the Lawrence case, and Ettor and

Giovanitti case, except that in this State accessories are guilty in the first
degree and liable to life imprisonment. . . .

The cases will be very costly too; we have a fine lawyer and a good
fighter, Mayor Powers of Hibbing for Carlo, and two other lawyers for the
rest. Judge Hilton will come for the trials. . . .

I do hope you can come. Wish Jack Reed would take it up too. Where is
Steffens? Carlo particularly inquired for him.

Mary Vorse arrived on the Range sometime in August, with
assignments from *Harper's,* the *Globe,* and the *Masses.* She was
shocked by her friend's visible exhaustion. Elizabeth, afraid to take
a room in a hotel, had gotten what sleep she could at the homes of
the strikers. Mary Vorse took a room at the Fay Hotel in Virginia,
where Elizabeth joined her without signing the register; that night
the women drove out to a strike meeting at Aurora. "Violence
seemed to be in the air," Vorse wrote. "The landscape is violent,
the seasons are violent." From time to time they passed the gunmen sitting around small fires along the road. At the sound of the
car the men rose and "shoved their unshaven faces inside"; seeing
only well-dressed, respectable women, they allowed them to go on
their way.

But the strike was going badly. The arrest of the leaders and the
relentless intimidation by the gunmen were taking a toll. Flynn
traveled ceaselessly from one end of the Range to the other, but
she had little support. Vorse noted that it was strange that Haywood never came to the Range. He not only did not come when his
presence might have lent inspiration, but he was critical of everything that was done and slow to send money. Twice Flynn left the
Range for Chicago to try to straighten out finances.

Vorse visited Tresca in jail. "Dear Mary," he wrote afterward,
"When you was here to see me was a great day for me. I am very,
very much thankful to you. Your generosity toward us is without
limit and I do not see the way to repay it in part. You are the best
friend I have in America. I never forget you Mary! Write to me
when you have time and please send to me the magazine in which
you will arise your voice for the poor miners of Minnesota. Kiss
your beautiful children, and respect to you from Your devotedly,
Carlo Tresca."

Once a week on visiting day, Elizabeth went to the jail. Almost
twenty-five years later, when she was on the Range again and

everything had changed except the Range itself, she remembered
those visits:

> I pity the young thing I once was here
> Who suffered so from love—divided and disarmed
> . . . I would go weekly to the
> County Jail; he'd hold my hand & sometimes kiss me on the throat
> If guards turned away a moment.
> The pain and joy of those hot fleeting caresses would
> Last a whole week thru.

"Very glad to have a cheering letter from you," Tresca wrote to
Vorse when Flynn had left the Range to raise money. "I was awaiting you today to get some news. Tell Elizabeth to write to me. I am
anxious to hear from her. I am very glad she is out. I feel now
much relief. When she was here I can't sleep. My poor girl! Cheer
her up Mary dearest, please!"

He gave Elizabeth a photograph of himself at this time. On the
mounting he wrote, "To the women who have constantly inspired
me, who have spent in the trench of class war her time, her energy,
her youth to rescue me from the capitalist bastille." He also received a photograph from Filomena. News of his imprisonment
had spread to Italy, where posters describing the case appeared in
various cities. The Italian Socialist party condemned the imprisonment, and a formal protest was lodged with the foreign minister of
Italy. Filomena had herself pictured seated on a large chair, reading a copy of *L'Avvenire*. "Go on son," she wrote.

The strike on the Mesabi Range ended less than four months
after it began. For the moment, at least, nothing had been gained.
Mine owners had refused to negotiate with the IWW or with federal mediators sent from Washington. By vote of the strikers the
strike was called off. In a circular letter to "Fellow workers and
Friends," IWW organizer James Gilday wrote, "we felt it would be
unwise to continue the struggle throughout the terrible cold of
Minnesota winter with eviction staring us in the face. The best
union men would be driven out of the country and the field would
be left to the scabs. The strikers are determined to devote themselves to organizing for the future and to defending the prisoners."

Trial was set for the prisoners for mid-December, six months
after their arrest. Flynn had said that it was the Ettor-Giovannitti

case all over again, but unlike the circumstances at Lawrence there was now something amiss between Bill Haywood in Chicago and the organizers on the Range.

Bill Haywood had been present at the founding of the IWW in 1905, had been a part of its early successes in the West, of its first eastern victory at Lawrence, and at its defeat in Paterson. Only a few men could claim, with justice, that but for them there would be no IWW, and Haywood was one of them. There had been too little growth and many defeats for the IWW in recent years, and Haywood decided to reorganize. As it functioned thus far, the IWW was decentralized; local unions formulated their own policies and printed their own newspapers. Haywood now proposed to centralize leadership. He rented a three-story building at 1001 West Madison Street in Chicago, bought an expensive printing press, and ordered all local IWW papers moved to Chicago for more direct supervision. He also proposed to put the treasuries of the locals under central control.

These proposals met with strong protests from the local unions and from some of the best of the Wobbly organizers. If there were weaknesses in the loosely federated autonomous organization, they seemed a lesser evil than the dangers of one-man rule. Some of the best of the IWW leaders were dropping out. Vincent St. John, the Saint, once the IWW's general organizer and a man who commanded intense personal loyalty, had become virtually inactive by 1916; Joe Ettor was at Mesabi, but he too was talking about leaving. Haywood was meeting wide opposition for the first time and he did not like it.

Tresca's tendency to opposition was by now well established in Haywood's mind. As early as the Lawrence strike, when Tresca's admiration for Haywood was greatest, they had disagreed. Haywood had opposed the organizing of a particular demonstration, saying that Tresca was a fool for courting violence. But the march had taken place peacefully, and Haywood behaved with grace. "Haywood," Tresca wrote later, "was not the man to sulk when his advice proved wrong." But that was 1912. By 1914, Tresca perceived Haywood as "a tired, broken man. The Paterson strike had crushed him physically and morally." And following that there was the matter of the funeral demonstration for Arthur Caron and an emerging difference in ideas: "Haywood was not in much sympathy with the Anarchists. He was an orthodox syndicalist. . . . I disagreed with him violently and we argued often and heatedly."

The imprisonment of the Mesabi organizers generated wide protest. There had been demonstrations of protest in New York, in Pennsylvania, and in Italy where the Socialist party demanded a fair trial for Tresca. But money was needed on the Range. The IWW's 1916 convention allocated $5,000, but it was far from enough; the defense costs would add up to $32,000. Flynn discovered that although there was response to her appeals for money, the money sent to the Chicago office was not being forwarded to the Range. Twice she went down to Chicago to ask for the funds, but she was apparently not successful. She began to send out letters for donations to be sent to the Range directly, bypassing the Chicago office. To Haywood this might have seemed a deliberate attempt to undermine his leadership. Already obstructive in the matter of money, he also objected to the lawyer Vincent St. John recommended to Flynn. "It was," she wrote later, "a very unpleasant situation."

Flynn was worried. The growing war fever, she thought, would surely affect the outcome of the trial. "The Trust may send thousands of guns and millions of shells to the slaughter house of Europe—that is business," she told fifteen hundred miners at the Virginia Opera House in early December. "But make a speech in free America and you are charged with murder. . . . You can—if the fight in the courts fails—down your tools in protest! How many of you will say, 'We will close the mines till the doors swing out for Scarlett, Schmidt and Tresca?'"

In fact, the danger was not so great as she feared; the state believed it had a weak case. In October the U.S. attorney for Minnesota, Alfred Jaques, wrote the attorney general in Washington that "personally I am unable to see how the state can make out a case against Tresca. . . . There were wild times on the Range during the strike and of course very many violent things were done and feelings ran high. . . . The evidence is very incoherent. To me, the prosecution of Tresca for this assault and murder seems to be far-fetched and I do not think a conviction can be secured."

But the defendants knew nothing of this correspondence, so when the trial was less than a week off and the state proposed a deal, they were ready to entertain it. The authorities proposed to drop all charges against the IWW organizers and against Mrs. Masonovich; Philip Masonovich and the other miners would plead guilty to first degree manslaughter, and the state would guarantee them a sentence of not more than three years, with release after one year. As *Solidarity* reported on December 23, the deal was thoroughly discussed with the miners and was welcomed by them. The outcome of a trial might be much worse (although, as it turned out, the miners would serve three years in jail).

On December 30, *Solidarity* reported a "celebration on Mesaba" at the release of the organizers. No hint of any discord appeared in IWW publications. But according to Flynn and to Haywood in their separate accounts, Haywood was furious. He ordered Flynn, Joe Ettor, and Tresca to Chicago headquarters and demanded an explanation of why the miners had been allowed to plead guilty.

"Ettor and Flynn said it was the best that could be done," Haywood wrote. "I told Ettor in plain language that when he was being held for murder in Lawrence I would not have permitted him to plead guilty to anything, not even to spitting on the sidewalk. . . . I did not expect much from Tresca as he was not a member of the organization though he had done effective work during the Lawrence strike. . . . Ettor and Flynn had long been connected with the IWW and were earnest and vigorous workers. They should not have allowed themselves to be entrapped by lawyers who would rather 'fix' a case than try it." Their part in the affair terminated their connection with the IWW.

Flynn was equally angry. She suspected that her friendship with Vincent St. John, who still had a loyal following in the IWW, had "aggravated our relations with Haywood." She believed that only her independent solicitation of funds had staved off collapse of the defense campaign, and she objected to Haywood's instituting bureaucratic methods. "Haywood," she wrote, "blasted us publicly without even waiting for our explanation. The whole episode determined the official relations of Ettor and Tresca with the IWW. I stuck for a while longer, determined to prove to my fellow-workers that my loyalty and devotion could not be shaken by my relations with Haywood. But it wasn't easy, and it became increasingly difficult in the next few years after 1916."

Chapter 8
War and Repression

SIX-YEAR-OLD Buster Flynn was the first to spot Carlo and Elizabeth on their return to New York. He threw himself into Carlo's arms, crying out to Annie Gurley, "Mamma! Mamma! Carlo and my mother are home!"

Tresca and Flynn were exhausted after their six-month ordeal, but they entered into a round of celebrations. Thousands of Wobblies gathered at the Manhattan Lyceum to cheer Tresca's release; Annie Gurley cooked turkey dinners; Carlo cooked spaghetti dinners; Italian anarchists threw parties. Soon after their return, however, the Seattle IWW sent for Flynn; she was needed to raise money for more than a hundred Wobblies imprisoned at Everett. Elizabeth was accustomed to going when she was summoned, and on this occasion she wanted to make it clear that the quarrel with Haywood had no effect on her IWW activities. But her decision to go to Washington led to a quarrel with Carlo, who was furious that she was willing to leave him after their long separation.

Elizabeth left for Washington with the quarrel unresolved. Matters were serious enough for her to record that Carlo did not write to her during the six weeks she was away and that she "suffered a great deal from loneliness and worry." Fred Moore was in Seattle, and she was comforted by his presence. She also met Dr. Marie Equi again, whom she had first met on her 1915 speaking tour. Together, the two women visited the men in jail, and Flynn was heartened to hear the enthusiastic shouts, "Gurley!"

Tresca's health had suffered during his Mesabi ordeal, and he continued in a weakened condition through the spring. On May 4, 1917, Ettore Tresca inserted a notice in the pages of *L'Avvenire:* "To all of you, the physical condition of Carlo is not unknown, caused by the conditions in Minnesota. . . . He asks the comrades not to ask for his participation in activities for at least three months."

In the summer of 1917, Carlo and Elizabeth rented a small bungalow on a wooded hilltop on Staten Island, a place to which they would return every summer for the next nine years. They spent their days swimming, picnicking under the trees, entertaining family and friends, and, during this summer, looking down at Coney Island's lower bay where the troop ships were loading.

The European war had come as a blow to American radicals— not so much the fact of war, but the response to it of most of European socialism: German socialists were the first to vote war credits, then the Belgians, the French, and the British Labour party capitulated. Even Peter Kropotkin acquiesced to the war. American socialists, virtually alone in opposition, feared the end of the international socialist movement.

In March 1917, news arrived of a revolution in Russia. On April 6 the United States entered the European war.

The IWW's position on the war was firm in 1916 when the general executive board stated: "We will resent with all the power at our command, any attempt to compel us to participate in a war that can only bring in its wake death and untold misery . . . and only serve to further rivet the chains of slavery on our necks." But in late July 1917, when the board met in emergency session to formulate a policy on conscription, the majority, fearing government repression, chose to leave the matter to the conscience of each individual member.

The caution, as Frank Little predicted, made no difference, and the IWW took the brunt of war fever. Arizona senator Henry Ashurst declared that its initials stood for Imperial Wilhelm's Warriors; in Jerome, Arizona, eighty striking copper miners were loaded onto cattle cars and deported to California by their employer, the United Vedde Copper Company; in Bisbee, Arizona, twelve hundred miners were rounded up by two thousand armed vigilantes, locked in cattle cars, and shoved out into the desert without food or water. A *Tulsa Daily World* editorial declared that the first step in whipping Germany "is to strangle the IWWs. Kill them, just as you would kill any other kind of a snake. . . . It is not time to waste money on trials and continuances and things like that. All that is necessary is the evidence and a firing squad." Eleven Wobblies, in jail for vagrancy in Tulsa, were taken from their cells by a mob and whipped, tarred, and feathered.

Carlo brought Elizabeth the news of Frank Little's death. It was August 2; she was at the stove at South Beach, cooking dinner for her brother Tom and his friend. Carlo arrived from New York with the newspapers. Bad news, Elisabetta, he said.

Frank Little had gone to Butte, where a fire at the Speculator mine had killed 178 miners. The remaining miners had gone on strike. On July 31, Little spoke to them at the Butte ballpark. Then, limping because he had one leg in a plaster cast, he went to his hotel room. Sometime during the night six men, masked and armed, broke into his room. First they beat him, then they tied a rope around him, tied the rope to the back of a car, and dragged him to a railroad trestle on the outskirts of town, where they hanged him.

Arturo Giovannitti wrote:

Six men drove up to his house at midnight, and woke the poor woman who kept it,
And asked her: "Where is the man who spoke against war and insulted the army?"
And the old woman took fear of the men and the hour, and showed them the room where he slept . . .
No one gave witness of what they did to him, after they took him away, until a dog barked at his corpse.
But I know, for I have seen masked men with the rope . . .
And they inflicted on him the final shame, and ordered that he should kiss the flag.
They always make bounden men kiss the flag in America where men never kiss men, not even when they march forth to die . . .
He did not kiss it—I swear it by the one that shall wrap my body . . .
To him who would not barter a meaningless word for his life, they said, "You are a traitor."
And they drew the noose round his neck, and they pulled him up to the trestle, and they watched him until he was dead.

Elizabeth stood at the stove, weeping.

"You will forgive me for not writing you before," Carlo wrote

Mary Vorse that summer. "You have to blame the war time and the glory of the democratic reign. I was, in the past weeks, very busy on account of my paper. I have decided to send out a monthly magazine and not give up the fight. The dead of Frank have impressed me very much. I can't forget him."

Tresca was being watched, not only by the Bureau of Investigation but by the League for National Unity, a private group whose chairman, Ralph Easley, reported to Washington. "Carlo Tresca, from four to six p.m. spoke against President Wilson [in Passaic] by saying he would protect capitalists and run down the poor people," an informant from the league reported. "He also said: we have got to be ready for a revolt, but I cannot say all I want because I am shadowed by detectives."

Military Intelligence examined Tresca's bank account in 1917, searching for a reported twenty thousand dollars in German gold. In September, Tresca wrote to a comrade in Boston: "We have never gone through an epoch so dark as this. I am kept under surveillance continually. I expect to be struck momentarily either by the Department of Justice in Washington which has many articles of *L'Avvenire* translated, or a conspiracy together with Haywood and others."

The blow came on both fronts. *L'Avvenire* was found to be full of violations of the Espionage Act and the Trading with the Enemy Act; the post office ruled issue after issue of the paper to be unmailable. "This publication from beginning to end attacks the United States and its Allies," the post office translator reported in August, "but in its anti-war arguments it is strangely silent in so far as Germany is concerned."

As *L'Avvenire* piled up at the central post office, Tresca allowed the paper to die. In October *Il Martello*, describing itself as a popular review of science, literature, and the arts, appeared under new ownership, although Tresca's name did not appear on the masthead until the following March and his articles were signed "Ego Sum" and "L'Homme Qui Rit." But it was not long before the post office began to note objectionable articles in "a general defense of the Bolsheviki and a condemnation of militarism." In June 1918 a memo was sent to the U.S. assistant district attorney complaining that the paper "carries an article on the Russian situation . . . in particular the coming of Lenin and Trotsky to power. . . . This article is itself objectionable as a defense of the Bolsheviki. I recommend that this issue be declared unmailable."

Beginning in July 1917 the Department of Justice, with the occasional cooperation of the War and Labor departments, began to collect information to indict the IWW under the Espionage Act of 1917. Detectives watched Chicago headquarters around the clock. In mid-July federal agents broke in, and on August 21, Attorney General Gregory informed President Wilson that the Department of Justice was ready to act. On September 5, agents of the Department of Justice, together with local police, raided the Chicago headquarters as well as local IWW offices in Sacramento, California, and Wichita, Kansas. They removed books, typewriters, boxes of papers, furniture, files—a total of five tons of material. Three weeks later a grand jury issued indictments for 165 IWW members charging them with, among other things, interfering with congressional acts and presidential procedures relating to the war; criminal conspiracy to strike and thus interfere with the right of employers to execute war contracts; and influencing others to refuse conscription and desert the military. On September 29, the day after the indictments were handed down, IWW counsel George Vanderveer advised all those indicted, including Flynn and Tresca, Vincent St. John, and Arturo Giovannitti, to surrender to federal agents.

Flynn was at home with her mother on October 1 when federal agents knocked at the door. Her response to the announcement that she was under arrest was reported to Washington: How was that possible? she asked the agents. She had not been active in the IWW for a year; during that time she had made no speeches. At the moment she was without employment at all: I have educated my two sisters, she told the agents, and now they are giving me a vacation. As to the whereabouts of Carlo Tresca, she could not say.

The federal agents placed Flynn between them and escorted her to the 134th Street "el" station. A local policeman named Harry Hand, who knew the Flynns well, accompanied them. As they waited on the platform for the train to take them downtown, an uptown train pulled in on the platform opposite. Among the passengers leaving the train Elizabeth saw Carlo and her sister Bina. She turned away quickly, hoping they would not see her, but Carlo spotted her and ran across. Harry Hand identified him, and

Tresca was informed that he was under arrest. Oh, yes, he responded, he had been expecting to hear from the Department of Justice. (That very morning the *New York Times* referred to him as "one of the most rabid IWW troublemakers. He recently declared that the organization was against all governments and that its war program included strikes.") Tresca now said to the federal agents: It's all in the game.

After a night in the Tombs, Flynn requested an interview with U.S. Attorney Harold Content. As a private lawyer Content had represented Tresca on matters to do with the post office; he now recommended that the defendants hire a lawyer who had no taint of association with radical causes and to have him make a case for severance. It thus became immediately clear to the other defendants that Flynn, Tresca, and also Arturo Giovannitti and Joe Ettor, who had been arrested the same day, would not submit to the mass trial endorsed by IWW attorney George Vanderveer and Bill Haywood.

The strategy devised by the IWW was an optimistic one, based on the weaknesses of the government's case. Haywood and Vanderveer were confident that the prosecution would be unable to prove conspiracy or illegal acts, and they believed that the IWW would win a propaganda victory in court. The government had named 165 people in a carelessly drawn indictment: one defendant had been named twice; Frank Little was dead; Vincent St. John, Joe Ettor, and Arturo Giovannitti had been inactive during the April 6 through September 28, 1917 dates covered by the indictment; Tresca had never formally belonged to the IWW at all. (And Flynn would argue that she had been inactive during that period because of the hostility shown her by other IWW leaders.)

Flynn's assessment of the times was more realistic than Haywood's. She saw clearly that the weaknesses of the case would not weigh against the hysteria of the moment. She thought it was foolhardy to abide by the government's strategy of a mass trial when they might use the legal system to their own ends, forcing the government to try each named individual separately, prove each charge in the indictment, and so draw the case out indefinitely.

With Tresca still in jail, Flynn hired a former assistant district attorney, George Whiteside, to represent her, Tresca, and Giovannitti. Anticipating criticism, a circular signed by Flynn, Tresca and

Ettor was sent "To Our Friends and Sympathizers," setting out the reasoning behind their demand for severance and stating that "our decision is not dictated by any lack of consideration for the other defendants. In fact . . . we believe that they too should follow the same course."

As a practical matter, however, the ability of other defendants to do so depended on whether they could raise bail money, as Flynn was able to do, and hire lawyers to fight their cases. Flynn's connections were uniquely her own. U.S. Attorney Harold Content, for example, who would a short time later prosecute Emma Goldman and Alexander Berkman in their fight to avoid deportation, was not generally available to advise radicals as to their best interests, nor were, among other influential people, Flynn's bondsmen, Edith Cram and Amos Pichot. That Flynn was aware of this may be reflected in the way her close friend Mary Vorse put the matter: "After much heart-searching Elizabeth, Carlo and Giovannitti decided to take the urgent advice of their friends and ask for a severance."

During the six months between their arrest in October and the beginning of the IWW trial in Chicago the following April, Flynn used all the considerable resources at her command. Her friend Edith Cram's husband, J. Sargeant Cram, prominent in Democratic party politics, joined George Whiteside in a memorandum to the attorney general arguing that, during the period covered by the indictment, Flynn had not been an officer of the IWW; that she "had ceased" her activities prior to April 1917, due to hostility shown her by a number of officers who were her co-indictees; that the one piece of material evidence against her, the pamphlet "Sabotage," had been written by her long before the war and that she had, in fact, objected to its continued circulation.

Flynn now called on her most powerful resource. In 1915 she had met President Wilson's secretary, Joseph Tumulty, who had been friendly to her on that occasion when the issue was the case of Joe Hill. She again asked Tumulty for help. He advised her on the sort of letter that would be most likely to move Woodrow Wilson, and in January 1918, Tumulty delivered a letter from Flynn to the president.

"An humble and obscure citizen who has struggled for democracy as her vision glimpsed it and who has suffered for espousing an unpopular and much misrepresented point of view, will surely be granted a hearing by you," Flynn wrote to Woodrow Wilson. She continued:

> I am compelled to appeal to you against what seems to me a grave injustice, and it is an embarrassing undertaking, since it is the first time in twelve years continuous service to the cause of labor that I have addressed anyone on my own behalf. . . .
>
> For seven years I have supported my child, and helped to educate two sisters (one of whom is now a teacher) and a brother, who is now eligible to the draft. This is, of course, only what other women are doing and has been a labor of love, but it is rather incompatible with the popular conception of "a labor agitator."
>
> . . . may I respectfully present for your consideration the reasons why the Department of Justice should grant a severance in my case? . . . I ask the Department of Justice to recognize the essential distinction between two groups of defendants. The first group are those who have been actively participating in the affairs of "The Industrial Workers of the World" since last April, who in all probability will not deny the overt acts or their responsibilities in them, but will affirm the legality of their conduct. Their defense can be made collectively and they are not requesting a severance.
>
> The second group consists of non-members of the IWW, and members who have been entirely inactive for periods ranging from one to five years. I, among others, deny all knowledge of or responsibility for the overt acts alleged and am convinced that I am being tried for past reputation rather than for conduct since war was declared. . . .
>
> I have not taken part in strikes or other IWW affairs since long before the war was declared, due to violent disagreements which arose within the organization last December. I have engaged in no anti-war agitation of any character. . . .
>
> The only conceivable basis for my indictment is a pamphlet on "Sabotage" written four years ago in defense of men arrested during the Paterson strike. I had no intention that it should apply to any other time or conditions . . . and long before my arrest had requested the IWW not to publish it further until I could rewrite it. . . . It will be necessary for me to call as witnesses certain other defendants whose credibility will be affected by and whose legal interests will be hostile to giving such testimony before a jury in a common trial. . . .
>
> I know some of my co-defendants and their unselfish devotion to labor is unquestionable. Others I do not know and some have possibly acted most foolishly. . . . I feel that my own acts and ideals, mistaken though they may be, are all for which I am justly responsible. . . .
>
> I do not aspire to prove my conception correct. I am only too willing to suspend judgment in these days of world upheaval, to watch the silent

progress of events, to hope that the world may be purged of tyranny and greed. . . . It is relatively unimportant that the puny efforts of people like myself may have all been sterile and vain. . . . To prove at least that such ideals are free from sordid motives . . . and that it is inconceivable and loathesome to one whose darkest moments are lit by dreams of freedom, to ally oneself with Green militarism and its fiendish autocracy is of such grave and vital concern to me that I can plead to you as one idealist to another.

Flynn was not proud of this letter; in any case, she never referred to it in her writings. And while the tone of abject pleading is disturbing, the letter also contained something not quite true. In August 1917, a time covered by the indictment, Flynn had written to *Solidarity* to counter the rumors that she had been dismissed by Haywood: "I am a member of the IWW at this writing and have never stated otherwise. . . . [I] now emphatically deny . . . that labor should not strike during war times . . . labor must protect itself against increased exploitation . . . under the guise of patriotism. . . . I would not have my friends believe me a quitter in a crisis. We have enough slackers in the class war already."

Flynn's letter to Wilson may not have helped her case, although along with intervention by Roger Baldwin and other friends, it surely did not hurt. By the time President Wilson received her letter, Attorney General Gregory had written to prosecuting attorneys in Chicago to "examine carefully as to the strength of the case against Elizabeth Gurley Flynn, Joseph Ettor, Arturo Giovannitti and Carlo Tresca. If you find we have no sufficient foundation to those, or equally clearly as to others, then gain the advantage of doing voluntarily what government would have to do at trial."

In February Tresca and Flynn were in Chicago, waiting for the disposition of their application for severance. According to a telegram sent on February 7 by the prosecuting attorneys to the attorney general in Washington, "strong pressure is being brought to bear upon New York defendants to go to trial at the same time as Chicago defendants and to cooperate actively in raising defense funds. You will appreciate our purpose in wiring this information."

Already inclined to sever the cases, the government's decision to do so had been made the previous day, perhaps with the idea of rendering the New York defendants ineffective for the defense of the Chicago defendants. The assistant attorney general, in a letter to George Whiteside on February 6, wrote that his application for severance "will not be resisted on the part of the Government. . . . While these cases are . . . held in abeyance, the Government . . . will be pleased and grateful to have you cooperate [with your clients] in order to influence them toward a patriotic course. . . . Especially is it desired that you influence these people in such a way that their writings may not be used by the offending IWW or others who would retard the Government." For herself and Carlo, then, Elizabeth's strategy worked. They were never brought to trial.

There was little Tresca or Flynn could have done to impede the prosecution of the Chicago trial which opened on April 1, 1918. Five months of testimony was followed by jury deliberations of less than an hour and verdicts of guilty on all counts. The sentences imposed on the 101 defendants ranged from one year to twenty years, with Haywood drawing a twenty-year sentence. "The big game is over," Haywood wrote to John Reed from his cell at the Cook County Jail, "we never won a hand. The other fellow had the cut, shuffle and deal all the time. . . . All in the world they had against us was morsels of fragmentary evidence, not enough to convict a ward-heeling politician, but we were off our field."

Haywood was released on bail during the period of the appeal. For a while, until the general executive board removed him, he conducted the defense committee. But for a number of years he had been sick, and he drank heavily. He had no way of knowing that all the convicted Wobblies would be released from jail by 1923, and in 1921, with a number of other Wobblies, he boarded a ship and sailed for the Soviet Union, leaving his comrades to read about his flight in the newspapers and his organization to repay a large amount of painfully collected bail money.

Haywood arrived in Moscow in time for two International Congresses. The Comintern and the Profintern (the Red International of Trade Unions) were meeting. In Moscow Haywood went to see Emma Goldman, who had been in the Soviet Union since her deportation at the end of 1919. He had made an agonizing decision, he told her, but it had not been out of cowardice: Moscow had urged him to come, and from Russia he would be able to help revolutionize the American masses. He had been assured that his bail would be repaid by the Communist party.

Emma Goldman was already out of favor in Moscow, and by the time Haywood saw her again at the opening session of the Profintern he had learned that fact. He pretended not to see her when she entered the chamber. By the time the congress ended, he had seen the majority vote for the liquidation of the IWW in accord with the new Comintern policy.

"Poor Bill did not realize that the captain of a ship has no right to run for safety and leave his crew behind," Emma Goldman wrote to a friend after she had left the Soviet Union, "but what will you when people are not strong enough to take the consequences of their ideas. They must pay the price. . . . At least if they suffer from their ideals physically they can claim their souls their own . . . but there is nothing more dreadful in the world than to pay a double price. . . . Bill's price is a double price and I feel deeply sorry for him."

Haywood died in Moscow in 1928.

Chapter 9
All of Them Anarchists

I<small>N</small> his diary for November 8, 1917, Alexander Berkman expressed the response of revolutionists to the news of the October Revolution: "Hurrah! Hurrah! Hurrah! Kerensky deposed! Bolsheviki in control! Land to be returned to the people! Armistice and peace! I am wild with joy!"

Two years later Italy, Hungary and Germany were verging on revolution and the United States itself was in the throes of strikes from the East to the West Coast. The U.S. communist movement was born in 1919, and John Reed edited the organ of the Communist Labor party from Tresca's office.

Opposed to this revolutionary fervor was the Red Scare, instituted by Attorney General Mitchell Palmer in 1919: mass raids and arrests of communists and anarchists, and the deportation of aliens, including Emma Goldman, Alexander Berkman, and Luigi Galleani. Further dampening of revolutionary optimism for anarchists came out of the new Soviet Union. "At the present moment," Peter Kropotkin wrote shortly before his death in 1921, "the Russian revolution is in the following position. It is perpetrating horrors. It is ruining the whole country. In its mad fury it is annihilating human lives. . . . And we are powerless for the present to direct it into another channel until such time as it will have played itself out."

Errico Malatesta, leader of the anarchists in Italy, also offered a caution. In February 1920, Tresca reprinted in the *Martello* an interview with Malatesta: "if by Bolshevism is meant popular initiative . . . then I am a Bolshevist. We anarchists, however, exclude all political authority that rules over the Soviets." A year later, as the Fascists gained in power, Malatesta warned, "We do not want and shall not tolerate gendarmes, neither red, nor yellow, nor black."

During the next few years Tresca himself wavered on this principle. He was opposed to centralized government, but was the dictatorship of the proletariat government in the accepted sense? "The Soviet government represents *only* the workers and cannot help but act in the workers' interests," declared an article in the *Martello.* "In time of strike every worker knows there must be a Strike Committee—a centralized organ to conduct the strike whose orders must be obeyed. *Soviet Russia is on Strike against the whole capitalist world. . . . The Dictatorship of the Proletariat is the Strike Committee of the Social Revolution.*"

Tresca was less certain by 1922. Persecutions of political dissidents in the Soviet Union, the disillusionment of Emma Goldman and Alexander Berkman, and the massacre of the rebellious sailors of Kronstadt had entered the equation. Challenged by a critic to declare where he stood, he answered in the *Martello:* "I am what I have always been—a syndicalist anarchist, body and soul with the revolution in Russia. But many new things have taken place in Russia since the time the communists in authority spoke . . . about the transitory dictatorship of the Proletariat. But the dictatorship is there to stay until the third revolution uproots it in the name of liberty which today, even in Russia, groans under the heel of government." The Russian revolution was not too revolutionary, it was not revolutionary enough. Anarchists and syndicalists had been persecuted by the government. The revolution and the government were no longer one entity: "They cry out to us! 'Bend your backs to the inevitability of history!' But we salute the soldiers of the Third Russian Revolution. We tip our hats to the martyrs of Kronstadt, and we still hope."

From the split between Marx and Bakunin, the anarchist movement developed along two paths, not always distinct. Followers of anarcho-syndicalism held to a belief in a mass movement of organized workers as the basis for the overthrow of the system. The individualist anarchists were opposed to mass organization, which in their view was itself destructive of liberty. The individualist anarchists offered the alternative of the insurrectionary activities of small, intimate groups, and the revolutionary acts of individuals—the *attentat*—the "propaganda of the deed"—which, by example, would inspire the masses to spontaneous revolt. "Permanent revolt by word of mouth, in writing, by the dagger, the rifle, dynamite," Kropotkin had once written: "Everything is good for us which falls outside legality." Acts of assassination and expropriation by anarchists were not uncommon in Europe. In France, when Emile Henry was put on trial for bombing a café and killing innocent workmen, he defended himself in the language of anarchism: "Are not those children innocent victims who, in the slums, die slowly of anemia . . . or those women who grow pale in your workshops. . . . At least have the courage of your crimes gentlemen of the bourgeoisie and agree that our reprisals are fully legitimate."

These two tendencies of the Italian anarchist movement, as they were transplanted to the United States, were represented by Carlo Tresca and by Luigi Galleani. Galleani, the individualist anarchist and the elder of the two, was also the publisher of a newspaper, the *Cronaca Sovversiva*. In the early years of the century Tresca and Galleani had been occasional collaborators. Galleani lectured at the Popular University established by Tresca in the Pennsylvania coal fields. Despite the differences that began to appear between them, Tresca retained affection and respect for the older man, suggesting in a letter of 1917 that Galleani visit him in New York.

But Galleani had little patience for a man who compromised every anarchist principle: Tresca worked with socialists and with labor organizations. While Galleani hailed the *attentat,* praised the assassination of McKinley, and published the memoirs of the French expropriationist Clement Duval, Tresca curried favor with politicians. It was true that Tresca was sometimes useful. Should an anarchist get into trouble, he knew the immigration agents and he had the contacts to raise bail money. But although he might be used, he was not to be trusted. In the years after Galleani's deportation in 1919, relations between Tresca and the Galleanisti became poisonous. The very fact that Tresca had not been deported told against him.

In later years Tresca's comrade Sam Dolgoff assessed the situation with the coolness of hindsight: "They hated Carlo because he was their link with reality. In reality, their ideas were not effective. Carlo was effective. So they concocted all kinds of stories about him—he was a counterrevolutionary, a police spy. And it was all done in the Italian style with plots and subplots and tangled webs."

But the worst of this feud was still to come when Nicola Sacco and Bartolomeo Vanzetti were arrested in May 1920.

A distinct trail leading to the arrests of Sacco and Vanzetti has its origin in the May 1919 deportation of Galleani. Galleani had exhorted his followers to take revenge. On the night of June 2, bombs exploded almost simultaneously in eight cities: in New York the explosion killed a night watchman; at 11:05 P.M. in Washington, D.C., a bomb damaged the home of the author of the Red Scare, Attorney General Mitchell Palmer. This bomb also blew to bits the man who carried it. A few clues to his identity remained: a soft gray felt hat; a railroad conductor's check showing that he had arrived in Washington by the 10:30 train; one gun and fragments of another; an Italian-English dictionary. Also found at the site of the explosion in Washington and other cities was a leaflet, printed on pink paper. Titled "Plain Words," it was signed "Anarchist Fighters" and it offered an explanation for the bombs: "We have been dreaming of freedom, we have talked of liberty, we have aspired to a better world, and you jailed us, you deported us, you murdered us whenever you could. . . . There will have to be bloodshed; we will not dodge; there will have to be murder; we will kill because it is necessary. . . . Long live social revolution! down with tyranny." Government informers in the anarchist movement were instructed to bend their efforts to locate the source of "Plain Words."

In March 1920, a Mr. Morgillo, owner of a print shop in Harlem, called on Tresca for advice. Federal agents had questioned him about the leaflet and his shop was being watched. Morgillo suspected that a man named Eugenio Vico Ravarini was behind it. Ravarini had visited his shop often and was urging him to print some material that was clearly provocative and inflammatory.

Tresca already knew something about Ravarini. He advised Morgillo not to print the material unless Ravarini and his associate agreed to sign it. Morgillo did put this condition to Ravarini, whose visits to his shop then ceased. But Tresca continued to gather information about Ravarini, and by June he had enough evidence to charge him, in the *New York Call*, with being an agent provocateur for the Department of Justice.

Ravarini soon disappeared, but he had already done much damage. In February he had informed the Department of Justice that a possible source of the pink leaflet might be Canzani's print shop in Brooklyn; Canzani's shop was raided. No evidence was ever produced showing it to be the source of the leaflet, but two employees, Roberto Elia and Andrea Salsedo, were taken into custody on February 25. Both were brought to Department of Justice offices on Park Row, where, for more than two months, they were held incommunicado.

Andrea Salsedo was a follower of Galleani's and publisher of a small clandestine newspaper that propagated Galleani's ideas. Shortly before his arrest, Salsedo had sent a special notice to his subscribers, warning them against Eugenio Ravarini. Among his subscribers was Bartolomeo Vanzetti. When the news of Salsedo's arrest reached Boston, a meeting of the Naturalization Club of East Boston was called, and Vanzetti, who had no regular job, was delegated to go to New York to see what could be done for Salsedo.

Leaving Boston, with forty dollars given him by his comrade Aldino Felicani, Vanzetti arrived in New York on April 25 and went at once to the *Martello* office on East Twenty-third Street. The office was also the headquarters for the Italian Committee for Political Victims, of which Tresca was chairman. Tresca told Vanzetti what he knew about Elia and Salsedo. Very little. He had been unable to see the two men in custody (Roberto Elia had once worked on *La Plebe*), and he suspected that their lawyer was in league with the Department of Justice. Vanzetti also talked to Walter Nelles, the ACLU lawyer who was counsel to the committee, and to Luigi Quintiliano, the secretary. Neither of them had any more information about the arrested men, but they told Vanzetti to warn his comrades in Boston that more raids on anarchists could be expected. They advised him and his Boston comrades to get rid of all incriminating papers.

On May 3, Salsedo's body was found on the Park Row pavement fourteen stories beneath his cell. According to Roberto Elia, who was quickly deported, Salsedo had been beaten during questioning. After their lawyer informed them that they were being charged with first degree murder, Salsedo had said to Elia: "We have done nothing but we are in a trap. . . . I will admit that I printed Plain Words because I cannot stand more and maybe I will help myself." But even after Salsedo's confession, when both men were given a clean room and decent food, Salsedo's mental state deteriorated.

He groaned all night long, refused food, complained of pains in his stomach and head. "He showed clear signs," said Elia, "of an unbalancing mind."

On May 5, while riding a trolley car between Brockton and Bridgeport, Massachusetts, Sacco and Vanzetti were arrested. Among the items in Vanzetti's possession was his handwritten draft of a leaflet calling a meeting to protest Salsedo's fate.

As chairman of the Italian Committee for Political Victims and an anarchist leader, Tresca naturally heard about the arrest almost at once. He knew Vanzetti from his own trips to Boston, and of course Vanzetti had visited the *Martello* office only a few weeks earlier. He did not personally know Sacco, although Sacco had been arrested in 1916 while demonstrating against Tresca's imprisonment on the Mesabi Range. Aldino Felicani, who had given Vanzetti the forty dollars, and who at once formed a defense committee for the two men, was an old comrade. The world of the Italian anarchists was small.

On June 15, the *Martello* warned its readers;

> Another Terrible Plot!
> Proletarians Beware!
> During the month of April on the public highway of Braintree, Mass., while the cashier of a construction company, accompanied by a guard was on his way to the factory with the money for the workers' payroll, he was assaulted, killed and robbed by highwaymen who escaped in an automobile taking with them twenty thousand dollars. . . .
> The innocence of these two men must be brought out. Sacco as well as Vanzetti are well known as veterans of the movement for freedom, always ready to support any worthy cause, always ready for the sacrifice. . . .
> Vanzetti and Sacco are worthy of the unconditional support of all the comrades and of all good workers, for themselves, and for the idea which unites us. Let us show that the blackest persecution against the "Reds" has not broken the ranks of the militants, has not weakened the spirit of proletarian vindication and that all are united to defend by word and deed the reputation and the life of Vanzetti and Sacco who may be guilty of political heresy, but not of a common crime.

Flynn was in Boston, and there she stopped in to see Aldino Felicani. She brought back to Tresca news that Vanzetti was first to be tried, separately, for a previous attempted robbery at Bridgeport that police had been unable to solve.

By August Vanzetti had been found guilty and would thus appear as a convicted felon at his trial with Sacco for the South Braintree robbery and murder.

After the conviction of Vanzetti on the Bridgeport charge, Tresca went to see Felicani. He thought the defense committee had handled matters badly. To defend Vanzetti they had hired a small-time lawyer with underworld connections and no sense of the political nature of the case. The case of Sacco and Vanzetti should be treated as a political case, Tresca urged Felicani in the late summer of 1920; the lawyer who could handle it was Fred Moore.

Tresca and Flynn trusted Moore. He had been involved in the IWW free speech fight in Spokane, where Flynn first met him in 1910. Tresca had met and worked with him in Lawrence in 1912. Moore had worked with Clarence Darrow on the case of the Mac-Namara brothers, who were convicted for the bombing of the *Los Angeles Times*. He had worked on the 1918 IWW trial. Moore had a reputation as an obsessive investigator who would overlook legal niceties on behalf of his clients. He was also developing a repu- tation, whether Tresca and Flynn knew it or not, for being oddly unreliable, given to unexplained disappearances: he had disap-peared for a time during the IWW trial, and Bill Haywood had sent desperate telegrams around the country in the attempt to find him.

Fred Moore entered the Sacco and Vanzetti case in mid-August 1920. He was a short, stocky man, then in his late thirties, given to wearing large Stetson hats over his long hair. As he drove north from New York, Moore carried three passengers, Lola Darroch, whom he later married in Boston, and two Italians who had been shoved into the car by Tresca at the last moment to save them from arrest by the New York police.

Before matters were settled, Moore was interviewed by Felicani, and by Sacco and Vanzetti. All were agreed on him. Vanzetti wrote to his father that "we now have a faithful, able man." It was ar-ranged that Moore would take charge of the legal strategy, the in-vestigations, and the publicity for the case. For the actual trial, a local laywer, more likely to get a sympathetic hearing from the judge and jury, would argue the case.

But it was not long before Felicani began to have doubts about Moore. Felicani was in charge of the treasury; the nickles and

dimes he collected from the Italian community he viewed as his
sacred trust to Sacco and Vanzetti. He gave Moore his first check,
for five hundred dollars, and Moore began to spend: a house, a
car, a chauffeur, investigators. Resources were limited, but there
seemed no end to the money Moore could spend.

Moore had nine months to prepare for trial. In the first months
after the arrest of Sacco and Vanzetti, the two men were unknown
to the general public. Felicani had early approached the Communists for help, but they would have nothing to do with what
they considered a simple criminal matter. Moore began to use
his connections with the AFL, the Socialists, and the American
Civil Liberties Union to build support. Flynn and Roger Baldwin
helped bring the liberal ladies of Boston to the cause. Moore hired
Eugene Lyons, Robert Minor, Art Shields, and John Beffel to pub-
licize the case. Beffel's piece, which appeared in the *New Republic*
on December 29, 1920, was the first article on the case in a national
English-language publication.

Moore "developed a fanatical zeal built on his absolute faith that
these two men were innocent," Flynn later wrote. "He was determined to save them at all costs." One way to save them would be to
find the real murderers. Moore hired investigators to follow every
lead. There were too many investigators, Felicani began to believe.
It seemed to him that Moore wanted to support all his friends
through this case. Moore also wanted to control the treasury, and
Felicani entered into a tug of war with him about money. They also
disagreed about the offer brought to Felicani by Angeline De Falco
in January 1921.

De Falco was a court interpreter who sometimes worked for a
lawyer, Percy Katzmann, brother of the prosecutor, Fred Katzmann. Before the trial, De Falco went to see Felicani; she told him
that for a sum of fifty thousand dollars Sacco and Vanzetti's acquittal could be arranged. She said it was a simple matter, that these
things were done all the time.

Felicani and the defense committee were ready to accept the
offer. In their experience, American justice was to be trusted
less than the greed and corruption of its agents. But Moore was
against it. He reported De Falco for offering a bribe, and she was
chastised in court as "imprudent . . . but not criminal." The story
made the front pages of the Boston papers, but it did Sacco and

Vanzetti no good. In later years Felicani believed that Moore's decision on the De Falco matter sealed the fate of Sacco and Vanzetti: he thought that Judge Webster Thayer never forgave Moore for impugning the integrity of the Massachusetts courts.

So even greater strain developed between Moore and the anarchists of the defense committee, who believed that De Falco might have saved their comrades and who were also opposed in principle to using the courts to do their work for them. They began to believe that Moore had more interest in having the case played out in court than he did in the fate of Sacco and Vanzetti.

The trial of Sacco and Vanzetti opened on May 31, 1921. It had been agreed that local lawyers would handle the trial work; two brothers, Jerry and Thomas McAnarney, had been hired as lawyers for Vanzetti; Moore appeared as Sacco's counsel. The McAnarneys were soon in despair over Moore's courtroom behavior. First, he challenged all prospective jurors who were middle class or educated—who were, in the McAnarneys' opinion, Sacco and Vanzetti's best hope. And at every opportunity he clashed with Judge Thayer. The McAnarneys offered to try the case for nothing if only Moore would stay out of the courtroom. Moore refused. They asked a colleague, William Thompson, to observe Moore's courtroom behavior. Thompson watched for a while and told the McAnarneys, "Your goose is cooked." Later, when Fred Moore was fired, Thompson took over the case and Felicani lamented, "If we'd had Thompson from the beginning, then we would have got them off."

Felicani was distraught. He would sometimes go to Moore's room and find the lawyer a wreck. "The thought came to me that he was using morphine or something like that," he said later; at the time he thought, I will kill that son of a bitch if he isn't good in court.

"Well, dear Tresca," Vanzetti wrote, "we have been found guilty. Why it would have been a great wonder if we had been absolved. . . . [But] after all they did not have the satisfaction of seeing us tremble, nor will they ever have."

Moore remained on the case until 1924. During that time he followed clues that promised to lead to the real killers, and he obtained recantations from prosecution witnesses. Felicani acknowledged that Moore was indefatigable: "Moore's investigations did contribute something. We had the Lola Andrews recantation, and the Goodrich recantation and the Gould. We had all kinds of investigations leading . . . to Atlanta where one of the Morelli gang of Providence was." Felicani added, "Those trips to Atlanta cost a lot of money. Moore didn't stop at anything."

Tresca supported Moore's efforts, but the anarchists of the defense committee were opposed. They argued that if Moore's investigations should lead to the prosecution of others for the crime, then anarchists would be implicated in securing the safety of their own by using the hated State. It may have been at this juncture that Moore began to wonder whether knowledge relating to the crime might have a part in the reluctance of the defense committee to give him a free hand.

There has been little in the way of direct testimony about Moore's personal and professional habits until, in late 1978, a woman named Mary Hunter spoke for the first time about her relationship with Moore and her role in the Sacco and Vanzetti case.

Mary Hunter met Fred Moore in 1914 or 1915 in Chicago, when he was working for a Chicago law firm and she was a legal secretary. Five years later, when Hunter was in personal difficulty and had to leave her job, Moore found her a job in Kansas City with Caroline Lowe, a lawyer for radical causes. It was during the summer of 1919, the year of the Palmer raids, and Caroline Lowe's house was a stopping place for traveling radicals. Hunter recalls driving Mother Bloor to meetings, and she remembers that Carlo Tresca turned up one night at dinnertime. Hunter had little interest in politics, but she had heard about Tresca; she was a very attractive young woman, and Tresca apparently paid her a great deal of attention.

Shortly after this, Hunter went to work at IWW headquarters in Chicago, again through Moore. Bill Haywood was then out on bail, conducting the IWW defense committee. The job did not last long, and Hunter came to New York where for a time she shared an apartment on Waverly Place with Fred Moore and Lola Darroch.

In the fall of 1921, after Sacco and Vanzetti had been convicted, Moore offered Mary Hunter a job as an investigator. She was to go to Quincy to find out what she could about Lola Andrews, the prosecution's chief witness: it was Andrews who had placed Sacco at the scene of the crime.

In Quincy, Mary Hunter set herself up as a public stenographer, taking rooms over a movie theater in the building in which Lola Andrews lived. Hunter lived in her office and, over a period of three months, developed a relationship with Andrews, whom she describes as "touching. . . . She wasn't young anymore but she had beautiful long black hair and black eyes. She cleaned up the movie theater once a day. She also kept a consumptive sweetheart who was dying. . . . She was the town whore and the town scrubwoman and the policeman's football. She was frightened of her own shadow."

During the day Hunter did some stenography and typing for the McAnarney brothers, and she nodded to Lola Andrews when they met in the hallway. In time the women began to spend some evenings together. Hunter learned that Andrews had a son whom she had placed in a Maine orphanage and had not seen for fifteen years. And one evening Andrews told her: You know, I was the star witness in the Italian case. Hunter pretended ignorance, and Andrews repeated her trial testimony: she had been in South Braintree that day looking for a job and had asked directions of a man whom she later identified as Sacco. Lola Andrews repeated the story a number of times, and Mary Hunter felt that Andrews believed it. Although she had been first bullied by police into giving testimony, she was a simple soul; something extraordinary had happened in her vicinity that had made her important. Cautiously Hunter began to raise questions about inconsistencies in the story, to which Lola Andrews replied, Well, I thought I saw him but my friend who was with me didn't think I did.

Mary Hunter persuaded Lola Andrews to take her doubts to Fred Moore, and Moore was ready for her. He had sent Lola Darroch, whom he had since married, to bring Andrews' son from Maine. With Moore's coaching, the boy pleaded with his mother to tell the truth. Lola Andrews recanted her testimony, only to later recant the recantation. It was an experience Moore was to have with other trial witnesses as well. His methods were spectacular but, as in this case, they sometimes did not hold up.

"I know people said that Fred was unreliable," Mary Hunter said of Moore fifty years later. "He *was* unreliable when he'd exhausted himself. Fred was a magnificent lawyer, a wonderful investigator. He lived his cases twenty-four hours a day until he collapsed. Then he'd hole up in a hotel room and stay there until he quieted down. He was a real labor lawyer. He got his people off. He'd have gotten Sacco and Vanzetti off if he'd stayed on the case."

Even given his initial zeal, it is more than doubtful that Moore could have gotten the men off. And there is no doubt that at least when he began the case he did believe in their innocence. In a letter to a former client in Pennsylvania, asking for support on the case, Moore wrote, "You know that for a long time I was in doubt with reference to yourself, equally for a long time I was in doubt with reference to them. Now I know, and I pledge you my word that they do not know anything more about this crime than you did about the Pew job."

But Moore was besieged by the defense committee on one side, and by his wife on the other. He separated from Lola Darroch, who, on December 19, 1922, wrote accusing him of leaving her in poverty while he spent money on entertainments and on other women. "The biggest curse that you have ever been inflicted with," she wrote, "is a pleasing personality and a glib tongue."

At some point Moore began to waver in his belief in the innocence of his clients. He mentioned to Roger Baldwin that he distrusted some of Sacco's alibi witnesses. Baldwin was not concerned. He expected that friendly witnesses would adjust their testimony even for innocent men. But while Baldwin believed Sacco and Vanzetti to be innocent, he also knew that the anarchist movement was infiltrated, "in a small way," with bootleggers and crooks of one kind or another. It was not inconceivable, it was possible in theory at least, that anarchist groups existed which staged robberies. Luigi Galleani had written of "the right to expropriate the bourgeoisie—which lives by theft—whenever the need presses or the struggle against the social order demands it." If such a group had been involved in the robbery and murders that took place in South Braintree on April 15, 1920, Sacco and Vanzetti might know who they were. In his concern about this matter, Baldwin, as secretary of the Garland Fund, opposed Moore's request to the fund for five thousand dollars to follow a promising lead. He feared that a connection between the real criminals and Sacco and Vanzetti might be established. When Eugene Lyons located Mike Boda in Italy, Boda, who had been with Sacco and Vanzetti on the night of their arrest, had refused to return to testify for his comrades. He said that his life would be in danger if he did.

Tresca had heard rumors of the possibility of Sacco's guilt at
least by 1922. Luigi Quintiliano, who handled all matters relating
to Sacco and Vanzetti for the *Martello* and the Italian Committee
for Political Victims, made a cross-country trip on their behalf that
year. He was asked about the possibility of Sacco's guilt, and he returned to New York to talk to Tresca about it. They spent a number of nights arguing the matter. Tresca was definite: the rumors
are false, he told Quintiliano. The men are innocent. To reassure
himself, Quintiliano visited Sacco in his cell. He did not come right
out with his doubts, but put the matter delicately: Should the comrades continue to assert Sacco's innocence? he asked. Or should
they defend him as an anarchist? Sacco took his meaning. He "took
my hand in his," Quintiliano wrote in the September 30 issue of the
Martello, "and with almost tears in his eyes said, 'Luigi, continue to
ASSERT our complete innocence. You will never regret it.'"

By October 1, 1924, all five of Moore's supplementary motions
for a new trial had been denied. By that time Sacco hated him. In
his frustration with the defense committee, Moore had tried to organize a New Trial League. He had also signed the papers commit-
ting Sacco to the Bridgewater State Hospital for the Criminally
Insane when Sacco had gone on a hunger strike.

"Sir," Sacco wrote Moore on August 18, 1924,

> I would like to know if yours are all the boss of my life! I would like to know
> who is this men that . . . take all the authority to do every thing . . . against
> all my wish. . . . I am telling you to stop this dirty game! You hear me? . . .
> If you please get out of my case, because you know that you are the obstacle
> of that case. . . . Of course it is pretty hard to refuse a such sweet pay. . . . I
> want you to finish my case and I do not want to have anything to do with
> this politics in my case because it does repugnant my conscience. . . . So tell
> me please why you waiting now for? Do you wait till I hang myself? That's
> what you wish? Let me tell you right now . . . I would not be surprised if
> somebody will find you some morning hang on lamppost. Your implacable
> enemy, now and forever, Nick Sacco.

Flynn was given the job of firing Moore; in November 1924,
Moore left Boston for California, alone and bitter. His wife had
left him, and he may already have been suffering from the cancer
of which he would die in the early 1930s. After Sacco and Vanzetti
were executed in 1927, Moore told Upton Sinclair that some anar-

chists did raise money for the movement by robbery, though, he added, neither Sacco nor Vanzetti had ever hinted to him that they were involved in such activity. Moore believed, so he said to Sinclair, that Sacco was probably, and Vanzetti possibly, guilty.

When Sinclair came East, he mentioned his conversation with Moore to Roger Baldwin. It was not news to Baldwin, but he brought it up with Tresca. Again, Tresca staunchly maintained the innocence of the two men.

If Tresca knew or suspected anything about the guilt of Sacco and Vanzetti in 1927, his conversation with Roger Baldwin would have been a logical moment to mention it. Sacco and Vanzetti were dead, and Baldwin was an outsider to the Italian circles where such news would have increased the hostility of the Galleanisti toward Tresca.

In the Sacco-Vanzetti case the hostility became evident at an early stage. On November 27, 1920, Tresca wrote an indignant note to the Boston defense committee demanding a "categorical" answer as to why contributors to the defense had received a notice instructing them to "send not a penny to Tresca, but to send all contributions directly to Boston."

By 1919, Tresca, in an isolated political position after his break with the IWW, was drawing attacks from a number of sections of the radical movement. On February 28, 1920, after a Department of Justice raid on radicals in Paterson, the IWW paper *New Solidarity* charged that the arrests were "made possible by the cooperation of Carlo Tresca and the officials of the Amalgamated Clothing Workers," with the federal agents. "It was an article supposed to be by Carlo Tresca . . . attacking [Louis Caminita, one of the arrested men] which gave government men the clue."

It was self-serving—there was a history of rivalry between the Amalgamated and the IWW—to charge Tresca with being in league with the Department of Justice. Tresca and Giovannitti, who had also been named by *New Solidarity*, sent a telegram to Bill Haywood at once about "this . . . moral assassination the indecency of which is beyond qualification." Haywood pleaded ignorance of the article, writing to Roger Baldwin, "If my feeling toward Tresca has changed somewhat I still have a personal love for Giovannitti."

The Italian-language weekly of the IWW, *Il Proletario*, continued the quarrel with Tresca through 1920, with accusations of "crook," "swindler," "spy," and "stool pigeon" and a rehearsal of the Mesabi incident and the 1918 trial severance.

"It's a shame, a real shame," Tresca wrote in the March 15 edition of the *Martello*.

> He who really has faith in his heart, he who has given to the ideal all his being, all his thoughts, all his brimming desires cannot remain indifferent [to] our periodicals which . . . instead of aiming at the one and only target—the enemy who persecutes and oppresses us—turn their best efforts to personal attacks. . . . A struggle of ideas is desirable and noble. But . . . these senseless controversies are doing more harm than the merciless persecutions on the part of the ruling classes . . . *it hurt me, and still hurts me* to polemicize against comrades whom I love. . . . Enough! Let us all rise above our miserable impulses of personal resentment . . . above our base sectarian passions and let us struggle for the ideal.

Joining the anarchist and IWW attacks, the Socialists now took Tresca to task for inconsistency to anarchist principles: he had expressed approval of the Soviet regime and of the electoral victory of the Socialists in Italy. To these charges Tresca replied in the *Martello* that he remained a syndicalist; the organization of society on the basis of labor unions, and the position of the Sparticists and the Italian Communists were all in accord with his concepts of revolutionary syndicalism. As for the Socialist victory in Italy, "it is preferable that they [the workers'] should indicate their orientation towards socialism rather than their servile submission to the clergy, to the employer and the Government."

Even some of Tresca's friends were dismayed by the position in which he now found himself. The young anarchist Sam Dolgoff taxed him with his association with the "Social Democrats" of the Amalgamated. With some sadness Tresca answered that since his break with the IWW, he had lost the former base of his activity; and without activity, he could not live.

In later years Dolgoff described his comrade as a firm anarcho-syndicalist: "He believed that the union of the workers must overthrow the system, and he also had a great deal of faith in insurrection. But he was given to a certain amount of opportunism. To make friends, to curry influence, Carlo would overlook ideology. Not because he was a hypocrite, but because he felt these contacts with the Socialists and dissident groups in the labor unions, these people were in a position to do a lot of good and help him when he needed it. Tresca's group was interested in daily struggles and he collaborated with people of different tendencies. It was not exactly by the rules, but he would bend the rules for humanitarian reasons."

Jack Frager, another young anarchist comrade, recalled, "Carlo was loved by a lot of people, not just respected, loved. He could mix with millionaires, he could mix with prostitutes. Maybe he mixed too much. When police would come to question him he took them out for a drink. I think that damaged him a lot. But like a fish needs water he had to be with people. It's the nature of every rebel not to be isolated."

Tresca's friendship with Aldino Felicani never faltered. But others on the defense committee, primarily Emile Coda, who became its secretary, were venomous in their hatred of him. Coda launched a violent newspaper attack on Tresca in 1925, but Tresca continued speaking publicly for Sacco and Vanzetti, the *Martello* remained at the service of the defense, and Flynn traveled often between Boston and New York; "our link with Tresca," Felicani called her.

On August 22, 1927, the day before Sacco and Vanzetti were to be executed, Tresca addressed an enormous crowd in Union Square and called for a general strike. His appeal prevailed no more than had the exposure of the glaring weaknesses in the evidence against the two men.

On August 22, Vanzetti requested an interview with his lawyer, William Thompson. Thompson found Vanzetti writing at a table in his cell. The two men shook hands. "The Harvard graduate, the man of old American traditions, the established lawyer," Thompson wrote shortly before this final meeting, "is now quite ready to say that nowhere in his soul is there to be found the faith, the splendid gentility which make the man, Bartolomeo Vanzetti." At this meeting, Thompson asked, as Luigi Quintiliano had earlier asked Sacco, about the rumors of guilt. He asked for Vanzetti's "most solemn reassurance, but with respect to him and with respect to Sacco. Vanzetti then told me quietly and calmly, and with a sincerity which I could not doubt, that I need have no anxiety about this matter; that both he and Sacco were absolutely innocent. . . . He asked me to do what I could to clear his name."

For more than a decade after their executions, the innocence of Sacco and Vanzetti remained an article of faith for their defenders, unblemished by the earlier rumors of guilt. But in the late 1930s, and until shortly before his own murder in 1943, Tresca would tell a number of people that Sacco had been guilty. At Norman Thomas's apartment, Tresca told John Roche, who asked his opinion of Maxwell Anderson's play based on the case, *Winterset,* that Sacco had murdered a good comrade. Vanzetti, Tresca said in great agitation, was innocent; Sacco had refused to plead guilty because he thought they could win.

More than once during this period Tresca repeated his accusation against Sacco: to Norman Thomas he said that he had known of Sacco's guilt from the beginning and had urged him to admit it in the defiant anarchist tradition. Late in 1942, in response to a question from Max Eastman, Tresca said that Sacco was guilty, Vanzetti was not.

Everyone who heard this assertion, first- or secondhand, was shocked by it. Yet it remained simply an assertion: to no one did Tresca offer supporting evidence, nor had he hinted at such a possibility during the seven years of the case or in the decade that followed. It is true however that two days before the trial of Sacco and Vanzetti had opened, he had addressed an audience of several hundred at Malnati's Hall in Quincy, and in the hearing of an agent who reported his words to the Bureau of Investigation he had said: "We defend Sacco and Vanzetti because they are innocent. We defend them because they are two men. If, instead of Sacco and Vanzetti, two other men, who were not comrades, were in the same circumstances, we would defend them just the same even if they were the true robbers. And do you know why? Because the money they would have stolen would have been the property of . . . the producing class. . . . That money belongs to the workers, belongs to you, belongs to all."

But if this statement of Tresca's was meant to imply specific knowledge of the crime, seventeen years would pass before he ever referred to it again. And when, in the late 1930s, Tresca accused Sacco, he at no point offered evidence for Sacco's guilt.

Even so, Tresca's statements have affected recent reappraisals of the case. One historian, assuming that Tresca, of all people, would know the truth, has used his word to make the case for Sacco's guilt. Another historian believes that the attacks by the Galleanisti against Tresca, which reached a height in 1938, may have left Tresca so bitter than he came to think that lies they told about him extended to their insistence on Sacco's innocence.

This smear campaign by the Galleanisti in 1938 reached Emma Goldman in London: "I don't know if you are aware of the feud that has gone on for years between Tresca and his comrades and the L'Adunata group," she wrote to a friend that year. "Some years ago they charged him with nothing less than being a spy. They actually wrote to us to pass an opinion on the matter which Sasha and I refused pointblank. They sent us no evidence of any character, besides which we have known Carlo so long we cannot imagine him capable of such a thing. I'd quite forgotten the whole business when lo and behold a few weeks ago the L'Adunata group started a new campaign."

For whatever reasons—bitterness and vindictiveness against those who should have been united with him in revolutionary solidarity or proof that has utterly vanished—toward the end of his life Tresca said, and no doubt believed, that Sacco had been guilty of the robbery and murders that took place in South Braintree on April 15, 1920.

Chapter 10
Sick at Heart

WHEN Sacco and Vanzetti were executed at the end of August 1927, Elizabeth Gurley Flynn had been in Portland, Oregon, for eight months. She made a note of the executions in her journal. At that time, and in all senses of the phrase, Flynn was sick at heart.

Flynn had worked hard in the years after the 1918 IWW trial. Under the auspices of the Workers Defense Union, a delegate body of the National Civil Liberties Union, she organized meetings, raised money, and made speeches for those wartime and Red Scare prisoners who still languished on Ellis Island and in other detention centers. "It seemed then like a hideous nightmare," she wrote of those years. She worked long hours in a small, dark room at the Rand School; in her office electric lights burned all day long, and fumes from nearby factories filled the room. "I lived in the Bronx, came down early to our office and stayed late, or spoke at night. I saw little of my family, my child or my husband. . . . [On a] Christmas day . . . I was at our family dinner, a festive occasion. . . . The phone rang. . . . I took a long breath before I returned to the dining room to announce that I had to leave. 'This is outrageous!' boomed Carlo."

Labor defense work was a dreary grind compared with Elizabeth's IWW days: "There is no period in all the labor history of America that is more picturesque, that has in it more gaiety and heroism than the early days of the singing Wobblies," Mary Heaton

Vorse recalled. "The very heart of this was 'Gurley,' not yet twenty, fearless and beautiful."

Flynn was a conscientious professional, and she put all her energy into her work. But it could not have yielded the same gratifications as being at the center of a revolutionary movement. And Flynn was no longer twenty, but thirty, still fearless but without the beauty of her youth. In only a few more years Albert De Silver would refer to her as "two hundred pounds of horse sense."

Her personal life continued much as before. She lived with her family and Carlo in the Bronx: her sister Kathie taught public school and studied for a master's degree at Columbia; Tom, her brother, had become an optician; her youngest sister, Bina, had left school to be an actress with the Celtic Players; Buster had been taken out of his local public school in 1917 when his teacher responded to Carlo's and Elizabeth's arrest by telling him that "only people who lie, steal and kill go to jail." From then on he went to Friends Seminary in lower Manhattan. Either Carlo or Elizabeth took him there each morning, and one of them put him on the el to go home in the afternoon.

Each summer they returned to the bungalow at South Beach, on Staten Island, where they had many visitors. Roger Baldwin was an occasional visitor in the early 1920s. He was very fond of Flynn. He considered her more than competent at her work, and never found her other than charming and cheerful. Tresca was always a treat: "Big, hearty, full of fun, explosive. He loved his food, loved his friends, he loved to explode in indignation," Baldwin recalled. "He loved to be alive. He enjoyed himself immensely. In fact, I think he enjoyed himself more than he enjoyed anybody else. He was so spontaneous, almost childlike in his spontaneity."

Baldwin liked the other members of the Flynn family, Bina in particular. She did not have Elizabeth's forcefulness, but she was witty, quiet, and very attractive. Buster was a sad little boy, plump, a little lost, not really understanding what was going on around him. And Baldwin also formed the impression, although no one said anything to him, that by the early 1920s Elizabeth and Carlo were no longer lovers.

In the summer of 1922 Flynn and Tresca entertained other visitors at South Beach. Vincent St. John, released from Leavenworth, where he had been confined since the IWW trial, came for a few days to recuperate. He brought James Cannon with him. Cannon, once an IWW organizer, had, along with other Wobblies, Earl Browder and William Z. Foster among them, joined the Communist party. In 1922 Cannon was deeply involved in the factional fight for leadership of the Party. He wanted St. John with him. "I remember the occasion when I made the final effort with The Saint," Cannon wrote later. "The two of us went together to have dinner and spend the night as guests of Carlo Tresca and Elizabeth Gurley Flynn at the cottage on Staten Island beach. We spent very little time looking at the ocean. . . . All through the dinner hour, and nearly all through the night, we discussed my thesis that the future belonged to the Communist Party; and that the IWW militants should not abandon the new party to the intellectuals, but come into it and help shape its proletarian character." Of Cannon's audience, it was Flynn, in the end, who had listened most carefully.

Mary Hunter also saw Tresca and Flynn fairly often during 1922 and 1923. She had returned to New York after her work with Fred Moore and was sharing an apartment with Lola Darroch, Moore's estranged wife. The two women frequently had dinner with Carlo and Elizabeth at a weekly institution called a round table, where for a fee dinner was cooked in the home of an Italian family. "Carlo and Gurley had a round table going somewhere on Thompson Street," Mary Hunter recalled. "My memory of Carlo is always sitting at the head of the table, having a beautiful time. Everyone always had the most marvelous time, good food, a little red wine, just good fun."

Sometimes Mary Hunter went to South Beach to see Tresca and Flynn there. The last occasion was during the summer of 1923. She had struck up an acquaintance with a handsome Italian naval officer named Luigi Paladini. Paladini, in disgrace in Italy for having gambled with his ship's funds, was making his way in the United States by various means, including selling advertising to importers of Italian foods. On a summer afternoon in 1923 he had an appointment with an oil and cheese importer on Staten Island. Mary Hunter accompanied him; afterward, at his request, because he had often asked her to introduce him to Tresca, they took the streetcar and rode out to South Beach. "The minute I introduced Gigi, I knew I had done something wrong. I knew Gigi was an ardent fascisti, but I was never very interested in politics and I never took Mussolini seriously. In my breezy, dumb, American way, I paid no attention. But Carlo got me alone. '*What* made you bring that man here?' I said, 'Carlo, I didn't think you'd mind; he's an Italian.' That was the last time I ever saw Carlo." (Tresca's instinct about Paladini was sound. Paladini later returned to Italy as a volunteer in Mussolini's Ethiopian campaign; he returned to New York and in 1941 was deported as a suspected agent of Italian intelligence.)

Mary Hunter, who had known Tresca for six or seven years, had strong feelings of affection for him. She was indifferent to Flynn, whom she found always perfectly civil but distant. Elizabeth must have been wary of Carlo's attractive women friends; she had reason to suspect that he was chronically unfaithful. In the summer of 1922 she learned that her sister Bina was pregnant with Carlo's child.

Of the three younger Flynn children who had grown up in Elizabeth's precocious shadow, Kathie seems to have been most free of resentment and was content for Elizabeth to have life on her own terms. She was also willing to deal with the consequences of Elizabeth's life: Buster was more Kathie's and Annie Gurley's child than his mother's, if time and effort are a measure. As for Tom, the "quiet" brother, he committed suicide in 1936, and that must speak of a lifetime of unease.

Bina was the baby, eight years younger than Elizabeth and determined not to be overlooked. She had helped Elizabeth with legal defense work now and then, and she had also helped out at the *Martello,* but by the early 1920s she had begun a promising career as an actress and was associated with the Provincetown and Celtic players.

Bina had married a James Martin, known as "Slim." But the marriage did not work out, and in 1922 she was again living in the family home, "in the apartment also occupied by Elizabeth Gurley Flynn and Carlo Tresca," as Bureau of Investigation files note.

Bina had known Carlo for almost half her life. Their relations almost certainly began in flirtatious teasing between the adolescent girl and her sister's powerfully attractive lover. Bina was twenty-four in 1922, almost twenty years younger than Carlo, and she had grown into a dreamy Irish beauty. But even Carlo's habits of sexual self-indulgence and Bina's impulse to self-assertion are not enough to explain this love affair: the particular cruelty of the betrayal at least indicates that strong feelings were involved. According to their son, Bina continued to love Carlo all her life.

But motivations aside, in March 1922, Bina became pregnant. On August 10, when the Italian steamer *Conto Rosso* sailed for Genoa, Bina was probably aboard. The Bureau of Investigation agent who examined the passenger list looking for a Bina Flynn failed to find her name since, most likely, Bina was using her full legal name, Lucy Sabina Martin. Whether on that ship or not, Bina did sail to Italy that summer, where she intended to remain until her child was born. Maybe she planned to leave the baby with the Tresca family; maybe Carlo meant to join her in Italy. But politics, on a large scale, intervened. When Mussolini ascended to power in October 1922, a frightened seven-month-pregnant Bina returned home.

Elizabeth now needed all of her considerable courage. No record remains of what took place between Elizabeth and Carlo and Bina. In her memoirs, Elizabeth alludes to separation from Carlo in vague terms. She writes about discovering love letters written by Carlo to a married woman (Bina was still legally married to Slim Martin) that were "of such a nature that I had no choice." She speaks also of growing political differences between herself and Tresca: "His preoccupation was with Italian affairs. . . . I became more and more immersed in my own field of labor defense work." He was an anarchist, she was a socialist, with no place or much interest in the Italian anarchist movement. "Carlo's Italian comrades realized we had drifted apart. . . . They tried to tell me that if I would only stay home and 'keep house' for Carlo, all would be well. . . . [But] they knew the answer and so did I then. Carlo had a roving eye that had roved in my direction in Lawrence but then, some ten years later, was roving elsewhere."

Still, no open breach occurred between Carlo and Elizabeth in 1922 or in 1923, though they saw each other less and less. In October of 1922, Tresca started on a propaganda tour of the Midwest, which kept him away from New York into the winter of 1923.

Il Martello published his schedule, advising comrades in Ohio, Michigan, Minnesota, Wisconsin, and Indiana that they might take their choice of lecture topics, including "The Class Struggle in America," "Fascism in Italy," or "The Russian Revolution and the Dictatorship of the Proletariat."

Flynn continued her legal defense work, including work on the Sacco-Vanzetti appeals. She and Tresca remained together formally until 1925. They would probably have separated sooner had Tresca not needed all Flynn's skills for legal defense when, in August 1923, he was arrested on a federal charge.

Chapter 11
The United States and Italy versus Carlo Tresca

As Italy verged on revolution in 1919 and 1920, Carlo Tresca and the *Martello* watched events unfold. "The bourgeois world vascillates," Tresca wrote in April 1919. "The eyes of all proletarians . . . the eyes of all rebels are now turned towards Italy." In the November 1919 elections the Socialists had emerged as the strongest party in Parliament; in July and August 1920, the metal workers of Milan and Turin occupied the factories and in Sicily armed peasants took over the land: "It is the ardent thirst for the land, the factory and for liberty," cried the *Martello*, "It is the road to communism."

For the Italian anarchists in 1919, communism, as exemplified by the Bolshevik revolution, was still indistinguishable from their own revolutionary ideal. Errico Malatesta, however, was already warning that in Russia "a new government has set itself up above the Revolution in order to bridle it and subject it to the purposes of a particular party . . . or rather the leaders of a party."

The moment and the distinctions were crucial for Italy. The *fasci*, organized by Mussolini in March 1919, had grown to about one hundred organized groups by summer 1920, still weak but supported by a broad spectrum of middle and upper classes. In the face of the Fascist movement, Lenin in September 1920 called on the "Italian revolutionary proletariat" to substitute its "old leaders by Communists in all proletarian organizations," a decision endorsed by the Comintern. When Socialist party members rejected the directive to expel reformists and parliamentarians, the left wing marched from the meeting hall, singing the "Internationale," to form the Italian Communist party.

Angelica Balabanoff, who was about to leave her post at the Comintern, spoke with Lenin about the Italian situation in September 1920. She told him that she believed Italy was better prepared for social revolution than any other European country, to which Lenin responded with "irritation." He said he wanted no repetition of the Communist defeat in Hungary: a revolution in Italy, he said, would have "fatal consequences" at that time. Balabanoff later wrote, "I have often been asked if Italian Fascism would have triumphed without the splits provoked by the Bolsheviks. . . . The splits . . . both facilitated and prepared the way for the victory of the Fascist terror." Furthermore, the splits were inexplicable without the "key" of Moscow's intolerance for anything but complete acceptance of Moscow's direction.

Thus was Italy's most powerful party opposing Mussolini weakened, and by February 1921 the *fasci* had grown to more than a thousand groups. "Every day armed bands selected from the dregs and scum of the Italian gutters and recruited from the jails, the most savage bloodthirsty gangsters go about . . . setting fires to the Chambers of Labor, Leagues and Circles," the *Martello* reported in April 1921. "These bands of assassins are known as the 'Fighting Fascisti.' In fact they fight the poor at the order of the rich."

On the morning of October 30, 1922, Mussolini stepped off the Milan-Rome night train to receive the government of Italy. A year later, Mussolini's chargé d'affaires in Rome wrote to Charles Evans Hughes, under secretary of state, enclosing a list of radicals in the United States about whom the director general of public safety in Rome wished to have information. To this request, William J. Burns, director of the Bureau of Investigation, was pleased to be able to reply that one of those radicals, Carlo Tresca, was at that moment being prosecuted by federal authorities in New York.

Apart from the Post Office Department, federal agents had so far been surprisingly lax in their attentions to Tresca. But in March 1922, William J. Burns sent a memo to his agents across the country. He instructed them to utilize all sources available to discover whether Carlo Tresca was a naturalized citizen. If not, Burns wrote, "it is, of course, our intention that every effort be made to bring about his early deportation, and I would care personally to call his case to the attention of the Secretary of Labor."

Bureau of Investigation agents spent weeks searching records of the Naturalization Bureau in various cities. It was pointless labor; Tresca freely admitted to anyone who asked, including a bureau agent posing as a reporter, that he was not a citizen. That fact being finally established, the bureau had now to find some published or uttered statement that would bring him under the net of the deportation statutes.

A bureau agent, Joseph Sposa, managed to get a job in the *Martello* office. *Il Martello* was then housed at 208 East Twelfth Street, next door to the stables of a milk delivery company and just behind a brownstone leased by the Workers' party. The possibility of breaking into the *Martello* was discussed and abandoned by the Bureau of Investigation. But they had a valuable source in Sposa. Sposa was able to report on all of Tresca's activities, plans, and many of his conversations. Early in May, for instance, Sposa reported on one of his own conversations with Tresca. Knowing that Tresca was looking for space to open a bookstore, Sposa asked him why he was having a problem. Why didn't he just rent a regular storefront? That's too risky, Tresca told him; a street-level bookstore would be subject to constant raids. He needed a store on an upper floor. Sposa changed the subject. Why not, he suggested, write an article attacking the president? Tresca must have been astonished, but he patiently replied to his new, eager comrade that it was not advisable to be too antagonistic to the administration. He had been granted concessions in the past. The road was hard enough to travel, he said, without making it more difficult: I have kept myself out of trouble this long by not declaring my paper to be anarchist. Such an admission would mean being barred from the mails, and the authorities would try to jail me. If I can help it I'm not going to jail. I can do better work outside.

With Sposa reporting Tresca's itinerary in advance, bureau agents and informers were prepared to follow him. In the middle of May, they followed him to Pennsylvania. At the railroad station in Hershey he was met by several men who drove him to a farm in nearby Swatara where a picnic was in progress. About forty-five Italians greeted Tresca warmly. He began to speak at once without introduction, promising that the real culprits of the crime of which Sacco and Vanzetti were accused would soon be produced. Sacco and Vanzetti, he said, were the victims of capitalist government. But all governments were corrupt. The Italian government was the worst of them, but even the government in Soviet Russia was no different; under its system, the laboring classes were starving to death.

Here Tresca was interrupted by one Tomasso Matrassi, who called out, Are you a socialist or an anarchist? I am an anarchist, Tresca replied; the informer present noted that he "cleverly refrained" from advocating violence, advising only that the laboring classes stick together in unions and educate themselves by reading the *Martello.*

A few days after the picnic, the bureau noted a positive side effect of their surveillance: the Mutual Beneficial Society, which had sponsored the picnic, was broken up by officials of the Hershey Company; the leaders of the society, all of whom worked for Hershey, were to be discharged on one pretext or another.

In early September, Tresca was followed to West Virginia. An informant watched as he got off the train at the Fairmont Station on Monday, September 4. He was carrying two bundles—the first, two-feet wide and almost as high; the other, half again that size. Six Italian men met him at the station and helped transport the bundles to an address on Market Street. Desperate to find out what the bundles contained the bureau informant went to the office of the local district attorney. He explained the situation and the district attorney promptly issued a search warrant for liquor. Five policemen rushed to the address on Market Street and confiscated the packages which, when opened, contained books—works by Tolstoy, books on evolution, anarchy, libertarian speech, the foreign policies of the Soviet Union, and a number of journals, including the *Martello,* "a hundred dollars worth of books," Tresca later complained. The police then broke into Tresca's hotel room. It was empty.

A chase began. The bureau informant stationed himself at the depot of the town's bus lines. As each bus driver arrived, he was asked: "Have you seen my uncle with the black beard?" Alas, no driver had seen him. From six in the evening until eleven, the distraught informant, in the company of local police, drove in the district attorney's Dodge coupe through the towns of Monongah, Rivesville, and all over the county, searching for the anarchists' meeting place. In vain: the quarry had escaped.

Back in New York, Tresca went to a restaurant with some of his staff. As soon as I arrived at the Fairmont Station, he said, I was shadowed. That means the government knew which train I would be on. And it means there is someone in the organization who is spying on me. Joseph Sposa, who was at the table and who reported the conversation, was apparently not under suspicion.

To his comrade Federico Arcos, Tresca wrote, "it is not worthwhile to stick one's head out of New York. I made a disastrous attempt to go to West Va. and I came out of it *miraculously*. I do not know how it will end up. I am waiting for their next move now. . . . Enough. We will see."

During the next year the bureau watched and harrassed. Tresca was traveling a good deal during the fall and winter of 1922–23, speaking in eastern and midwestern states. "Carlo Tresca leaving New York November 4, 1922, 12:25 A.M. for Detroit," an informant reported. "Tour expected to last two months. Description: Italian. Age 45; Height 5′11″; Weight 230; well built; black Van Dyke beard; olive complexion; very dark brown eyes; may be wearing glasses; usually wears blue serge suit; black fedora hat; light grey coat; carries new leather suitcase, flowing black tie."

In the various cities and towns of Ohio, Illinois, Michigan, and Pennsylvania, where the police chiefs were notified of his presence, Tresca spoke often about Fascism. "Most all of you have read something concerning the actual state of things in Italy," he said at the Roma Theatre in Cleveland. "And in spite of the fact the press, mercenary and dishonest, gives the savage inhumanity of the Italian fascisti an appearance of justice, I am here tonight to tell you that the press lies. . . . Fascismo . . . is an army of degenerate, perverted criminals who are trying to kill the spirit of revolution in Italy."

In February, bureau director Burns informed the State Department that "Carlo Tresca recently addressed a meeting [in New York City] at which was discussed the Fascisti and in which it was stated that it might be desirable to write to some friends in Italy to take action against Mussolini. . . . This matter will be given very careful attention by the Bureau."

The bureau successfully prevented Tresca from speaking in Waterbury, Connecticut, by making its wish known to the superintendent of police. Tresca returned to Waterbury three times during February and March 1923, bringing Roger Baldwin for legal support. Three times he was prevented from addressing the audience. But despite the activities of so many agents, the bureau apparently still did not have evidence that would stand up in a deportation hearing. They began, however, to set the stage for one.

In April the bureau requested a reporter, Frank Hopkins, to sign an affidavit swearing that, in 1914, within his hearing, Tresca had said: "I believe in violence. Nothing can make me feel any other way than Caron did." Hopkins was reluctant; he was not sure whether Tresca had actually spoken the words in his hearing or whether he had copied them from another reporter. He was nevertheless persuaded to sign. Two Minnesota reporters also agreed to testify, in the event of a deportation hearing, that on the Mesabi Range in 1916 Tresca had made remarks inciting violence. A bureau agent returned to Swatara to ask Tomasso Matrassi to testify that Tresca had answered his question by stating, "I am an anarchist." Matrassi was not so helpful. He denied that he had ever asked such a question or heard such a statement. Nothing could persuade him otherwise.

The post office was helpful to the bureau, keeping a careful eye on the *Martello* for language that might fall under the deportation statutes, but they could find nothing specific enough. Agent William Palmera bought a copy of "Rationalist Propaganda," an eighty-seven-page booklet written by Tresca and advertised in the *Martello*. The best he could report was that it was atheistic propaganda: "As long as a man expects justice from God . . . as long as the faithful laborer gazes at God and speaks to him of earthly miseries there will always be someone who will cheerfully exploit him and lighten his almost empty pockets. . . . God is the broker of the rich, he orders you humility."

By May the Italian ambassador, Prince Gelasio Caetani, was becoming impatient. Caetani wrote to Secretary of State Hughes that "the notorious labor agitators Carlo Tresca, Arturo Giovannitti, the Amalgamated Workers . . . and other social-communist elements in New York" were defaming the Italian government. Particularly objectionable was a recent article in *Il Martello;* it was "most desirable" that this publication be barred from the mails and its editor prosecuted.

The article in question was called "Down with the Monarchy," and appeared in the May 5 issue. It dealt in some scatological detail with the purported sexual habits of the Italian royal family. Not only was the monarchy guilty of embracing Mussolini, but "the Savoyan monarchy, dripping with blood and dirt . . . the king, the princes, the princesses and the queens . . . able to pass their days in bacchanals of passion and debauchery . . . the animal love affairs of Victor Emmanuel II [who gets] up in the morning from the bed of adultery and goes to the royal chapel to purge himself. . . . These love affairs, these orgies and these royal adulteries have cost the people tears of blood. . . . We who know that every gem worn by Yolanda in her wedding crown is made of tears and blood, and of the flesh of the people are once more raising the outcry with all the strength of our soul: Down with the Monarchy!"

Secretary of State Hughes, acting on Prince Caetani's complaint, met with the postmaster general and the New York district attorney. They agreed that as soon as a formal complaint was received, they would cooperate to vigorously prosecute a deportation case.

In July, Prince Caetani returned to Washington from an official visit to Rome. He attended a banquet for Judge Elbert Gary, president of U.S. Steel, who was about to be installed as an honorary Fascist. Prince Caetani made a little speech in praise of the judge and went on to voice his concern about opponents of fascism among Italians in the United States. There is, the prince said, "a certain Italian paper in New York [which] ought to be suppressed."

On July 21, the post office seized all copies of the current issue of the *Martello*. On August 14, Tresca was arrested by a U.S. deputy marshall, on the charge of mailing and delivering unmailable matter. "Down with the Monarchy," the article that was the basis of the complaint, was so obscene, the government maintained, that parts of it had to be omitted from the formal charge so as not to sully court records.

But in its eagerness to please the Italian regime, the U.S. government had been overhasty. Inspector Keen of the post office "seems to think this case is somewhat weak," a bureau agent noted, "and is preparing another case . . . charging subject with sending certain books through the mail, both of which contain obscene matter, and one of them treating on methods to prevent conception. These books bear the following titles: *Chastity and the Virgin State, The Art of Preventing Childbirth.*"

Nor would this case wash. The post office translator noted that *The Art of Preventing Childbirth,* which was written by a physician, was "on the whole instructive and rather educational. . . . It sounds more like a paper being read before a convention of medical authorities" than like an obscene book. Still, if the books had been sent across state lines, an illegal act had been committed. The bureau made sure that this occurred "by having Italian operatives . . . send orders to Tresca for these obscene books . . . with a view to securing evidence to obtain a successful prosecution."

The Bureau of Investigation tried to cover all bases, arranging for the agents to give an address in some small town, "otherwise Tresca might write to them and state that they could purchase these books at certain bookstores located in large cities." Director Burns himself added a flourish, suggesting that "in order to divert or allay possible suspicion," another book offered by the *Martello* library should be ordered at the same time and the writers should request the books to be sent in "a plain envelope."

Letters ordering the books were duly mailed to New York, where an agent was stationed at the *Martello* post office box to ascertain that the letters were received. All outgoing packages from the *Martello* were inspected to be sure the books were mailed out. By October 11 the agent in Pittsburgh had received his books, which he then mailed back to New York, where they were to be translated for the hearing. To divert suspicion from what was going on, the post office held up the October 27 issue of the *Martello,* citing an objectionable article dealing with the Fascist practice of dosing adversaries with castor oil.

Tresca apparently had no notion of what was going on. While waiting for his hearing—originally scheduled for September 25, but postponed while the government tried to build a stronger case against him—he made speeches in Pennsylvania, attended a dance in Philadelphia to raise money for his defense, and began a series of anti-fascist meetings in New England.

Flynn and Giovannitti joined him for a meeting at Eagles' Hall in Providence on October 28, where the audience was swelled by a large number of plain clothes detectives and Department of Jus-

tice agents. "We have come here tonight," Flynn told them, "for
the purpose of discussing with the American workers and those
workers of Italian birth who live in America, the question of the
Fascisti movement in America. It attempts to get a footing here
and I ask why it is, and why we don't fight it." The next afternoon,
Ambassador Caetani arrived in Providence as the honored guest of
a convention of the Sons of Italy. An honor guard escorted Caetani
to the convention hall where hundreds of delegates cheered him.
Arturo Giovannitti and Luigi Antonini, who were in the hall, were
forced to kiss the flag when they objected to a resolution before
the convention.

Tresca's hearing was held on November 1. Represented by
Harold Content, he entered a plea of not guilty to eight counts of
violation of the postal laws. The trial was set for November 26; the
government had only three weeks to get its case in order.

With so much preparation, it was astonishing how many things
had gone wrong. In the first place the agent in Pittsburgh, who
had received the books, turned out to be unavailable as a witness.
J. Edgar Hoover, Burns's assistant, was extremely irritated: "The
Pittsburgh office obtained evidence but it cannot be used in court
and is of no value," he wrote to Burns. "It is a most exasperating
incident. . . . As a matter of fact, now the entire case against
Tresca may fail, which will bring down upon this Department considerable criticism and Tresca will become more blatant in his activities and statements than ever before."

Letters and telegrams flew back and forth between Pittsburgh
and Washington. Washington insisted on being told the name of
the informant who had received the books; the bureau agent in
Pittsburgh apologized but refused to compromise an undercover
source. "The Bureau is seriously embarrassed," Burns wrote to
Spencer, the Pittsburgh agent in charge. "I cannot too strongly indicate to you my disapproval. . . . It is imperative that the person
receiving these books be used as a witness." "I am more embarrassed than you are," Spencer replied. "I have taken the case up
with the man who . . . handles this informant. . . . He stated that
while he was only too anxious to help the Department, he could
not as a matter of honor disclose the name of this informant. I do
not personally know the name of the informant or his present address." "Too unfortunate for words," J. Edgar Hoover thought.

Assistant U.S. Attorney Mattuck, who was prosecuting the case, also thought it very unfortunate, since the Pittsburgh count was probably the strongest of the eight counts in the indictment. As late as November 12, an agent was sending for books to be mailed across a state line, but his postal order for $2.35 was returned by the *Martello,* with the apology that "it is impossible for us to fill any orders of the books you requested because their mailability is at present questioned by the U.S. Post Office Dep't."

Prosecuting Attorney Mattuck, however, remained optimistic about obtaining a conviction. When the trial opened at 2:30 on the afternoon of November 26, 1923, he had dropped two counts of mailing books to Pennsylvania, but he had added another charge. The jury was asked to consider seven counts of mailing indecent books and, in addition, the publication of a two-line advertisement in the *Martello* for *The Art of Preventing Childbirth.* This was a strange charge; the advertisement had indeed been printed in the September 8 issue, but that edition had been held up by the post office and accepted for mailing only after the offending advertisement had been crossed out by hand in each copy of the paper.

The jury heard evidence from post office employees, a Bureau of Investigation agent from Boston, and from the bureau's "special employee" Joseph Sposa, who revealed that he had been privy to all goings-on at the *Martello* office for almost a year. Tresca took the stand in his own defense. In response to Mattuck's questioning he denied that he was an anarchist. He denied that he had ever advocated forcible overthrow of the government or agitated for a general strike. Yes, he admitted, he knew Alexander Berkman, but had never been associated with him. And as for the mailing of the books, he was not responsible for that. His partner, Umberto Nieri, was director of the *Martello* library and took care of that end of the business. Nieri, who also took the stand, confirmed this.

The jury deliberated for three hours. While they were debating, Bureau of Investigation agents mingled with spectators in the corridors, "for the purpose of noting the various Anarchists known to be in attendance at the trial." At 7:30 the jury returned with a verdict of guilty on the eighth count alone—that of publishing the advertisement, "a compromise" vote, the bureau was informed.

"The jury could not do otherwise," the *Martello* reported on December 22. "They were told by the District Attorney that Tresca was a bombardier, anarchist, a dangerous agitator, sly. . . . Do not let this man go or he will climb up on the roof of his house and will cry out with all the strength of his voice that he has beaten the government once more."

It was not only to the government that Tresca had to answer, but to some of the Galleanisti who attended his trial and were angered at his denial of anarchism. "Oh, yes," he wrote in the *Martello*, "Tresca said he was not an anarchist. Well, Tresca is not an imbecile. You know it. The District Attorney knows it also. . . . He had to state he was an anarchist to oblige spies like you and the Fascists in Italy and here? The Department of Justice was there in full force . . . to grab Tresca by the neck and say, 'Ah, you state you are an anarchist. Well, then, Ellis Island for you.'"

Sentencing took place on December 8 in Judge Goddard's chambers in the Woolworth Building. In addition to his lawyer, Harold Content, Fiorello LaGuardia and George Gordon Battle were present to plead for leniency for Tresca. Elizabeth Gurley Flynn sat silently as Mattuck argued that, in view of Tresca's entire notorious career, the most severe sentence allowed by law should be imposed.

Judge Goddard turned to Tresca. Are you a married man? he asked. Carlo said that he was, and turned to indicate Elizabeth.

Goddard was not satisfied. Is this a legal marriage?

A common-law marriage, Tresca replied. He was separated from his legal wife and contributed to the support of their daughter. He hoped that the sentence about to be pronounced would be a lenient one.

Mattuck had been waiting for this opportunity. The government, he stated, would not object to a lenient sentence provided that the defendant voluntarily agreed to leave the country.

If I return to Italy I will be killed, Tresca said.

Judge Goddard handed down the most severe sentence allowed by law—a year and a day in prison. A few days later the Bureau of Investigation noted that "concerning the possibilities of instituting deportation proceedings against Carlo Tresca, I am informed, according to Immigration rules, Tresca cannot be deported as the result of his recent conviction."

But the ideal of deportation remained, and the government continued to try to find the evidence. On December 8, Tresca was taken to the Tombs, where he was held overnight until bail of five thousand dollars was furnished. He remained free during the year of the appeals process. The end-of-year-statement sent out by *Il Martello* to subscribers stated, "Mussolini has become a sacred and inviolable person also in America." The paper showed a deficit of almost three thousand dollars for the year, and also the amounts collected from subscribers to aid political victims: for political prisoners in Italy, more than two thousand dollars; for Sacco and Vanzetti, more than one thousand dollars; for Tresca's right to free speech at Waterbury, Connecticut, one hundred and eighty dollars.

Chapter 12
Women and Children

BINA Flynn gave birth to a son on January 6, 1923. He was named Peter, called Pete, and carried the surname of Bina's legal husband, Slim Martin.

She tried to keep the baby a secret at first, at least from Annie Gurley. Shortly after his birth Pete was sent to a country place where infants were boarded; when he was a little older he was boarded with a German couple in Queens who had a number of other foster children. In a story he wrote many years later Pete recalled his foster mother as a fat, bad-tempered woman who invariably wore a polka-dot housedress; her husband, small and thin, cursed constantly. New babies arrived and departed quickly in this house; older children stayed for longer periods. Each child, so it seemed to Pete, had some distinct flaw: there was a boy whose parents were not married; another's were married but were Jewish; one little girl had no father at all. As far as he could determine, he himself had parents who may have been married but no longer were.

Bina came to see him on weekends. She always asked if he was happy, and he always answered that he was because the fat woman in the housedress, whom he was told to call "mama," listened. He was miserable.

From time to time during those years the woman said to him: Your father is calling for you. She took him into Manhattan where a tall, bearded man met them on the corner of Twelfth Street and Second Avenue. He took Pete across the street, to the speakeasy above John's Restaurant, where John's son, Danny, played with him. At five in the afternoon "mama" called for him and took him back to Queens.

"I must have seen Carlo no more than eight times between the age of six and eight," Pete said a half century later. "My memory is of a marvelous man. I loved the sight of him very much. He was tall, he had a marvelous beard. And this *hat!* He didn't look outré or strange on the street. His dress so became him. And I loved him. It was a pleasure to be with him. He was very good to me. Once he gave me a little child's desk; I suppose he wanted me to have a desk like he had. Even though I saw later that he had just ditched me, I loved him then. I was delighted with having him as a father. At least it meant that I didn't belong in this little world I was being boarded out in. Later, I sort of forgot that Carlo was my father. But I knew it then."

Pete saw Carlo for the last time in 1931 when Carlo came to Pennsylvania Station to see him and Bina off on their journey to Arizona. "I've always extended a lot of understanding to Carlo," Pete said. "There were things he just couldn't do anything about."

Both Carlo's children extended understanding to him, although Beatrice, since she never lost touch with him, had to forgive him more often.

Beatrice did not get along well with Helga; her mother was domineering and self-righteous. And when Beatrice turned to her father for comfort, he offered something more complicated. In the summer of 1919, when she was thirteen, she wrote him an angry letter. Her own letter has not survived, only his answer, written on August 22, while he was on board a train heading toward Topeka, Kansas:

My dear Beatrice:

Just before leaving New York I received your letter. I was at that time thinking of you very much and I was coming to see you. Was impossible for me to write to you because you and your mother have left me without address. In fact I had to learn the same from your Uncle Mario just five days previous of the date of your letter to me.

Now I want you to consider first your action in not writing to me for such a long time. You said I was mad at you because you have not waited for me the day we supposed to have gone together for lunch. Have you, before you decided to punish me so hard, asked me why I was not in the office that day? Is not a good thing to find guilty any man without letting him to defend himself. In fact I was forced that day to leave the city for a speaking date at Syracuse, New York. Amalgamated Clothing Workers of America called me sending a man after me and when I saw him he told me to go to Syracuse. I rushed to the station and before the train sent a telegram to you addressed to my office begging you to excuse me. . . . If you had asked me like a good girl, if you had knowed the reason for your disappointment you would have excused your father. But you are a quick tempered little girl.

Now for the promises I made to you, is true. You are right. I have promised many times to do things for you and I have disappointed you. So truth and I earnestly ask you to forgive me. And I will try in the future to be more correct with you my darling little girl.

As for the money question, you are wrong when judging the situation without knowledge of the facts. You said to me: don't say you have no money, for if you have no money how you have kept the bungalow? Well dear, this is the truth. Elizabeth is paying for the bungalow for the sake of her son. I have paid only twenty-five dollars this year. Elizabeth, instead to put the money in bank as some other mothers do, she prefer to spend it for her and her son, and I think she is doing the best she can to help me. Really, little darling girl I am at the present in very bad financial condition on account of the war and the money issue of the paper held by the authorities. I am going through a very hard time. Why your mother who is well fixed financially don't help you, instead to let you judge me so severely and let you write to me such harsh letter?

Well, Beatrice! I have decided not to reply to your letter. But here I am. I must write to you because I am thinking of you constantly. I want to ask you to forgive me, and to forget all the misery existing between us. Let the past go and look at the future with the hope to be more in love with each other. I will do all I can in this line and you do the same. Soon I will be back in New York. I will come to see you, or I will call you and will give the money you need.

With love and devotion and best thoughts, I remain you affectionate father,

Carlo Tresca

However hurt Beatrice might be, there was no residue of coldness between herself and her father. In the early 1920s she was a student at Washington Irving High School, only a few blocks from Tresca's office. Twice a week she walked over to the office after school, often taking two or three of her girlfriends with her. She was proud to show Carlo off. Her friends were crazy about him. He was handsome and charming, and there was always an atmosphere of excitement surrounding him: don't go near Union Square today, he might tell the girls. The police are there; you'll get your heads cracked. He put them to work helping Mario roll up newspapers for mailing and sent them off with a dollar bill.

Beatrice wanted to go to Barnard, but Carlo said no: he might pay the tuition for one semester and then forget or, more likely, be unable to pay. So Beatrice went to Hunter College which was free. She yearned for a raccoon coat. Earn it for yourself, Carlo said. The saving grace for Beatrice was that Carlo admitted his faults: Look, baby, he often said, I'm sorry if I hurt you, but I have to do what I want. I'll try to do better next time.

As she grew older, Beatrice became increasingly disturbed by the newspaper stories. It sometimes seemed to her as though every reporter in town who was at a loss for material went to Carlo and came away with a feature story. It began to affect her social life. For a while she went out with an Italian boy until his mother put an end to a relationship with Carlo Tresca's daughter. Then she became interested in a Jewish boy, but he was Minna Harkavy's nephew and Carlo was then living with Minna Harkavy. This boy's mother was also displeased with the idea of her son and Carlo Tresca's daughter.

Beatrice was confused and angered by Carlo's personal life. *Why* did he have to have so many women? Elizabeth was one thing—*that* had been a great love affair. But Bina? Whom she had admired and taken as a model! And now Minna and this inexplicable arrangement! Look, baby, Carlo said to her when she taxed him, I have to live my own life.

One day early in the 1920s, perhaps 1921, Bina went to the Rand School to meet her sister for lunch. In Elizabeth's office she met a former IWW organizer named Romolo Bobba, recently released from Leavenworth and needing Elizabeth's help to find a job. Bobba fell in love with Bina at sight; as he was leaving the office he thanked Elizabeth, adding that he would no doubt see her again since he was going to marry her sister.

A number of years and events intervened before he did. Bina fell in love with Carlo, gave birth to Pete, and took a job editing pulp magazines, one of which was called *Ranch Romances*. Her friends were drawn from the Greenwich Village literati. Allen Tate worked in her office, editing a confession magazine called

Telling Tales. After work they often met Hart Crane and other writers in a tiny West Fourth Street speakeasy.

As Bina was forging a life for herself outside the political movement that consumed Elizabeth and Carlo, Bobba, tall, handsome, Italian-born, not unlike Carlo in looks, devoted the boom years of the 1920s to making money. One of his enterprises was the illegal importation of Italian refugees. He also soon owned a manufacturing company in Brooklyn, a Stutz Bearcat, and two houses on Jane Street in Greenwich Village. He continued to court Bina and, in the mid-1920s, they bought an old farmhouse with 160 acres of land near Sherman, Connecticut. In 1927, when Bina's divorce from Slim Martin became final, they married in an elaborate ceremony in Montreal. Bina's friends liked and admired Romolo: "Romolo's a great guy isn't he?" Hart Crane said to a mutual friend. "He knows what he wants and what needs to be done, and then he does it."

On January 6, 1925, Carlo was put on a train and taken to the Atlanta Penitentiary to begin serving his sentence of a year and a day. Elizabeth saw him the day before he left, and from then on, according to her journal, she plunged into nonstop activities. On January 7 she left New York for a Sacco-Vanzetti meeting in Boston. On January 23 she recorded Bina's presence in Boston. It can be assumed that the sisters tried to repair their broken bonds, but it was not a successful meeting for there is no indication that they met again until the 1930s. The betrayal had been too great, and the balance of strength between them had shifted so much. Elizabeth was worn out. She was thirty-five, grief-stricken, and buried under too much weight, while Bina had youth and resilience. She also had Carlo's son and she was rebuilding a personal life.

During the next nine months Flynn made thirty-four speeches and attended twenty-one meetings. There are some personal entries among the list of her activities: "Letter from Carlo," she noted on January 10 and 17. On February 16 she learned that "Carlo's sentence reduced to 4 mos." She took Buster to watch the St. Patrick's Day parade, had dinner with Vincent St. John and Romolo Bobba at the end of March, and took Buster to see *Quo Vadis* in early April. On April 9 she attended an IWW defense meeting. The same day she received a "Letter from Carlo re separation."

Tresca was released from Atlanta on May 6, and a gap then occurs in Flynn's journal between the 7th of May and the 24th. "Sick several weeks here," she noted later.

Early in January 1926, the seven-month-long Passaic textile strike began. It was a mass strike, as in the old IWW days—twenty thousand nonunionized workers—but this strike was led by the Communist party in line with the policy, recently formulated in Moscow, of dual unionism designed to build communist-led unions to challenge the AFL.

Flynn threw herself into the strike. It was particularly brutal— mass arrests and police violence against both strikers and press. Flynn made as many as ten speeches a day; she organized a food distribution program. There is a photograph that shows her demonstrating the use of gas masks for use on the picket line.

But almost at the moment the Passaic strike began, U.S. delegates to the Comintern's American Commission were gathering in Moscow in bitter contention for the leadership of the U.S. Communist party. One result of their quarrels was a change in the Comintern's trade union policy: the policy of dual unionism was now incorrect; the new policy, decreed from Moscow, demanded that the Passaic strike be handed over to the AFL. According to Vera Weisbord, wife of Albert Weisbord who had led the strike for the Party, "The Comintern became purely an apparatus by which Russia could obtain recognition in the capitalist world and expand its own industries. To this end was sacrificed support for workers in other countries. The Communist Party of the USA had to make it clear to its government that there would be . . . no challenges to capitalism." Flynn wrote in her scrapbook: "A foolish move! *No settlement.*"

Her work for the strike had gone for nothing, and for the first time in her life she was living alone, in a large basement room in Greenwich Village. She confided in only a few people. Early in February 1926 she wrote to Joe Ettor in California. Ettor replied: "We have had no indication of the 'long story' you write about. I have an idea that I could guess however. But whatever it is, we both say good luck to you."

On Saint Valentine's Day 1926, the League for Mutual Aid gave a dinner to honor Flynn's twenty years in the labor movement. It was a grand occasion. Jane Addams, Eugene Debs, Sidney Hillman, and Morris Hillquit were some of the sponsors. Those who could not come to the dinner at the Yorkville Casino sent messages—Emma Goldman and Alexander Berkman from Paris, Clarence Darrow and Felix Frankfurter. From prison Vanzetti wrote: "I am holding a tin cup of water to drink and to toast at your good health and to your life." Arturo Giovannitti hailed the three great Elizabeths, "The first a queen, the second a poet, the third a revolutionary." The staff of the *Martello* sent a twenty-dollar gold coin and a card "for the disinterested help you have given." And Ben Gitlow, representing the Communist party, made the Party's interest in her clear.

Flynn had reservations about the Party; there were people in the Party whom she could not bear and tactics she could not stomach. Still, in the fall of 1926, without a center to her life, she made out an application for Party membership.

There may have been another factor in her application for membership. She had begun a love affair with Albert Weisbord during the Passaic strike. Weisbord was about ten years her junior, and there is a strong suggestion in the tormented letter she wrote to Mary Vorse that September that Weisbord's interest in her was calculated—the interest of a young man in an older woman who could be of use to him in his Party career: "Everything went to smash between us as a result of our discussion on the way back [from an International Labor Defense conference in Chicago where Flynn had been elected national chairman] . . . from the time we arrived in Chicago I completely overshadowed him which made him very peeved."

Weisbord, at the same time, was continuing an affair with Vera Buch, whom he later married. Flynn expected he would end that affair, but Weisbord did not, perhaps realizing that Flynn could or would not serve his ambitions. "I told him that I would not stand for such a triangular situation, that I had suffered too much from a similar one. I am sorry I told him as much as I did now. But I thought he loved me and would really understand. . . . I am terribly hurt, Mary dear. Life surely pummels me pretty badly. I really do love him a lot . . . [but] he has insulted me so grossly and seems so unconscious of it, that I don't know if I could forgive him. My pride, my self-respect were violated. . . . I can't help my standing in the movement . . . can I?"

So a relationship she may have entered to restore her self-esteem undermined her further. It did, however, serve at least one purpose: to Mary Vorse she could speak of Carlo as "an old dear" who wanted her to take a vacation with him. She was thinking about doing so to "tell him my troubles and weep on his shoulder [which] doesn't seem to bother him and helps me a lot. It's a funny situation or else I'm a bit off myself."

She was. Things "went to smash" for her. Mary Vorse came down to New York from Provincetown to find her friend in a hysterical state: "you can see her terrific will crashing against circumstance," Vorse wrote, "and her talking like some girl, a jealous pitifully unbalanced creature."

"Sick. (Exhausted.)" Flynn wrote in her journal on September 21. She nevertheless began a speaking tour for the ILD on behalf of Sacco and Vanzetti, stopping in Pennsylvania, Chicago, and Colorado on her way to the West Coast. On the train, somewhere between Chicago and the Rocky Mountains, she felt "sharp pains in my spine, breathlessness, and a heavy feeling around my heart as if it were as large as a football."

She spoke in Denver, Salt Lake City, and Los Angeles. In San Francisco, Ella Reeve Bloor took her to a hotel to rest for a few days, and then Joe Ettor and his wife drove her north to Portland to keep another speaking date. "I had too many emotional shocks in the past few years," she wrote to Mary Vorse. "They have left me tired and empty way inside myself."

In late December and early January she spoke in Seattle and Spokane, but returned to Portland "too ill to go on with trip." Her journal remains blank from January 5 until March 31, when she "went out first time for ride." But this was not yet the beginning of recovery.

On January 11, 1927, a concerned, perhaps guilty, even distraught Tresca telegraphed Dr. Marie Equi at whose home in Portland Flynn lay ill. "Elizabeth should give up immediately and stay under your care even for months. Will take care of Buster. Paying weekly allowance and rent Mamma. Agree if she return job as Director American Department Auto [*sic*] Fascisti Alliance with sixty weekly. Awaiting advise by wire. Thanks your kindness."

"Even for months" seemed a generous estimate for Flynn's recovery; that ten years would pass before she returned to normal life was inconceivable. "Thanks your kindness" Tresca had wired Equi, but there is some ambiguity about Dr. Equi's motives.

In later years Flynn wrote of having an "enlarged heart," but a doctor's examination and X ray at the time showed her heart to be of "normal" diameters. She was, however, advised to have complete rest at the risk of a "heart lesion." A more serious problem may have been an infected tooth that, when pulled at Equi's direction, released the contained pocket of infection to flood Flynn's system. In the early months of 1927 Flynn was critically ill. Delirious, "bordering on madness," she later wrote, she heard "the rushing of angel wings."

In April, Equi wrote to Flynn's anxious friends in the East: "While I cannot report a recovery I can at least give you the good news that she is making progress and gradually improving. . . . During the last weeks she has been able to sit up a short time daily."

Flynn was actually doing better than Equi reported; she had been out for a ride on the last day of March. In July Buster came out to see her, and by August she was well enough to take a trip with him to Crater Lake. Elizabeth went back to New York for Thanksgiving. She probably intended her return to be permanent. At Christmas, however, she received a telegram from Marie Equi's adopted daughter, informing her that Equi was now ill and needed Flynn's care. "Should have stayed home and never gone back," Flynn noted in her journal.

A local Portland newspaper published a photograph of Marie Equi in 1934, when she was sixty-two years old. She was a formidable-looking woman with white hair, light eyes, and a firmly set mouth. The article accompanying the photograph reported that although Equi had been confined to her bed during the two previous years, she was now taking up the strike action on the waterfront.

Marie Equi, half Irish, half Italian, had a long history in the radical movement. Flynn met her first in 1915; in 1918, when Equi was convicted under the Espionage Act and sentenced to prison, Flynn raised money for her defense and telegraphed: "Just received the bad news you must go. I cannot express amazement and sorrow. I have supreme faith in your courage and spirit."

Equi was indeed a strong and courageous woman—a physician,

she had been a hero of the San Francisco earthquake when she or-ganized a trainload of doctors and nurses to help with the injured. She was also a lesbian and, in Bina's view, probably in love with Elizabeth. "What's wrong with Aunt Elizabeth?" Bina's daughter Jane asked her in the early 1930s. "Nothing, really," Bina said. "It's like Elizabeth Barrett Browning and her father. There's a domi-nant person trying to keep her sick."

In Portland, neither sick nor well, by 1928 Flynn was overcome by lassitude. "It isn't that I'm so busy either," she wrote to Mary Vorse on April 18, 1928, "it's just that I am not so well and seem to have lost the knack of writing letters." She was full of nostalgia for the past: "I do think of all my friends, especially you, Mary. . . . I was reading Eugene O'Neill's 'Strange Interlude' and I thought of that strange play we saw together years ago." Her old friends were aging and dying: "How about Bill [Haywood] being ill in the hos-pital in Russia—I guess he's about done for. And poor old St. [Vincent St. John] is ill in Cal . . . I'm afraid he's about done for too. I met Jim Thompson on the street here a few weeks ago and he looked so weak and weary. Time flies and we all change don't we?" In a way she was glad to be removed from life: "It is so beau-tiful out here . . . I really don't care much when I go back."

A year later, when she wrote to Vorse again, her lethargy had increased: "I have the hardest time forcing myself to write letters. I got so bad that actually I only wrote to my mother and Fred for about six months, and that was an effort." She planned a trip to California, but Equi became ill and she had to put it off.

"Suddenly, with the coming of Spring . . . I feel better," Flynn wrote Vorse in 1929. "Of course the heart specialists told me two years ago that it would take that long to get the streptococcus in-fection out of the bloodstream, and I simply had to be patient. But I am glad to say I have spoken at two meetings, one in Seattle for the Centralia IWW men and one here for [Tom] Mooney . . . and did not feel any the worse for it except a little tired." She intended to go back to New York. "But of course I'll have to take it a little easy at first and not overdo. And I can never go at the pace I used to—that's certain. I guess it won't delay the revolution any either!"

In the summer of 1929, Flynn was back in New York. Her family had moved from the Bronx to Brooklyn, into an apartment near her brother Tom's optometry business. She moved in with them.

Kathie was teaching and helping to pay Buster's way through the University of Michigan. Buster had been raised by Annie Gurley and Kathie, and it was not surprising that they made decisions about his life, nor that Elizabeth resented it. "He's a good enough boy from all conventional standards," she wrote Mary, "doesn't drink, smoke, run around with girls, etc. I guess he's a reaction from my own wild youth. But my family, as usual decided what he is to do. My father and mother are too old to quarrel with—but the others should know better. However, they sent him off to the University of Michigan—tho where they expect to get the necessary funds to see him through is beyond me. And they do not seem to realize the importance of him getting a job and helping to pay his own way through. So I've been quite upset by it all. . . . Buster will never be a radical, I fear. He heard too much of it when he was a child."

From the summer of 1929 until the spring of 1930, Flynn remained in New York. She saw only a few friends. The political atmosphere distressed and confused her. At a party with Roger Baldwin, Arturo Giovannitti, Ben Gitlow, and Jay Lovestone, the talk was about Communist party politics. "Such a mess!" she wrote Vorse. "I'm glad to be out of it all." She was helping her mother with the housework, trying to write her memoirs, and all in all "I'm pretty well—except that I still have the strep heart and must be very careful." And she added in what may be a reference to the storms of her love life, "My mental troubles are pretty well eliminated—I've got them out of my system I believe."

If Flynn was to see any of her old friends during this time, she could not stay away from politics altogether. Once again she wrote to Vorse in February 1930: "The [Party] is certainly a wreck. That awful nut [Israel] Amter is local organizer and if he doesn't precipitate a butchery it will be a miracle. My grandfather used to say, 'Damn a fool. A drunken man will be sober!' and it surely applies to several of these people. Trouble is they damn others!" In May she wrote again: "The movement is a mess—torn by factionalism and scandal and led by self-seekers, with one or two exceptions."

Soon after, Equi fell ill again. Just before she went back to Portland, Flynn wrote to Mary Vorse once more. She was not sorry to be leaving, she said; if not for her mother she wouldn't go near the city again: "It's a nerve-wracking place and too *Jewish* for me, Mary." But later she wrote in her journal: "Dope not to stay."

There is no sign that Tresca and Flynn saw each other during her visits to New York though she surely heard news of him. At that time Tresca was as closely involved with the Communist party as he would ever be, an involvement based more on proximity than ideology.

In the early 1930s he was living in a menage à trois with Minna Harkavy and Moissaye Olgin. Minna Harkavy was a sculptor and, from descriptions, something of a coquette. She wore her short black hair in bangs, and she had a flirtatious manner that, although Beatrice never understood why, attracted at least three men: her husband, Louis Harkavy, Moissaye Olgin, editor of the Yiddish-language Communist newspaper *Freiheit*, and Carlo Tresca. Louis Harkavy, a pharmacist by profession, often wrote for the *Freiheit*, and while he may not have been pleased by the idea, he seems to have been extremely civil about the fact that early in the 1930s, his wife was living with both Olgin and Tresca in the Harkavy house on St. Luke's Place.

Earlier in Olgin's political career, he had been a supporter of Trotsky's, but he had taken careful note of what happened to dissidents within the Party. He soon became an official guardian of each turn of the Party line, known for the vitriolic style in which he denounced deviations from Party policy. In this talent for vituperation at least he and Tresca had something in common.

An incongruous assortment of people passed through the Harkavy house on St. Luke's Place: Minna's brother, a judge and a pillar of the Democratic party; Mayor Jimmy Walker, who lived a few doors away; Party friends of Olgin's, at least one of whom, Schachno Epstein, was a GPU agent.

In the winter of 1931 a young man named Irving Ignatin arrived at the Harkavy house for a visit of a day or two. He recalled meeting Tresca: "Heavy set and with one of the rare beards of the period. He seemed to be wandering around the apartment, partially pyjama clad." Ignatin, who had recently joined the Communist party, felt called upon to lecture Tresca about his indifference to the proletarian cause. Tresca was amiable. "He only remarked briefly that many had tried to proselytize him without success." Ignatin referred to the dictatorship of the proletariat. The dictatorship of the *Party*, Tresca corrected him. Ignatin liked Tresca, but he thought it odd that Olgin and Tresca, ideological opponents, not only lived in the same house, but in such circumstances. The Party was not tolerant of such "dangerous bourgeois liberalism." As for Tresca, he laughed at the ironies of the affair. At breakfast, with the table set for three, Minna sat between Carlo and Moissaye, trying to calm Moissaye as Carlo made jokes about one or another of the Party's positions.

Minna Harkavy was designated to represent the John Reed Club at a Conference against Imperialist War, held in Amsterdam in 1932. On her travels she stopped in Moscow. The New York police discovered that a telegram had been sent to her there and sent a copy to the State Department, which in turn forwarded it to the FBI for decoding. On the face of it the telegram wished Minna a happy birthday and was signed with love from "Louis/Carlo."

Beatrice Tresca was not happy about this latest affair of her father's. Minna Harkavy's attractions were lost on her, but still she often went to dinner with her father, Olgin, and Minna and Louis Harkavy. "Carlo and Minna would walk together, with Moissaye holding on, and dear Mr. Harkavy, who loved his wife dearly, walked behind with me."

The affair did not last very long, for Tresca would soon be involved with Margaret De Silver. "It may be an apochryphal story," James Farrell recalled, "but I was told that when Carlo broke up with Minna, she picketed his office."

When Beatrice graduated from Hunter she took a job teaching school in Queens, not far from where she lived with her mother and her stepfather. One day she was surprised by a visit from Elizabeth's son. She had not seen him for many years. Fred had turned into a nice-looking fair-haired young man. They took the subway into the city and talked about their lives, agreeing on the difficulties faced by the children of parents who lived life by their own rules. Then Fred said, "Look, we've both suffered from the consequences of our parents' lives. If we got married, we'd understand each other." Beatrice felt very sorry for him; Fred seemed to be suffering in a way she was not. She refused the proposal as nicely as she could.

In 1933 Beatrice married Ted Canzanelli. Ted's father had been Ettore Tresca's boyhood friend in Sulmona, and he had befriended Carlo during his first days in Philadelphia. It was a marriage Beatrice greatly desired, but she found the adjustment difficult and she was troubled by jealousy of one of her husband's earlier affairs. She confided something of her feelings to her father. Three months after her marriage, when she had moved with her physician husband to a suburb of Boston, Carlo wrote to her:

> My darling . . . The problem you whispered to my ears was already there: you know that daddy has the sixth sense to understand things and people. . . . It is quite natural my dear Beatrice that the sudden change of your life makes your present situation a little hard. Accustomed to do creative work in the classroom, having created for yourself an economic independence, makes quite difficult for you to accept ready and gracefully your present status. Unconsciously your own ego rebels against it, but you must let reason to say the last word . . . the word of your own heart, your love for Teddy. Where he is there is your place, as long as the love is there too. . . .
>
> You have time now: read, study, follow the genius, get interested in the multitude, see with your own eyes, get your mind alert and ready to receive, but also prompt to give. . . . You want books. I will send you or bring you some. I want to suggest to you the buying every Sunday the New York Times and Tribune. . . . Be a modern woman; intelligently and seriously interested in every problem of the life, charming and attractive without being presumptuous. In this way Ted, who is an intellectual, will admire you, and every man like to love someone you can admire also.
>
> As for your jealousy: it will never have a justifiable base if you know how to be less and less a wife and more and more a sweetheart. . . . I am sure you have no reason to worry . . . that flame is a dead one. Watch for other flames. They will burn if you forget to be always a sweetheart, a charming one, the one who make life cheery and not a burden. . . .
>
> Well, darling! I guess I have said too much . . . I miss you in New York. It don't matter if we used not to meet very often but the fact that you were here was much better. . . . I will step into some dentist office very soon and get all the bad teeth pulled out, they are so many.

If these are strikingly bourgeois sentiments for a man of Tresca's beliefs and experiences, they have the ring of sincerity. Flynn had noted, with some acerbity, that in the Italian anarchist households she visited with Tresca, "the women were always in the background." Apparently Carlo wished a traditional life for his daughter, and in fact it was what she wished for herself. Beatrice thought that her father had written her a wonderful letter.

When Flynn reluctantly returned to Portland in 1931 she resigned herself to a long stay. She began, at this time, to write her letters on stationary printed with her initials and Equi's address. But, "I'm so lonely at times for my past activities, my old friends and the places where life was so full—that I don't even try to think about them," she wrote to Mary Vorse in 1931.

Once in a while she heard news from her old friends. Arturo Giovannitti was in Hollywood writing screenplays; Fred Heselwood, from early IWW days, was living in Vancouver; and Bina Bobba, in 1931, had moved with her family to Miami, Arizona.

Romolo's considerable wealth was wiped out in the stockmarket crash. But he still had connections in Arizona from his IWW days, and, with the offer of a job with the Arizona Highway Department, he rode the rails to the once-flourishing copper mining town of Miami. Bina followed, bringing Peter and their three-year-old daughter, Jane.

Once in Arizona, Pete's memory of Carlo became confused. Romolo forbid the mention of Carlo's name, and Bina and Romolo's children—Jane and Roberta, who was born in Miami—knew nothing about Pete's father; Pete soon forgot.

In any case, life in Miami was strange enough to obscure the memory of his previous life. The town, one of a cluster of mining towns, was situated in the middle of a desert. Many of the mines were abandoned by then. Sulfur fumes leaked from them, covering the sun with a noxious yellow fog, turning the light into perpetual late afternoon. "I never saw anything like Miami until I saw the moon on television," Pete recalled. Jane, describing the 120 degree summer heat, said that "the railroad cars carrying relief provisions would back up on the sidings. The food inside was steaming, full of fungus, the meat had green things growing on it."

Romolo lost his job with the Highway Department in 1932 and went back to work as an organizer with the Mine, Mill and Smelter Workers Union. But the few operating mines closed almost at once, and the union had no money to pay him. The Bobbas lived in the town's former whorehouse and went on relief. "To be on relief in Miami, Arizona, was the end of the world," Jane Bobba says.

Elizabeth and Bina were in touch again in the early 1930s. The Bobbas had no telephone, and Jane recalls Bina being summoned to the sheriff's office to take a call from Elizabeth. In the summer of 1933 Elizabeth came to visit for a month. Her unhappiness was apparent. In their changed circumstances the sisters were reunited, and Bina tried to persuade Elizabeth not to return to Portland. But Elizabeth did not yet have the strength to break away.

She was thinking about it, however. Mary Vorse was working for one of the New Deal agencies in Washington, and Flynn wrote to her wistfully in 1934 that Washington "sounds like an interesting place at present. Are we revoluting or not? What has happened to the comrades since recognition of the USSR?" Again she noted the deaths of old friends—Fred Moore of cancer, Caroline Lowe, Red Roan: "I feel completely out of and ignorant of everything."

"You ask me what I look like today," she wrote Agnes Inglis in July 1934. "Well, I am older, of course, lots of grey hairs now and *too* stout, probably from a rather inactive indoor life. Not active at present, though always hoping to be."

"Am 44 years old today," she wrote Mary Vorse on August 7. "It seems like yesterday that I was 22 in Lawrence."

By 1935, Bina had had all she could take of Arizona. The children's teeth are rotting, she told Romolo. The schools are terrible. You're organizing miners in a ghost town. She left for San Francisco where she got a job with the police department, as an inspector of dance halls. Her salary of one hundred dollars a month was more money than the Bobbas had seen in a long time. Romolo soon arrived with the children and got a job selling Italian food products.

Having liberated herself and her family from the wasteland of Miami, Bina was now determined to save Elizabeth as well. On a weekend in 1936, she and Romolo drove up to Portland. Jane had the sense of a rescue mission: "They were going to 'spring' Elizabeth. Equi was a very powerful person. My father hated her. He used to say, 'Between Marie Equi and the Catholic church, they own all the whorehouses in Portland.' And my father and Elizabeth were very fond of each other."

Bina waited in a Portland hotel while Romolo made the assault on Equi's house. He was not leaving, he shouted at Equi, until Elizabeth came with him. And Elizabeth, overripe for saving, returned to the hotel with him. The three of them drove nonstop down to San Francisco.

Elizabeth stayed in San Francisco for about three months. Then she took up her courage and went home for good.

Chapter 13
Fascists Home and Abroad

Not long after Carlo Tresca arrived in the United States in 1904, Italian consuls began to keep track of him and report his activities to Rome. The volume of reports increased in 1916 when agitation resulting from Tresca's imprisonment on the Mesabi Range crossed the ocean to involve Socialist parliamentarians, then decreased until Mussolini took power. After that Rome's interest in its dissident citizens abroad grew intense. Mussolini counted heavily on the friendship of the U.S. government and on the support of U.S. financiers; antifascist propagandists, small in numbers as they were in the 1920s, were intolerable annoyances in an atmosphere of much good will.

For Otto Kahn, for instance, representative of the banking house of Kuhn, Loeb, Mussolini was "a great man, beloved and revered in his country and much misunderstood abroad." In his memoir, Tresca recalls a meeting with Kahn, who approached him in a restaurant, saying, "in good Italian, 'I am glad to meet you personally. Each time I met Mussolini in Rome, he asked me about you. Now I shall tell him that I have met you and like you."

"This man and I," Tresca wrote, referring to Mussolini, "did look at each other across the ocean."

In its desire for Tresca's deportation to Italy, the Fascist government had the eager cooperation of many agencies of the U.S. government. Only a few scrupulous officials unwilling to bend immigration law, and the fact that the government was sensitive to the opinion of the press, stood between Tresca and deportation in the early 1920s.

Tresca's sentence of a year and a day had raised a minor scandal: the advertisement for which he had been convicted had not even been circulated; moreover, punishment for such offenses usually consisted of a twenty-five-dollar fine. Margaret Sanger and the ACLU took up the case. The *Baltimore Sun* of January 12, 1925, wondered if "the time had come for an inquiry as to where the Federal Bureaucracies derive their power—from Mussolini or from the American people." On February 16, Pres. Calvin Coolidge announced a reduction of sentence to four months.

During those months, however, while Tresca scrubbed the prison floors, made the acquaintance of dope smugglers, and enjoyed the two hard-boiled eggs flushed up into his toilet by an admiring inmate in the kitchen, the government remained busy on his case.

Atlanta's district director of immigration wrote to the commissioner on Ellis Island: "Please cause an investigation to be made which will bring this alien within the anarchistic class and thus enable me to bring about his deportation." The Department of Labor also requested the attorney general to search his files for confirmation of a report by "another prisoner in the Penitentiary, who was an official of the Department of Justice and active during the years of 1919 and 1920, [who] states that he personally knows that during those years Carlo Tresca was a member of the Communist Labor Party; was a member of the Union of Russian Workers in Chicago, and was run out of Waterbury, Connecticut."

On March 20, 1925, an application for a warrant of arrest was made out, to be enacted on Tresca's release. But because the attorney general's files confirmed only the information about Waterbury, on May 5 Tresca stepped out of prison a free man.

On May 7, Tresca told the *New York Times,* "When Mussolini came to power several years ago, he and his agents set out to crush me. They have failed, miserably failed. It is true they got me on a petit charge. . . . I do not mean," he added with caution, or with sarcasm, "that the United States Government or its agencies knew of the persecution and surely they had no part in it, but they were the unwitting allies of the Fascisti."

To reporters from the *World* on May 11, Tresca recounted a visit to the White House on his way home from Atlanta: "A group of students from a college were there to shake hands with the President. I formed in line with them. A moment later I was in the executive office. . . . We went by with a quick handshake. . . . I

wanted to stop and say: 'Mr. President. I am the man you par-
doned from the Penitentiary.' But I didn't say it for fear some State
Department agent might rush up and say . . . 'For God's sake be
careful Mr. President. He may have a bomb in his pocket.'"

But this good humor was for the Americans. In *Il Martello,* on
May 23, he wrote: "I continue to remain on this side of the barricade, like an oak tree, the leaves of which are not stirred by the
winds, under the red flags which are the immaculate flags of the
anarchist ideal . . . which I have not recanted. . . . The Department
of Justice, in order to please Mussolini, has persecuted me. . . . You
will find me always the same—against god and the master, against
the church and the state, and against the international bourgeoisie
which always keeps hay at hand to satisfy the belly of its bailiffs."

The barricade was barely a metaphor. By the mid-1920s there
was open warfare between fascists and antifascists on New York's
streets. Mussolini's regime was viewed with favor by the U.S. government, by the financiers who invested in his Corporate State,
and by almost the entire American press, including such liberal
journalists as Lincoln Steffens and labor leaders like Samuel Gom-
pers. Italian immigrants, so long despised, swelled with new self-
respect.

By 1926, Mussolini had effectively silenced opposition at home.
He had shut down all independent newspapers, abolished all political parties except the Fascist party, ordered the assassination of
the Socialist Giacomo Matteotti, imprisoned many other opponents. Only a few noisy instigators in the United States cast a small
shadow on "The Man of Miracle."

In 1924, Count Thaon di Revel received a mandate from Rome
to take charge of the Fascist League of North America. He was to
organize Italian immigrants into a coherent force for Mussolini
and silence Mussolini's opponents. Thus began a conflict that lasted
into the middle 1930s. Meetings of fascists and antifascists were
stormed by opponents. In Newark, in August 1925, six men were
stabbed when fascists burst into an antifascist meeting. In November 1926, the printing presses of the *Martello* and *Il Nuovo Mondo*
were smashed by armed men. Antifascists led by Tresca and Pietro
Allegra burst into the ballroom of the Hotel Pennsylvania during a
celebration of the third anniversary of the March on Rome; a cor-
don of one hundred policemen prevented what would have been

certain bloodshed. Despite the presence of more than one hundred police and government agents, three men were shot on the occasion of a visiting group of Italian delegates in November 1926. Police protected all fascist marches and demonstrations each Columbus Day and Garibaldi Day; they were present at the funeral of Rudolph Valentino, which was made the occasion of a fascist demonstration.

On September 10, 1926, after an attempt had been made on Mussolini's life, Tresca received a phone call at the *Martello* office: You people tried to kill Mussolini. We are going to get our revenge. That night, on 116th Street and First Avenue, where Tresca was scheduled to speak at a meeting, a car carrying three men was seen circling the block several times. As it returned once again, it exploded; the bomb had gone off too soon, killing its three passengers.

"We don't argue with the Fascists," said Tresca to Max Eastman. "When they offer to debate, we say we'll debate when our brothers in Italy have a free press and the right to speak and meet in the streets. Until then, we do our arguing with guns. You Americans think this is very Latin and very far away. You fool yourselves. Fascism is already here in embryo and it can't be stopped except with out-and-out war. Either they get the drop on you, or you get it on them. And if they get it, you can wait for the Resurrection."

"There was no group that fought so resolutely and at greater personal risk, than Carlo's group," Tresca's friend and comrade Sam Dolgoff said, recalling those days. "Carlo had groups in all parts of the country. Here in New York there were maybe several hundred. They'd break up fascist meetings with baseball bats." In 1943, Alberto Cupelli wrote of "the open air meetings which were held until 1936 on the lower East Side, in Harlem, and the Bronx . . . generally held on a Saturday evening in the summer months [where] Tresca was surrounded by a 'general staff' of very active anti-Fascist youths belonging to the Socialist, Communist and [Italian] Republican parties, and those of the Martello group. . . . Militant anti-Fascism was then compact and solid as a wall against the spreading evil plant of Fascism, and the Fascists didn't dare go through the streets of New York."

In March 1926 the Italian government began proceedings to deprive Tresca of his Italian citizenship. During the following months the ambassador informed the State Department that Carlo Tresca, among several other antifascists, had been engaging in anti-Italian propaganda. Should these men apply for U.S. citizenship, the ambassador wished the State Department to know that he was in possession of evidence proving that they were receiving money from Soviet sources.

Tresca wrote a play, a satire, *The Attempt on Mussolini*. The Fascist League of North America registered formal objection to it as ridiculous and deriding a government friendly to the United States. Once more, in April 1927, the Italian ambassador presented his "greetings to his Excellency the Secretary of State and has the honor to call his attention to the following: the weekly newspaper of Il Martello of New York (77 E. 10th Street) edited by . . . Carlo Tresca has published [an] article [that] contains a vulgar and violent attack on his Majesty the King of Italy and incites the readers to assassinate the King . . . [this] represents a criminal activity. . . . The Italian Ambassador will therefore be grateful to His Excellency the Secretary of State if he will inform him of any steps which the American government deems are useful to take in this matter."

On May 14, 1927, the *Evening Post* reported, "Carlo Tresca Held on Fascist Charge." According to the *Post* Giacomo Caldora, president of an organization known as the Alliance Fascisti Il Duce,

> declared that Tresca menaced him with a pistol and attempted to seize the contents of a safe in the office of the Fascist organization. . . . When arraigned before Magistrate Bernard J. Douras in West Farms Court, Tresca said that he was the victim of a plot. He said that he met Caldora and Baptiste Cozzitoro, another fascist . . . at the restaurant of Pio Susi . . . and was invited by the men to sit with them and have a drink. Tresca was accompanied by his friend, Ferro de Carro. Tresca said that Caldora offered to furnish him with documentary proof that a Fascist leader was engaged in dishonest dealings in this city and that he accompanied Caldora to a house in the neighborhood. Tresca learned later it was the local Fascist headquarters. He said that Caldora locked him in and called police saying he had been menaced by the editor with a pistol. . . . Caldora's story resembled Tresca's except that he denied offering papers to the editor, and said that Tresca demanded them at pistol's point.

This was a minor incident with no casualties (although sixteen years later, after Tresca's murder, police would search for Caldora).

But on Memorial Day, two weeks after the Caldora incident, two members of the Fascist League of North America were killed. It was 7:45 A.M. The two men, Joseph Carisi and Nicholas Amoroso, dressed in black shirts and riding breeches, carrying steel-tipped whips, were on their way from 183rd Street to join a Memorial Day parade downtown. At the el station, Carisi was stabbed and Amoroso shot. As it happened, Giacomo Caldora was standing about ten feet away.

Il Popolo d'Italia, Mussolini's official organ in Rome, called for revenge for "the double assassination of the fascisti perpetrated by the refuse of Italy. . . . We must crush the traitors as we would a viper that bites at our heel."

On July 11 the police moved, raiding the offices of the *Martello* and *Il Nuovo Mondo,* smashing furniture and breaking open files. Everyone present in the *Martello* office was arrested, including Mario Tresca and a recent Italian refugee, Mario Buzzi. No evidence was found to charge anyone at the offices with the murders. Buzzi was held in jail and badly beaten, though in vain, to persuade him to implicate Tresca, Vincenzo Vacirca, editor of *Il Nuovo Mondo,* and Dr. Charles Fama, who had protested the inclusion of the fascisti in the Memorial Day Parade.

Early on July 12, Donato Carillo and Cologero Greco, both tailors, both members of the Amalgamated Clothing Workers Union, both antifascists, were arrested for the murders. They were promptly identified as the murderers by members of the FLNA. With the executions of Sacco and Vanzetti only a few weeks away, on August 6 the *Martello* called for a mass meeting for "the two new candidates for the electric chair. . . . The battle must be fought by all anti-fascists. We have to . . . pass to the attack and put on trial the Fascist government, the government of assassins in black shirts."

"I accuse," Tresca wrote, "[Count Thaon] di Revel not only of being Mussolini's emissary in America, but also of heading a criminal association. . . . The bomb exploding at 116th Street with its terrible consequences was the work of the members of [the FLNA, who are] alone responsible for the infamous attempt to send . . . Greco and Carillo to the electric chair with the help of perjured testimony. . . . I will prove before an American court that all of you of the Fascist League are . . . what you must be in order to be Fascists—that is, criminals."

The defense committee formed for Greco and Carillo included Norman Thomas, Arthur Garfield Hays, and Vito Marcantonio. Jack Frager, Tresca's anarchist comrade, was on the committee, but Tresca himself was excluded according to a report sent to the Division of Political Police, in Rome. The informant reported: "We know that Tresca was excluded from the committee . . . because there was someone who said . . . that Tresca was a spy, an agent of the Department of Justice. . . . Today another anarchist, a certain Coda, accuses [Tresca]."

Greco and Carillo were anarchists of Galleani's persuasion, and the *L'Adunata* campaign against Tresca was continuing. But Tresca acted through other members of the committee, and, as Tresca and Norman Thomas wished, Clarence Darrow was hired for the defense.

Carisi and Amoroso, the two slain fascists, were given an elaborate martyrs' funeral. Ten thousand New York Italians turned out; sidewalks were lined with flowers, and white roses spelled out Mussolini's name. Giacomo Caldora made a brief speech, and the bodies were shipped to Italy for another spectacular funeral.

Arthur Garfield Hays and Clarence Darrow appeared for the defense of Greco and Carillo after Darrow's fee of ten thousand dollars was personally guaranteed by Tresca. The trial lasted several weeks. Defense witnesses, family and friends, gave Greco and Carillo alibis; witnesses for the prosecution, Giacomo Caldora chief among them, and members of the FLNA, identified Greco and Carillo as the murderers. But Caldora was a vulnerable witness. Tresca knew about the internecine quarrels within the fascist movement; he informed Darrow that Caldora had been expelled from the FLNA and had organized a dissident fascist group, the Alliance Fascisti Il Duce.

Under Darrow's cross-examination Caldora broke down. He swore that Greco and Carillo were innocent and that the FLNA were "a bunch of criminals." Caldora testified that di Revel had offered him twenty-five hundred dollars to identify the defendants and that he had agreed, fearing that if he refused the FLNA would brand him as a renegade and he would meet the fate of Carisi and Amoroso. Caldora also testified that one prosecution witness, Alexander Rocci, had once given orders for a bomb to be placed in Carlo Tresca's office.

At the acquittal celebration, after much eating and drinking, Tresca turned to Norman Thomas. This would be a good time, he murmured, to speak to Darrow about his fee. Thomas was a little embarrassed, but he agreed. Thomas said to Darrow, I know that Tresca promised you ten thousand dollars, but actually we only have two thousand dollars, and there are a lot of other bills to pay. Made magnanimous by victory, praise, food, and drink, Darrow agreed to take one thousand dollars. At the final meeting of the Greco-Carillo defense committee, Tresca boasted of his talents as a treasurer.

Throughout this period of the 1920s, reports from agents of the Italian government were being forwarded to Rome: "Carlo Tresca sends a package containing one hundred copies of the newspaper *Il Martello* each week to a certain Chiarina Borgognoni, resident in Locarno, "an informant noted in 1926. "The above-mentioned woman, according to what has been referred to me, was, several years ago, the lover of Carlo Tresca. They manage to get copies of *Il Martello* into the country by giving them to some sailors."

Since 1922 the Fascist government had been pressing for Tresca's deportation, and in March 1926 it seemed for a moment that luck had placed him within their grasp. The Italian consul in Nice reported that on "Friday morning, the 19th, an Italian gentleman arrived here, tall, robust, about fifty, dressed in black . . . wide brimmed hat . . . grizzled pepper and salt beard, long, manelike hair. The man went from the station to the store of Racanti. . . . Present at the meeting was an informer . . . he believed that he heard a name which resembles Tresca."

It was not Tresca, of course, and Rome was disappointed; by 1928 they had lost faith that his deportation could be effected. Their best hope in rendering him ineffective seemed to lie not with the U.S. government, or even with the fascist organizations in America, but with the Galleanisti anarchists. Reports of *L'Adunata*'s campaign against Tresca were transmitted to Rome:

"The anarchists of New York are making ferocious attacks on Carlo Tresca whom they have even accused of being a spy of the Italian consulate," the consul in New York wrote to the Division of Political Police in Rome, on May 14, 1928. A month later the consul reported that "the antifascist movement in America which has Carlo Tresca as its leader has taken a terrible blow. Its principle exponent has been definitely liquidated. Due to the initiative of the newspaper *L'Adunata dei Refrattari* . . . on last May 13 there met in Hartford, Connecticut, the anarchist components of an honor jury set up to judge Carlo Tresca. . . . [They declared] after the serene documented exposition made by [Emile] Coda . . . and the confirmation given by the absence of Tresca himself . . . that they found the accusations to be true."

Reports of the feud crossed the ocean all during October 1928: "the feud . . . has caused considerable confusion . . . in the anarchist and antifascist movement. . . . The antifascist alliance of Italians in America is dying because of the serious schism in the heart of the subversive element."

The subversive element may have been small and divided, but Rome noticed that it was having a certain effect. An editorial in the *New York World Telegram* had condemned as criminal the tactics of representatives of Italy against the antifascists. Also, "We have verified that the antifascist propaganda . . . has had the effect of making Italians, resident in America, abandon the Italian banks. Thus it is said that last year the money sent back home by Italian immigrants diminished by a billion lire."

On October 22, the director of political police in Rome noted that although the anarchists were denouncing Tresca, "This does not mean that Tresca and his antifascist entourage have been liquidated, because there are too many people who, despite all the public denunciations, swear by the innocence of Tresca. . . . It is certain, however, that this is a rather important matter, for the . . . definitive liquidation of Carlo Tresca . . . would give a mortal blow to the antifascist movement which depends much on Tresca. . . . Naturally the local fascists are fanning the anti-Tresca flame to finish the tribune."

In 1928 Mussolini gained a valuable ally in New York. Generoso Pope, who had become rich and politically influential in the city, bought the Italian-language newspaper *Il Progresso Italo-Americano;* shortly afterward he also bought, with help and approval from Rome, *Il Corriere d'America*. Both papers remained at Mussolini's service until the outbreak of the Second World War. Pope supported Fascist activities in the United States, raised money for Mussolini's invasion of Ethiopia, and disseminated Fascist propaganda to a very large audience. If Fascism needed more official support in the United States, Pope, with his connections in Tammany Hall and his influence in Washington was in a position to provide it.

Toward the end of 1928, a shrewd analysis of Tresca's position in the antifascist movement was received in Rome. According to the consular informant in New York, it was Tresca's "equivocal" attitude toward Moscow that was the cause of attacks on him by the Galleanisti. His failure to publish anti-Soviet propaganda in the *Martello* was, the analyst believed, a crucial factor in the enmity of the anarchists. Tresca himself was

> a socialist with little dabs of anarchist cosmetics who, by necessity . . . "plays the communists"; he is however certainly an antifascist with a large following among the Italian immigrants . . . and with some influence in the Italian-American community and in the labor unions. . . . [To] strike at him through his rivals in the same political area would be an excellent undertaking. Who are his enemies? the first and most ferocious is the anarchist Armando Borghi [who has assumed Galleanti's mantle]. Why? I suspect he has intentions of replacing Tresca. Borghi is sustained by the paper *L'Adunata dei Refrattari* . . . ; in its pages a certain Cova [Coda] keeps accusing Tresca of being a spy; the latter defends himself but is losing ground. . . . The communists, aside from their party organizations, have created an antifascist alliance that, although it gathers together different elements from various camps, is maneuvered by the Party. . . . Tresca with his ambiguous maneuvering and his *Martello* enjoys among all a privileged position. . . . Let us look at the defects of our adversaries. . . .
>
> The individualist anarchists . . . want only one thing, to destroy *Il Martello* and the man who edits it, Tresca.
>
> *Il Lavatore*, the communist organ, wishes for the death of the [socialist] *Nuovo Mondo*, [calling it] a nest of spies in the service of fascism. . . .
>
> This is the most opportune moment for fascism to unleash an attack to the very core of this political area; it would not be difficult to use the anarchists to create friction between Tresca and the communists, to kill off *Nuovo Mondo*, and then the vanquished will take up the fight against the victors . . . one wouldn't need a *squadrista* but a psychologist who would know how to exploit all the low ambitions and passions of these people.
>
> Certainly if this brief, but exact, description could reach Il Duce, he alone would understand the importance of what I am saying. I am certain that if the battle were fought with cleverness and bad faith . . . we could have the suppression of at least two or three newspapers with several leaders knocked out of the game, with hundreds of followers disgusted and disillusioned.

Il Martello started 1927 with a deficit of almost seven thousand dollars. Tresca sent out a handwritten appeal for funds: "Lay a snare for fascism that considers the Martello and those who write for it, the most effective enemy of the black-shirted tyranny. . . . [But] if you believe us to be spies, agents of the fascist government, a liability to the *propaganda,* do not send your contributions. . . . We await your word. The life or death of the newspaper depends on you."

The *Martello* survived; *Il Nuovo Mondo* did not and died in 1929. But plots by Fascists were not required to create chaos in the antifascist movement. The moment when the movement was "compact and solid as a wall," as Alberto Cupelli later described it, had passed. The Galleanisti, now led by Armando Borghi, bore much responsibility, but the Communists were also effective as disrupters of a coherent antifascist movement. In the mid and late 1920s, Tresca's relations with the Communist party were indeed "ambiguous," as Rome's informant had noted: at the time he made his report, the Communists had gained control of the Anti-Fascist Alliance of North America. An understanding of the relations between Communist and noncommunist radicals, and how these evolved over the next decade, can best be gained by examining Tresca's relations with one man: Vittorio Vidali.

Carlo Tresca in Sulmona, ca. 1902–1903.
Courtesy of Beatrice Tresca Rapport

Carlo Tresca. The photograph was taken in
a Philadelphia studio about 1910, and later
inscribed and presented to Elizabeth Gurley
Flynn. Courtesy of the Elizabeth Gurley Flynn
Collection, Tamiment Institute Library, New
York University

Elizabeth Gurley Flynn, ca. 1910.
Courtesy of the Elizabeth Gurley
Flynn Collection, Tamiment Institute
Library, New York University

Helga Guerra Tresca and
her daughter Beatrice, 1912.
Courtesy of Beatrice Tresca
Rapport

Elizabeth Gurley Flynn speaking at Paterson, 1913. Courtesy of the Elizabeth Gurley Flynn Collection, Tamiment Institute Library, New York University

From left, Patrick Quinlan, Tresca, Flynn, Adolph Lessig, and Bill Haywood at Paterson, 1913. Courtesy of the Archives of Labor and Urban Affairs, Wayne State University

Tresca, with an unidentified laborer, probably about 1916. Courtesy of the Archives of Labor and Urban Affairs, Wayne State University

Tresca, handcuffed to another prisoner, being taken to the Atlanta Penitentiary, January 1925. UPI, Bettmann Newsphotos

A Union Square rally for Sacco and Vanzetti, probably 1927. UPI, Bettmann Newsphotos

Vittorio Vidali, taken by his companion Tina Modotti, as they sailed from Mexico to the Soviet Union in 1930

Elizabeth Gurley Flynn and her sister Bina, Miami, Arizona, 1933. Courtesy of Peter Martin

*Juliet Stuart Poyntz speaking at City Hall in 1934. UPI,
Bettmann Newsphotos*

Tresca, with Margaret De Silver, about 1940. Courtesy of Peter Martin

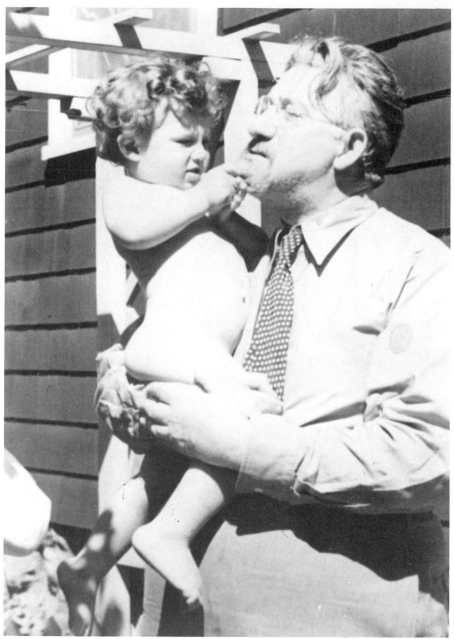

Tresca with his grandson and namesake (ca. 1935). Courtesy of the Archives of Labor and Urban Affairs, Wayne State University

Generoso Pope between Gov. Thomas E. Dewey and U.S. Attorney General Francis Biddle, at the 1944 Columbus Day parade. UPI, Bettmann Newsphotos

Carmine Galante in 1930. UPI, Bettmann Newsphotos

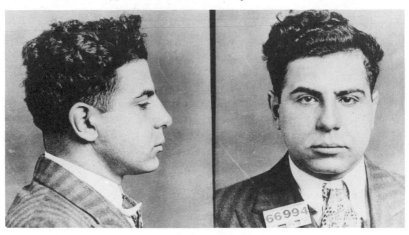

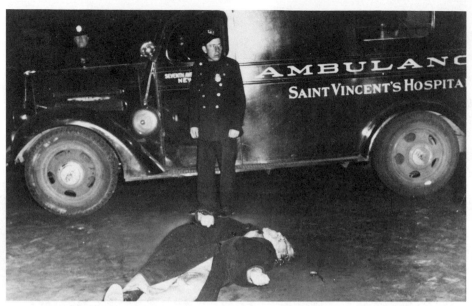

Approximately 10 P.M. on January 11, 1943, at the corner of Fifth Avenue and 15th Street. Courtesy of the Archives of Labor and Urban Affairs, Wayne State University

July 12, 1979, Galante's body lies in the backyard of a Brooklyn restaurant. UPI, Bettmann Newsphotos

Chapter 14
Vittorio Vidali, alias Enea Sormenti, alias Carlos Contreras

Vittorio Vidali arrived in New York Harbor as a stowaway aboard the *Martha Washington* on August 22, 1923. He was twenty-three years old, not a tall man but impressive, strongly built, intelligent, and an entirely political creature.

Vidali, or Enea Sormenti as he would be known in the United States, was born in Muggia near Trieste in 1900. By 1917 he was active in the socialist movement and had had his taste of street confrontations with police. He was attending Bocconi University in Milan, studying accounting, when Mussolini came to power. He then fled Italy and wandered through Europe: he visited Berlin, where he spent some time in prison, and then Austria, Czechoslovakia, and possibly the Soviet Union. In Algeria Vidali learned that the Italian consulate was looking for him. With the help of some sailors he was smuggled aboard the *Martha Washington*.

Once in the United States, Vidali made contact with the Communist party. After traveling around the country for a while, he returned to New York to become secretary of the Party's Italian branch and editor of its organ, *Il Lavatore*. He also became active in the Anti-Fascist Alliance of North America.

In 1922, Tresca organized a General Anti-Fascist Committee,

which was succeeded the following year by the Anti-Fascist Alliance of North America, or AFANA. As described in the *Martello* on October 31, 1925, "This United Front organization is composed of all organizations, parties, and associations that believe in the right of the people to win liberty. This organization proposes to fight fascism."

AFANA, which began as a coalition of Socialist, Communist, anarchist, and unionist delegates, split in 1926, when the labor union delegates charged the Communists with setting up fictitious branches of the organization in order to increase their voting strength. Tresca remained with AFANA; Vidali replaced Arturo Giovannitti as secretary. James T. Farrell later recalled Vidali as "one of Carlo's boys."

On October 18, 1926, the Department of Immigration, perhaps spurred by the disaffected labor unions as well as by the Italian consulate, took Vidali into custody as an illegal alien. The International Labor Defense took up his cause. In the *Labor Defender*, Tresca wrote in January 1927, "The cause of Enea Sormenti . . . is the cause of liberty of all people. . . . We have here in the United States thousands of Italian workers who have escaped from death . . . [but] the republic of Washington and Lincoln . . . has placed itself in the services of the tyrant of Rome by deporting them when denounced by the emissaries of Mussolini. They are seized . . . to be returned to Italy where death awaits them."

Vidali's deportation hearing was set for December 3. He did not appear for it. Clarence Darrow, the ACLU, and Tresca sent appeals to the secretary of labor on his behalf, and when the hearing was held in February, Vidali was given permission to leave the country voluntarily. He claimed that he had taken out Soviet citizenship in the course of his flight from Mussolini and could no longer be deported to Italy.

Vidali was still in the United States in April. In the *Labor Defender* he exhorted the U.S. government not to "spot with shame one of the best traditions of this people: the right of asylum for the political refugees. . . . The enemy is not only Italian fascism . . . but also the capitalist regime of this country which is deaf and blind. . . . It is the Federal government with its policy of deportation that has aided Mussolini to plant new crosses in the cemeteries of Italy. . . . The refugees want neither pity nor mercy. They are fighting men who have fought and know how to die. But they have a right to know once and for all time whether or not they can remain in America. If not, the government of this country should put the Statute of Liberty in its archives of antiquity and substitute for it a new symbol of the American Empire: an Electric Chair crossed with the littoral bundle of fascism."

Vidali was ordered to leave the country on the S S *France* which sailed in July. An agent assigned to the ship to make sure that Vidali was aboard reported that he did not see Vidali there. But when the Department of Immigration demanded an explanation, three affidavits were filed with the department from friends who swore that they had seen him off, and a photograph of Vidali on board the ship was presented as additional proof. His lawyer said that he was on his way to the Soviet Union.

Vidali arrived in the Soviet Union in July 1927. Shortly before his arrival, his compatriot Ignazio Silone had been attending a meeting in Moscow of the Executive of the Comintern. Silone left the country bewildered and aghast at Stalin's manipulations. The Russian party had already become a battleground in the struggle between Stalin and Trotsky.

Silone was not the first revolutionary to leave the Soviet Union with such feelings. Angelica Balabanoff, the first secretary of the Comintern, had left with a heavy heart in 1921. Emma Goldman had also departed with "nothing left but the ashes of my fervent dreams," and Alexander Berkman with her: "One by one the embers of hope have died out. Terror and despotism have crushed the life born in October." For them, Bolshevik arguments of "revolutionary necessity" had worn themselves out in the face of the Soviet reality.

Vidali had a different response. He remained in the Soviet Union for two months, and by the time he left, the logic of "revolutionary necessity" was his own. He followed where it led for the rest of his life. Vidali has left a remarkable document testifying to his spiritual birth as a child of the Comintern.

On September 10, 1927, from the port of Riga, still in a state of exultation from his recent experiences of the Soviet Union, he wrote to a friend in the United States:

Dearest Nino:

For the first time since I left New York, I feel the need to write. It seems as though the absence of skyscrapers and the tumult of the great American Babylon had paralyzed me in monomania and sterilized my will. . . .

I regretfully left Moscow three days ago. After two months of being there I had gotten used to loving that great village, almost oriental. . . . For these past three days I have gone through various states. Leaving America had become for me not only a necessity, but also a pleasure. The spirit of the gypsy powerfully awakened in me and almost extinguished the anxiety of awaiting my departure. . . . I wanted to see new things, new countries, new people. And if, during my trip, I indulged in dreams and became almost romantic, it was due to the fact that in my still young veins there flowed the desire to conquer the new.

But Europe disillusioned me. I know that seeing America four years ago provoked a tremor of joy in me, feeling as I did then that the old European continent was almost worn out. . . . And yet, there was my family, an old father who wished that I was closer to the tomb of a mother who had saved her last words for a faraway son; my adorable city. . . . The most fiery part of my youth that had passed through many challenges and battles. . . . I felt sick then. I believed I was ungrateful.

I arrived in Moscow on a Sunday morning filled with sunshine and sounds. In the evening I went to see the great Master in the Mausoleum [Lenin's tomb] under the walls of the Kremlin. . . .

I will tell you my impressions when I talk to you. Writing them down seems to truncate them, or to repeat what others have said. I love Russia, I love its heroic and good people, I love its revolutionary tradition and I believe in its emancipating function for the international proletariat. They will follow me always, even to the tomb, if a tomb I will have, those great visions I beheld in the heart of Bolshevist Russia.

And if, during the first days, I had some small, brief disillusionments in touching reality, I later felt that it was due to the petit bourgeois atmosphere that still had not disappeared from my soul. . . . But then, even this voice from the past . . . disappeared, torn away by larger horizons. And I saw the Red soldiers marching with their rebellious songs, with proud, intelligent faces; and the armed youth and the children who discuss politics: I like serious men. A new society, great, magnificent, raises its superb towers above the old and decrepit.

One leaves Russia more happy to fight. If I had stayed I could have entered the army with excellent prospects; or I could have entered school to give my experience a theoretical basis. But to study for one or three years, while outside the struggle rages on with falling comrades, seems a cowardly act. I would go mad. And so I left. . . . Sometimes I think my life is made up of stations of arrivals and departures.

Today I am at Riga, in the shanties of the immigrants. Tomorrow I will be in Berlin, which I got to know in prison. But this time I am leaving with a preestablished plan. These two months have served to coordinate my ideas and purposes. I want to usefully use these last three years before I turn thirty. . . . I have to apply myself, especially to languages: English, German, French, *Italian,* and Russian.

Before leaving Russia I attended the program of one of the best academies. It is good to go to Russia also to understand to what extent one is ignorant. Many go there and understand. And those that do not understand, and do not want to, return home to fight against her. I have understood. . . .

It is not enough to read Das Kapital or know the history of the revolutionary movement. One must become an iron revolutionary with a creative mind. . . .

I want to enter a factory. I believe that we cannot comprehend deeply the proletariat if we do not live with it, in its own suffering and aspirations. A revolutionary compelled to wander in the world cannot be an accountant only! . . . I'll join an evening industrial class and work in a factory. I also know that I'm assuming tasks which may be too great for the next three years, but I shall fulfill them in any way I can. Maybe when I reach these goals, duty will throw me into battle and instead of enjoying the fruits of labor I shall fall side by side with the others. It doesn't really matter; maybe an honorable death will turn out to be my prize.

Tomorrow I will be leaving for Berlin. Sunday next I will be in Paris: after that toward Mexico in the bowels of a ship together with the other third class immigrants. Around October in Mexico, I'll think about what to do. If given the chance of becoming a Mexican citizen on the basis of being a political refugee, I'll try to enter the United States legally. Otherwise I'll arrive in the United States earlier. . . .

As for you, dear Nino, listen to my advice. . . . A Marxist has got to be a cold rationalizer. A Leninist must aim straight to his own goal. . . . Write for our newspapers. . . . Sacrifice your point of view for that of the Party. . . . Deserve the love of the comrades: it is not that difficult. In a few months you will see that all doors will open. . . .

I suffered greatly in the political movement. I could tell you terrible stories that poisoned my youth. But I forged ahead of everybody else. I'll tell you one of the stories: I was 19 and had been in the movement for two years. A "rival" group wanted to eliminate me and my comrades: it was easily done. One week later we had been expelled as thieves. Disgusted and humiliated, my comrades left the movement for good. . . . I wept in rage. My family tried to convince me to give up. Not I. I did not ask help from anybody. . . . And for an entire year I carried the label of thief. Finding myself on the front line of battle, pretending indifference, I went on with my anguished soul. In various meetings doubts arose. The federation opened a commission of inquiry which found me innocent. A general assembly asked me to rejoin. A regional congress elected me secretary, and the national congress wanted to nominate me for the central executive. So I was very happy the day in which I became a cardholder and my accuser was expelled for theft. I was the executioner of justice. In political life you need strength of will. . . .

I have finished this letter. I would like to write more but it is late and I realize that I have strayed in other directions and maybe bored you. My best to your woman, your children. . . .

Your comrade,
Enea Sormenti

From Riga, Vidali found his way to Mexico, then back to the Soviet Union, then to Spain. During the years of the Spanish Civil War, Tresca began to follow Vidali's career closely.

Chapter 15
Wheels within Wheels

O N September 10, 1931, the Mafia boss Salvatore Maranzano was in his office at the Grand Central building waiting for a visit from Lucky Luciano and Vito Genovese. When the knock on the door came, Maranzano found four strange men outside. They identified themselves as government agents. Maranzano, who knew that he was under investigation by several government agencies, led the men into his inner office, where they stabbed him, shot him, and cut his throat. As it turned out, they were not government agents, but agents of Luciano's.

At the time of his murder, Maranzano was under investigation for the illegal importation of refugees from Italy. According to newspaper reports his organization, with headquarters in Montreal, was responsible for bringing in upwards of eight thousand aliens at a charge of up to five thousand dollars each.

In addition to making the alien pay this initial charge, indications are that the Mafia profited further by selling the names and whereabouts of the aliens. "In this city there are at least 15,000 militant anti-fascists," Tresca told a newspaper reporter in 1923:

All hate Mussolini very much. Positively I know at least 3,000 who are here in clandestine. They are living day by day in fear, exiles all. They change their homes two, three times a month. You see, those who live in clandestine are aliens. If they get deported it means death in Italy. So they live in horrible fear. A racket goes on based on fear. The Fascists hunt the exiles out.

A Fascist finds an alien. All right. One night a man knocks on the door. He comes in and says, "I am from the Department of Justice. We have to deport you now." Then he says, "$200 will straighten this little matter out." It's a shakedown, see? I stopped that little racket three times, but up it springs again. For a time everything is quiet and then one of my boys comes in and says they are shaking down again in the Bronx, on Staten Island.

Tresca's credentials as an adversary of organized criminals go back to his early battles with the camorra in Philadelphia. Yet he was a fixer, and he maintained connections, and even commanded loyalty, from some individuals within Italian criminal circles. A number of memorandums in FBI files record that in 1931 the bureau was informed that Tresca had been placed on Mussolini's "death list." In 1931, according to a story Tresca often told, he was approached by a man who identified himself as a bootlegger. The man said he wanted to return to Italy but he needed money. He had been offered four thousand dollars to do a certain job. The stranger was circumspect: It's a political job, you understand? he said to Tresca. I heard you speak in Paterson many years ago and I don't want to do this job. But I need the money. What do you say?

Tresca replied that he would think about it. He bought a gun with which, Sam Dolgoff reports, he promptly shot himself through the foot. When, after a month, he was able to walk again, the bootlegger returned for his decision. There was no way for Tresca to raise four thousand dollars; instead he turned to his own underworld connections for help. The bootlegger, summoned to dinner at a restaurant with Tresca and four high-ranking mafiosi, was informed that Tresca was under the protection of a high-ranking Sicilian Mafia chief and was thus protected from Mussolini's agents. The bootlegger was instructed to kiss Tresca's hand.

Fascist and antifascist clashes continued through the early 1930s. The battle of Staten Island occurred on July 4, 1932, when the Lictor Federation (which had taken the place of the disbanded Fascist League of North America) and the Sons of Italy attempted to claim Garibaldi as a forefather of fascism. In response, several hundred antifascists "headed by Carlo Tresca," the *New York Times* reported, protested the desecration of Garibaldi's memory. In the course of the day one profascist demonstrator was killed—the result, subsequent events showed, of quarrels within the Fascist movement. The following year, on July 14, 1933, a young anti-fascist, Athos Terzani, was accused of the murder of another anti-fascist, Anthony Fierro. A defense committee was formed by Tresca and Norman Thomas. Terzani was acquitted in April 1934, after the defense committee presented evidence showing that two members of the Khaki Shirts of America were responsible for the murder.

With so many murderous fascists in the city, Tresca was in danger. Indeed Max Eastman, in 1934, described the *Martello* office as "an armed camp" and Tresca "sleeping in a different house every night and never stepping into the street without a bodyguard." FBI files contain a report of an incident that never found its way into Tresca's fund of stories, nor is it confirmed anywhere else. The incident involves a known Fascist agent, Dr. Francesco Cerbini, who was involved in the Staten Island shooting of 1932 and charged at that time with attempting to bribe and threaten witnesses to the shooting.

In 1934, according to Cerbini himself (who spoke in the presence of an FBI informant), Count Thaon di Revel, by then returned to Rome, sent word to an employee of the Italian consulate, one Umberto Caradossi (an identification confirmed by Gaetano Salvemini), to "deliver" Carlo Tresca to Rome. Caradossi enlisted Cerbini's help, and Cerbini turned to the underworld for additional aid. Several years after the incident, Cerbini boasted that he, together with a group of Italian criminals in New York, "had Tresca tied up and ready to place in two bags for delivery to the Italian ship which was going to Rome, when Count Thaon di Revel cancelled the orders." Tresca was told, the report continues, that Cerbini's associates would kill him if he made a complaint to the police.

"Wheels within wheels" said Sam Dolgoff. "Carlo was a man of action. He was involved in all kinds of enterprises. He knew so many people—people from the underworld, politicians, judges. I don't know what kind of dealings he had which he never said anything to me about."

In 1935, Tresca invoked his underworld connections to issue a warning to Vito Genovese. Genovese had spent his 1933 honey-

moon in Italy and formed friendships with important Fascist officials there. Back in New York, in 1935, he was planning to open a
club for Italian sailors whose ships were in port. According to
Nino Mirabini, Genovese's chauffeur who later reported the incident to the New York district attorney's office, Tresca sent word to
Genovese that he would not tolerate the enterprise. Genovese
abandoned his plans, saying: I don't want trouble with Tresca.

Chapter 16
Carlo at Fifty

THE year the stock market crashed, Carlo Tresca turned fifty. He had never had much money so the Great Depression had little effect on his personal circumstances. But the *Martello* suffered: between the depression and *L'Adunata*'s smear campaign, subscriptions fell off; friendly creditors were now unwilling to wait for their money, and even Ettore could no longer make his brother the loans that had kept the paper afloat in bad times.

Tresca could count his riches in friends—250 of them forgot their political differences to give him a banquet on May 24, 1931. But in his twenty-seven years in the United States, he had never been free of money worries. And for a man in his fifties, his private life offered little ballast. He was still attached to Minna Harkavy in 1931, but that arrangement, though entertaining, was coming to an end, and he was involved in other love affairs as well: "he is in an intimate relation with a certain Panillo, Teresa," the usually accurate informant for the Italian consulate reported to Rome, "Woman of easy virtue who could help him in his propagandistic aims."

But Tresca no longer had a young man's insouciance. In April 1932 the Italian consul general in New York told Rome that "an informer of this office who has given repeated proof of being on excellent terms with Carlo Tresca [says] Tresca has been for some time in poor health and appears rather depressed, also because the contributions of his 'comrades of the faith' are becoming increasingly scarce. He complains continually and says that 'I have never gone through such a dark period in my life.'"

In June 1932, Tresca declared the *Martello* bankrupt.

Margaret De Silver never forgot the impression Tresca and Elizabeth Gurley Flynn had made on her in the early 1920s. She had been with her husband at a public dinner when they made an entrance, and she thought them the most romantic, exciting, and attractive couple in the world. By 1931, De Silver had been widowed for six years. She was a rich woman, the well-educated, cultured, and passionately liberal daughter of a Philadelphia Quaker family. Her husband, Albert De Silver, had been a founder, with Roger Baldwin, of the Civil Liberties Union, which became the ACLU. When Tresca approached her, probably late in 1931, to ask for support for the *Martello*, their relations soon passed beyond business. "Guess who's come back into my life?" Margaret wrote her son Harrison, then at school in Colorado.

Tresca moved into De Silver's house at 98 Joralemon Street in Brooklyn Heights, and their alliance lasted until his death. He called her "Big Mama" and "my little scamatsa"; she was indeed very like that Italian cheese, with a ballooning lower body and a small head. But, as Edmund Wilson noted, she was not unattractive: "If the hands and feet don't puff up, the women can get quite fat and still be all right—as in the case of Margaret De Silver."

Margaret was a happy woman. She confided her sexual happiness with Carlo to James Farrell's wife, Hortense. Carlo was also a good stepfather to her three children. "I just want to meet you man to man," he wrote to Harrison. The seventeen-year-old boy, shy and suspicious when he met Tresca at a little Italian club on Barrow Street, felt at ease almost at once. Carlo made a difference to life at the Joralemon Street house: parties, pots of spaghetti sauce simmering on the stove, boisterous talk, and laughter. He often argued with Margaret's stockbroker brothers, but there was never any anger. Harrison felt that there was no meanness in Carlo's nature.

At the end of 1932, Tresca left New York to give a series of lectures in Los Angeles: "violent outburst against fascism," as the Italian embassy in Washington reported to Rome. On the way back East he stopped off at the Fountain Valley School in Colorado, where Harrison was a pupil. You young men, he said to the students, especially those of you who come from conservative families, don't be too angry at your President Roosevelt. He has saved the capitalist system for you.

In the summer, Margaret took a cottage in Chilmark on Martha's Vineyard. The house, a shack on Menemsha Pond, had no indoor plumbing. Roger Baldwin's house nearby provided showers. Felix Frankfurter, Walter Lippmann, Max Eastman, and Thomas Hart Benton were among the summer residents who formed themselves into an association they called The Barnhouse.

Carlo spent most of the week in the city, arriving at the Vineyard on the weekend with his briefcase full of spaghetti, cheese, and wine. In the evenings he cooked with Thomas Hart Benton's Italian wife, Rita, and played poker. Days were spent on the beach. Baldwin thought it remarkably amusing to see the plump forms of Carlo and Margaret jumping naked into the waves. Max Eastman's wife, Eliena Krylenko, painted Carlo's portrait that summer. It now hangs in Beatrice's house—a large bearded man wearing a blue pyjama top and a beret. Carlo had only one complaint about this life: the fucking beards, the fucking beards, he repeated, by which Harrison understood him to mean that the noisy birds woke him too early in the morning.

Chapter 17
Vidali Goes to Spain

IN the winter of 1930, Vittorio Vidali was back in Moscow. No longer the itinerant revolutionary, he and his talents had been noticed; from this time on he acted as a direct agent of Soviet policies.

Tina Modotti was with Vidali in Moscow that winter of 1930–1931. The two had met in Mexico where Modotti was renowned as much for her beauty as for her talent as a photographer. Once in the Soviet Union with Vidali, Modotti put her camera aside. "I cannot use the camera when there is so much work to be done," she told a visiting colleague. She was assigned to work for Yelena Stasova, once Lenin's secretary, at the office of International Red Aid; less officially she did secret courier work. But Modotti took at least one last photograph that winter. It is of Vidali, standing beside the low, curved railing of the Dutch ship *Emden*, on which Modotti and Vidali had sailed from Mexico: he is a short, husky figure, at his ease, one hand in his pocket, the other holding a cigarette. His large head, in three-quarter view, looks into the far distance.

In 1931, five years before Franco's revolt against the Popular Front government, Vidali was sent to Spain. The reasons for his assignment are of interest in the conduct of the Spanish Civil War.

When the Bolsheviks took power in 1917, they believed their revolution could not long survive if Russia remained a lone revolutionary state. In 1919, when almost all Europe verged on revolution, Russian leaders could feel some confidence in the possibility of a Soviet Europe. But the European rebellions were put down, and by 1926, though Leon Trotsky called it a betrayal of the international proletariat, Stalin's new doctrine of revolution in one country prevailed.

As it would concern Spain in particular, Stalin's policy implied that the principle of revolutionary solidarity now took second place to the survival and defense of the Soviet Union. Soviet Russia's defense was best assured, in Stalin's view, by alliances—whether with the democracies of the West or with Fascist Italy; thus, Soviet foreign policy was bent on the preservation of the existing world order.

In 1931, when the Spanish monarchy fell and the Spanish republic was proclaimed, the *New York Times* correspondent in Moscow, Walter Duranty, reported the official reaction: "The organ of the Russian Communist Party seems none too jubilant over the prospects of the revolutionary struggle which it clearly expects will follow Alfonso's downfall. . . . It is believed here that the peace of Europe hangs literally on a thread . . . and that Spanish fireworks might easily provoke a general conflagration. . . . It may almost be said that if the Spanish revolution 'swings Left' as Moscow now expects, Moscow will be more embarrassed than pleased. One would naturally have expected *Pravda* to salute the chance of a Spanish proletariat's struggle. . . . *Pravda's* first reaction was a dismal editorial, stale as a damp squip."

Thus it is not unreasonable to conjecture that when Vidali was sent to Spain in 1931, his instructions concerned a mitigation of any leftward swing. The Communist party had small influence in Spain. Bakunin's ideas had taken root there. The anarcho-syndicalists were organized into the powerful National Confederation of Labor—the CNT, which was directed by the militant Iberian Anarchist Federation—the FAI. The Socialists rivaled them in power, organized into the General Workers Union, the UGT.

Between the proclamation of the republic in 1931 and Franco's revolt in 1936, the CNT demonstrated its dissatisfaction with the republic. Strikes and uprisings grew longer and more violent, culminating in the rising in Asturias in 1934, which placed the province in the control of the iron miners. Franco's troops put down the rising; two years of repressive government followed until, in February 1936, an alliance of Socialists, Communists, and Republi-

cans elected a Popular Front government, half-heartedly supported by the anarchists. Six months later, the military rose against
the Popular Front government, and the revolution, simmering for
decades, began.

Emma Goldman arrived in Barcelona that September. A com-
bination of CNT and UGT militias had fought off Franco's troops
from both Barcelona and Madrid, and the city fluttered with anarchist flags. "I have come to you as to my own," she cried to the
crowd of ten thousand that greeted her, "for your ideal has been my
ideal for forty-five years and it will remain until my last breath."

There were problems within the anarchist revolution: terror
erupted in its first few months—killings of priests, nuns, suspected
fascists, or simply personal enemies. Simone Weil, who had arrived
in Barcelona a month before Emma Goldman, in deep sympathy
with the CNT-FAI, was appalled by "a sort of intoxication" of killing. "The very purpose of the whole struggle is soon lost in an atmosphere of this sort," she wrote later. But still, when Weil left the
country, she planned to return to the war that began as "a war of
famished peasants against landed proprietors and their clerical
supporters." That she did not go back to Spain was because, in her
view, only a few months later the revolution became "a war between Russia on the one hand and Germany and Italy on the
other."

Because of the complicated nature of his policies, Stalin's position in relation to Spain was delicate. On the one hand, he had to
give at least token consideration to the obligations of revolutionary
solidarity. This obligation was consistent with his fear of a Franco
victory and a Spanish alliance with Hitler. But Stalin also badly
wanted alliances with the West against Hitler. To this end he had
signed a Pact of Friendship with Mussolini in 1933; concluded a
pact with France; had entered the Soviet Union into the League of
Nations; and had announced, in 1935, the Comintern's new policy
of a popular front against fascism. If Franco's forces won in Spain,
France's fear of Germany would make the country worthless as an
ally in case of a German attack on the Soviet Union. On the other
hand, a Left revolution in Spain would cause Britain to draw back
as an ally to the Soviet Union. If Stalin could help it, Franco would
not win, nor would there be a Spanish revolution.

In July 1936, a special meeting of the Comintern and the Profintern was held in Prague. Hitler was openly supplying Franco with arms and Mussolini flagrantly violating the nonintervention agreement Italy had signed, as had the Soviet Union, Britain, and France. The Prague meeting temporized: a fund of a billion francs would be created for the aid of the Spanish republic, and efforts would be made to organize volunteers to fight in defense of the republic. But no mention was made of sending desperately needed war materiel. And no materiel was sent until October. Then, while Franco received his arms from Germany on credit, Stalin demanded Spain's gold reserves: "Two ships crossed on the high seas," Jesus Hernandez, then a Communist and a minister of the Popular Front government wrote later, "one coming from Russia headed for Loyalist Spain with its hold almost empty, one from Cartegena bound for Odessa with 7,800 coffers of Spanish gold."

Because of the nonintervention and neutrality agreements in which Britain, France and the United States were joined, Spain had only the Soviet Union to turn to, and Soviet policies became determining for the course of the Spanish war.

Almost a decade earlier in Riga, Vittorio Vidali had written of his newfound determination. Phrases from his letter now spring to mind: "One leaves Russia more happy to fight. . . . One must become an iron revolutionary with a creative mind. . . . Maybe duty will call me into battle. . . . I was the executioner of justice." Vidali had long since exorcised the "petit bourgeois atmosphere" that remained in his soul, silenced what "small, brief disillusionments" he had felt in the Soviet Union. He was the iron revolutionary he had set out to become. The collectivization of agriculture, workers' control of the factories—in short, the revolution in Spain—was contrary to the policy of the Comintern. When the CNT-FAI declared that "it should be clearly understood that we are not fighting for the democratic republic. We are fighting for the triumph of the proletarian revolution. The revolution and the war are inseparable," *Pravda* responded on December 17, 1936, that in Catalonia, "the purging of the Trotskyists and the Anarcho-Syndicalists has begun; it will be conducted with the same energy with which it was conducted in the U.S.S.R." Vidali was among those Communists in Spain prepared to carry out what he had called the Soviet Union's "emancipating function."

In Spain, Vidali was known as Carlos Contreras, Commandante

Carlos. He was an organizer and the political commissar of the most impressive of Communist-led regiments, the Fifth Regiment. Both he and the regiment represented the professionalism the Soviet Union brought to chaotic Spain. Foreign journalists sought him out.

Claud Cockburn, in Spain to cover the war for the British *Daily Worker,* was introduced to a "husky, bull-necked man who combined almost superhuman driving power with an unbreakable gaiety . . . all I knew of his past was that he had once been a steelworker in Chicago. Later he turned out to be an Italian called Videla [*sic*] who was supposed to have organized the assassination in Mexico of Leon Trotsky." Cockburn spoke with Commandante Carlos in the chapel of a convent in northern Madrid where Vidali was in the process of organizing the Fifth Regiment. When a group of armed militia men began shooting outside, Carlos rushed out, a pistol in each hand: "By an effort of domination and the help of the pistols Carlos held them at bay long enough to get them sufficiently calmed down. . . . 'You see,'" he told the admiring Cockburn, referring to the problems of organizing an army from a rabble of backward peasants, "'You see, our problems are not quite simple.'"

Other journalists, in particular those with Soviet sympathies, were impressed by Vidali's personal force, his physical strength and courage, his brilliance as a speaker. Anna Louise Strong questioned him about the formation of the Fifth Regiment and reported his answers in the *Moscow Daily News:*

> We had at first just groups of comrades, old and young, men and women, many of whom did not know how to use a rifle. . . . We had only enthusiasm, determined people seizing any weapons they could find, following any leaders that arose, rushing to any front which they heard it was necessary to seize from the enemy. In those days we took anyone who knew anything and made him an officer. Sometimes it was enough just to look into a face and see that the eyes were intelligent and determined and say to the man, "You are a captain. Organize and lead these men." . . . [Then] we decided to create a special company which should give an example of discipline. We called it the "Steel Company." . . . For this company we established special slogans designed to create an iron unity: "Never leave a comrade wounded or dead in the hands of the enemy." . . . "If my comrade advances or retreats without orders, I have the right to shoot him."

The Soviet Union's prestige in Spain largely depended on the performance of the Fifth Regiment. In March 1937, along with the Italian Communist Luigi Longo and the Actionist Randolfo Pacciardi, Vidali led 500 men of the Garibaldi Battalion in a victorious battle against 5,000 Italian Fascist troops. In 1938, during the battle of the Ebro, he was with the Eleventh Brigade which fought off Franco's troops. "The majority in that battle were Communists," Vidali recalled at his eightieth birthday celebration in 1980, "members of the International brigades. . . . I too was part of the general staff. In fact I was responsible for propaganda among the enemy troops and for the organization of the resistance behind enemy lines." After a bombardment by 500 airplanes that "completely destroyed and changed the . . . configuration of the earth in that area [where] there had been a pine wood, now it had completely disappeared . . . we had already begun to say: 'It's all finished [the men] are all dead; there isn't one soldier left to fight; we have no reserves; this area is lost to us.' . . . But suddenly we saw living bodies arise from that mud, as if from nowhere: men covered with mud and with blood at the heels of a young lieutenant who yelled: 'Prepare your bayonets!' And those men formed a company and marched once more against the enemy. . . . Look, those are the Communists. When you think they are dead, they turn out to be more alive than ever!"

Vidali was a brilliant military commander and political commissar. By 1937 he had earned a reputation as an enforcer. Ernest Hemingway told the journalist Herbert Matthews that the skin between the thumb and index finger of Vidali's right hand was badly burned due to the frequency with which Vidali fired his pistol in a campaign against deserters, cowards, or fifth columnists. "I believe, myself," Matthews later wrote, referring to the massacre of hundreds, perhaps a thousand prisoners, in Madrid's Model Prison on the nights of November 6 and 7, "that the orders came from the Comintern agents in Madrid because I know for a fact that the sinister Vittorio Vidali spent the night in the prison briefly interrogating prisoners brought before him and, when he decided, as he almost always did, that they were fifth columnists, he would shoot them in the back of the head with his revolver."

The term *fifth column,* coined by General Mola, one of Franco's top commanders, was intended to describe the hidden presence in

Madrid of partisans to Franco's cause, ready to become active as Franco's four military columns advanced on the city. The term, however, was soon appropriated by the Communists, to be applied not merely to Franco's undercover agents, but to all who objected to Russian conduct of the war.

In Moscow, Stalin had begun the purges. He had already forced Trotsky into exile, and the trials and executions of the old Bolsheviks were now to follow. In Spain, the "uncontrollable element," meaning the anarchists along with the anti-Stalinist POUM party, were labeled "fifth columnists" and "agents of the Gestapo and Trotskyites." La Pasionaria, Dolores Ibarruri, called for their extermination "like beasts of prey."

"The only dilemma is this," wrote Camillo Berneri, Italian scholar, anarchist, and volunteer in Spain: "either victory over Franco with a revolutionary war, or defeat." Berneri's rooms were raided, his papers confiscated, and he and his comrade Giovanni Barbieri were placed under arrest. Their bodies were found on a Barcelona street on May 6, 1937. "I had occasion to meet and know Berneri," Emma Goldman wrote to a friend. "He saw what was coming and he warned the leading comrades against it."

The disappearance of Andrés Nin aroused more international attention. Nin was political secretary of the Partito Obrero de Unificación Marxista, the POUM, damned by the Russians as Trotskyites. "In short, what really concerns Stalin," *La Batalla*, the POUM newspaper stated in November 1936, "is not the fate of the Spanish or international proletariat, but the defense of his government by seeking alliances with some states against others." The Communist deputy, Miguel Valdes, replied in *Lérida:* "It is necessary to exterminate Nin and his little group of friends."

La Batalla was suppressed in early June 1937, the POUM itself on June 16. Andrés Nin (formerly secretary of the Profintern, expelled from the Soviet Union in 1930 after siding with Trotsky against Stalin) was arrested on June 16, with forty leading members of the POUM. Nin was taken from Barcelona to the city of Alcalá de Henares where the GPU, under the direction of Comdr. Alexander Orlov, had set up a prison. Nin was told to sign a confession stating that the POUM worked actively with the Nazis. When he refused he was interrogated and tortured for several days, but no signed confession was obtained. Orlov became concerned that Moscow would see Nin's refusal as a reflection on his own competence.

Orlov consulted his comrade Carlos Contreras. It was apparently at Vidali's suggestion that a faked Nazi attack was staged on the prison to "liberate" Nin. This tactic would enable the Communists to get rid of Nin and, at the same time, make it clear that he was indeed a Fascist spy. Ten German members of the International Brigade were assigned the job. They attacked the prison, calling loudly to one another in German, and scattering German railroad tickets and other like documents to connect Nin with the Nazis. Nin's body was never found. Enrique Castro, who, with Vidali, was a leader of the Fifth Regiment, later told Julian Gorkin of the POUM that Contreras had personally executed Nin.

The story of Nin's disappearance and death created enough of a scandal so that two months afterward, an international delegation arrived in Spain to investigate the Communist charges against the POUM and Nin's disappearance. Spain's minister of national defense told the delegation that "the arrest of the POUM leaders was not decided on by the Government, and the police [who arrested them] are not the heads of the police, but their entourage which has been infiltrated by the Communists according to their usual custom." The incriminating documents the Communists had presented to connect Nin to the Nazis, the Spanish government pronounced "valueless," obvious forgeries.

Emma Goldman returned to Spain in September 1937. "Well dear Roger" she wrote to Baldwin on the eve of her departure, "I am going into the cage of mad dogs." Two months later, to another friend, she wrote, "For the present I only want you to know that the prisons are filled with political CNT-FAI, POUM men and women without any charge against them except the most despicable invention . . . that the revolution lies gagged and fettered. . . . I do not know of any such instance of betrayal. Judas betrayed only Christ, the Communists have betrayed a whole people."

On her final visit to Spain in 1938, Goldman witnessed the October trial of the remaining POUM leaders, including Julian Gorkin. Emma Goldman was not partial to the POUM, a Marxist party to which she was "absolutely opposed." But of Gorkin and his comrade Juan Andrade, she wrote, "Their stand in court was magnificent. Their exposition of their ideas clear cut. There was no evasion or apologies. In point of fact the seven men in the dock demonstrated for the first time since the demoralization of all idealists in Russia how revolutionaries should face their accusers. . . . [They] rose to full stature with their clenched fists held high in the air, sure of themselves and defiant against their enemies." After the collapse of Catalonia in 1939, Julian Gorkin (whose real name was Juan Gomez; he had been exiled from Spain in 1922 and served as a Communist functionary in Moscow until he broke with the Bolsheviks in 1929) escaped from Spain and made his way to Mexico.

In the outside world, the Soviet view of the Spanish conflict prevailed. At a party in New York, at Muriel Draper's fashionable house, the British novelist and Communist Ralph Bates, just landed from Spain, told the gathering that the Spanish situation could not be more simple: a magnificent people, under the guidance of the Communists, were defending their republic against fascism. His own function as a political commissar was, in part, he said, to assure that the anarchists, Trotskyites, and other assorted fifth columnists did not stand in the path of victory.

Few people paid attention to those with more complicated stories to tell. Hugo Oehler, who had gone to Spain as a volunteer, was arrested in Barcelona and accused of stopping to visit Trotskyites in Paris: You visited Trotskyites, Trotskyites are Fascists, you are a Fascist, his Communist interrogators insisted. Oehler reported that an American named George Mink had been present during the questioning.

Liston Oak, a former editor of *Soviet Russia Today*, ran into George Mink at the Hotel Continental in Barcelona. Oak, who knew Mink to be an agent of the GPU, took him seriously when he boasted of plans to destroy the POUM and the CNT and execute the "Anarchist-Trotskyist-Fascist traitors . . . as agents of Franco." Oak warned Andrés Nin of these plans, but Nin, Oak later said, refused to take Mink seriously.

Carlo Tresca took Mink seriously. He had named him in *Il Martello* as "the murderer of our comrades Berneri and Barbieri." Before John Dos Passos left for Spain where he planned to make a film with Ernest Hemingway and Joris Ivens, he had dinner with Tresca. Tresca warned him, Dos Passos recalled: John, the Communists are going to make a big monkey out of you. Dos Passos protested, saying that he and his friends would have complete con-

trol of the film. Tresca laughed. In the first place, he said, your
director is a Party member; everywhere you and your crew go,
you'll be supervised by the Party; everything you film will be in the
interests of the Communist party. If the Communists don't like a
man in Spain, right away they shoot him.

Dos Passos was unconvinced until he arrived in Valencia, where
he tried to locate his old friend José Robles, a man he knew to be
devoted to the republic. He was first told that Robles was being
held for trial, then that Robles had been convicted and shot. "The
higher-ups in Valencia tried to make me believe that he had been
kidnapped and killed by anarchist 'uncontrollables.' . . . The impression I came away with was that the Russians had put him out
of the way because he knew too much about negotiations between
the War Ministry and the Kremlin and was not, from their very
special point of view, politically reliable."

Ernest Hemingway discouraged Dos Passos from making too
much of a fuss. Besides, Dos Passos "didn't want to add to the immense propaganda against the Spanish republic. . . . At the same
time you wanted to tell the truth. . . . There were things you suspected you couldn't yet be sure of." He was relieved to meet
George Orwell in Madrid: "Orwell referred without overemphasis
to things we both knew to be true. . . . He knew everything."

"I remembered Carlo Tresca's warning words," Dos Passos wrote
later, "the communists were liquidating every man they couldn't
dominate. I kept my eyes and ears open. By the time I left the
country there was no doubt in my mind that the case of [Robles]
was no exception. Carlo Tresca, as he always did, had his facts
right."

"In his heart and soul Carlo never left the anarcho-syndicalist
position," Sam Dolgoff says. "When he had no allies, nobody to
work with, he felt he was doing the right thing by getting influence. But with the Spanish war he became active as an anarchist
again. He got guns. Hardware. For the CNT. We had people coming over on the ships from France and other places. Carlo gave
them guns. He had connections. He did not support the republic.
He raised money and got arms for the CNT.

"I remember a fellow came to Carlo and asked for help to go to
Spain and fight. Carlo said, Why do you want to go to Spain? They
got plenty of people to fight. They need arms. Stay here, make

propaganda for our side, get money together for arms. If you go the Communists are going to get a hold of you; they'll find out you're an anarchist, put you in the front line and shoot you."

Finding arms for the Spanish anarchists was of necessity a secret activity, but Tresca's public speaking found few listeners. It was difficult to gather an audience of any but the convinced to hear about the anarchist position on Spain; it was even hard to get speakers. In March 1937 the anarchist Walter Starrett Van Valkenburgh was trying to organize a meeting. In a letter to John Nicholas Beffel, he ran down a possible list of speakers: Giovannitti was out of town; Flynn "has succumbed to the communists to my surprise and deep regret"; Angelica Balabanoff was afraid to speak "lest the government send her back to Europe . . . she is not an anarchist, after all, but her name would lend a certain prestige . . . for she is an old rebel. . . . Baldwin is . . . non-committal. . . . We have however the assurance of Carlo Tresca that he will come. Personally I like Carlo immensely and he draws from the Il Martello crowd but at the same time his presence on the platform will keep most of the Italian anarchists away because of a long standing feud. . . . Anyhow we have to have someone and Tresca is [an anarchist] come what may."

This particular meeting was held on April 4, 1937, at the Irving Plaza, with four speakers, Carlo Tresca, Sam Dolgoff, Van Valkenburgh, and M. Monoldi. About two hundred and fifty people attended according to Van Valkenburgh, "a lot from the C.P. who made nuisances of themselves by scuffling feet, getting up and sitting down, calling out unintelligent remarks." Fifty-four dollars was collected. "Even *L'Adunata* gave us space in spite of Tresca being one of the speakers."

In 1938, Luigi Antonini sent out a memorandum to members of the largely Italian Local 89 of the ILGWU asking for contributions: "There are two groups of Italian volunteers fighting for the Government in Spain: (*a*) a column operating in Catalonia composed mainly of anarchists and liberals commanded by Prof. Rosselli and emanating from the Italian Anti-Fascist organization 'Giustizia and Liberta'; (*b*) the 'Garibaldi Legion' over one thousand strong, which is part of the International Brigade operating in Madrid and is composed of socialists, communists, democrats, trade-unionists etc. . . . *Carlo Tresca* has repeatedly urged Brother Antonini to send some help to the 'Giustizia and Liberta' column."

Tresca introduced David Dubinsky to the wife of an arrested POUMist. "He was tortured, jailed and prosecuted in the famous trial of Barcelona," Tresca wrote Dubinsky after the meeting. "His wife succeeded to escape in France and organized a successful International Defense Committee for her husband and all the other victims of GPU. [She] know by personal experience what Stalinism mean."

On Tresca's part, his tolerance for Communist policies had ended with the murder of Camillo Berneri. To the Party and its sympathizers was now "Carlo Tresca The Enemy of Republican Spain," so characterized in a pamphlet by his former comrade, Pietro Allegra. The pamphlet titled "The Moral Suicide of Carlo Tresca" was a long catalog of Tresca's political sins: "Russia," wrote Allegra,

> with all its merits and faults presents the only ray of light in the fascist world. . . . It is a terrible crime to want to extinguish that light. . . . And Carlo Tresca, instead of fighting the fascists . . . fights the anti-fascists. . . . This is a saboteur's crime, it is treachery.
>
> Imagine dear reader . . . one day at Madison Square Garden, a crowd of 25,000 people, with another 30,000 outside, were demonstrating against invading fascism and collecting millions of dollars to help the glorious loyalist forces. Well then: Carlo Tresca at the same day and time was talking to about a hundred misled people, in the 14th Street Square in New York, suggesting to them that they should not give a dime to the forces of the Madrid government, because that government supposedly spends that money to kill anarchists. Can one be a greater saboteur, more stupid than this?

"The truth about the C.P. policy in Spain is gradually leaking out here," John Dewey wrote to Emma Goldman in February 1939, "but of course not adequately. Two or three C.P. people who went over and some who had been sympathizers came back disgusted, but of course they don't get much chance at publicity. . . . The C.P. are trying to hold their position by claiming all they want is union with democratic-anti-fascist elements, but it is becoming clearer all the time that what they really want is simply military union to protect the U.S.S.R. and that their democratic pretentions are only a pose. . . . My good friend Carlo Tresca has kept me somewhat in touch with the real conditions in Spain."

In January 1939, Barcelona fell to Franco's troops. As the population fled just ahead of the approaching army, Tina Modotti sat alone at an outdoor café. She had been in Spain since 1935, enlisted in the Fifth Regiment as "Maria." An old friend from Mexico passed by on the road: What are you doing here? he asked. She was waiting, she said, for Carlos to come through with the regiment. The friend, Fernando Gamboa, later recalled: "It was more or less about six in the evening, the sun was shining but gave no warmth . . . the winter sun, the peasants escaping from the mountains, the army retreating and the image of Tina, sitting alone . . . sitting alone and waiting." He wished her luck and sent regards to Carlos.

Modotti and Vidali were in Madrid when the city fell in March 1939. Vidali was wounded and lost the thumb of his right hand. With the help of the Mexican artist David Siqueiros, they managed to get out of Spain. On April 16, Vidali was waiting at the dock in New York harbor to meet Modotti aboard the entering *Queen Mary*. He had been in New York for a month, using the identity Carlos Contreras, Spanish professor of history. Together he and Modotti returned to Mexico, where Tina Modotti would die in January 1942. Vidali had many admirers by then and would have many more in his long life. But he was grieved by his detractors. "Even in Spain," he complained to a reporter in 1950, "Even in Spain Vidali was held to blame for every military or political leader who disappeared." By then, he was also blamed for involvement in the assassinations of Leon Trotsky and Carlo Tresca.

Chapter 18
Home Again

IN mid-July 1936, Elizabeth Gurley Flynn left Bina and Romolo Bobba in San Francisco and, with trepidation, came home. She was forty-six when she arrived at her mother's apartment. While her own life had been at a standstill for ten years, change was apparent everywhere. Annie Gurley Flynn was now a frail seventy-seven. Elizabeth's brother, Tom, had committed suicide the previous January. Her sister Kathie, who had never married, had a daughter. Her son, Fred, had quit college in Ann Arbor and was working in Washington, D.C. "We hit it off allright now," she wrote to Agnes Inglis in September, 1936. "There was too much interference when I was in Portland and he stopped writing to me, to my great sorrow. But we are allright now I am happy to say." She added that she still felt "so out of touch with everything and everybody . . . I feel quite at a loss."

But when Flynn ventured out in public she was welcomed warmly. Old friends gave cocktail parties in her honor. In November she went to Norman Thomas's fifty-second birthday party at the Hotel Edison. Tresca was also a guest. On January 21, 1937, she noted in her journal that she went to "Party Mrs. De Silver—Brooklyn. Ettor, Arturo—Carlo there."

Flynn cast about for work. She consulted Fiorello LaGuardia who was now mayor of the city. He told her that she could have a future in Democratic party politics. It must have been a temptation to her in this period of the Popular Front. But Flynn's identity had been forged in revolutionary politics, so on February 10, with Ella

Reeve Bloor and William Z. Foster as her sponsors, she made her second application to join the Communist party. (The first, in 1926, had never been acted on.)

A number of people were appalled by her move. Romolo Bobba had been a Party member for a little more than a month; the Party had sent him to Berlin to report on the possibilities of an alliance with the National Socialists, and he had returned home in disgust. Hearing the news about Elizabeth, Bina screamed, Oh no! I can't believe she did it! At John's Restaurant, Flynn ran into James Cannon, who had broken with the Party since his 1922 recruiting visit to Staten Island. His wife, Rose, accompanied Flynn to the ladies room: Oh, Elizabeth, she said. We were so sorry to hear the news.

But Flynn "yearned to plunge back into my old exciting life to make up for the dreary days of inactivity"; only the Party could offer her a sense of her life's continuity. On March 6 she went to Paterson on Party business, and "the workers remembered," she told a *Daily Worker* reporter. "Women with children in their arms came up to me and said they had heard me speak when they were kids. They insisted on giving me a party. . . . It was wonderful."

She tried to revive all the old feelings. When she met Minnesota congressman John Bernard, she wrote excitedly to Mary Vorse: "He was a boy on the Range when we were there. . . . He told me he plans to help organize the miners in the CIO. . . . I would be so glad if I could help in *that* job. . . . It may be a crazy idea—but I feel so strongly moved to do it. What do you think? We are living in great days—dreams coming true—I feel sorry for people like Joe Ettor and Carlo who are living in the past and can't see the CIO and what it means to American labor. We can't go on forever on past reputations and dead organizations. Life goes on."

Two weeks after making her application to the Party, Flynn spoke at the Hunts Point Palace in defense of the Moscow trials. In April, at the Mecca Temple, with John Dos Passos, Josephine Herbst, and Joris Ivens broadcasting from Spain by radio, Flynn spoke "for the first time as a member of the Communist Party," as the poster for the event advertised. From then on the Party used her as a speaker constantly. In early January she was sent on a tour to St. Louis, Chicago, Cleveland, Milwaukee, and Indianapolis.

And in late September 1939, she fulfilled her wish to return to the Mesabi Range. "Dearest Mary," she wrote from the Virginia Hotel where they had stayed twenty years earlier, "Being here in this same old hotel where you still walk up two flights of stairs, I was bound to remember our experiences here together I wonder where you are now? Here am I, still at it, barn storming for the C.P. and struggling for free speech as ever. . . . I feel as if the pages are turning back and we are fast approaching 1917 again."

For a brief time, at the age of forty-nine, she fell in love again, with a red-haired Party organizer from New Orleans, ten years her junior. She was wary: "I try to keep my dual minds apart," she wrote in one of her poems in the summer of 1939, "the mind of reason and the mind of heart . . . Not to be torn again by gaping wounds, not to be anguished by a feverish longing for a most beloved . . . Not to be possessed and once again be lost." But she was too eager and had been unloved too long: "Won't you unlock your warm and tender lips, whose kisses are so sweet, To say some words of love, once in a while? . . . Dear Comrade, stay a little while with me. Fold up your tireless wings and light within my arms." The affair didn't last, and in November she "burned with the sharp hurt of anger. . . . How well I know the anodyne of time. . . . I lock my heart against you—throw away the key."

But this unhappy, brief affair only seemed to reawaken old feelings. On some unspecified month in 1939, she went to South Beach on Staten Island, where she wrote sad and bitter poems: "To Carlo." "I am alone—and being alone am brave. Gone are the nights of lonely waiting and of tears, of anxious worries and a comrade's fears, for him who did not come so long ago. The same tide beats against the waiting sands. The same moon glides from Coney's lurid crown. Red Mars, nearer yet far, shines peaceful down. My heart is free—tonight I do not care. . . . I do not miss the kisses and the tears. Only the faith that died so slow and hard."

Her public meetings with Tresca were cordial. She invited him to her mother's birthday party in 1937. Once, at John's Restaurant with her sister Kathie, Kathie said: There's Whiskers! Tresca sent a bottle of wine to their table.

But there was no question of easy friendship between them. Flynn still suffered too much for this man who had been "so long the other half of me!" And she was further distanced from him by her political choice. The Party's denunciations of Tresca comforted and strengthened her against him. Only when he was dead did she forgive him for "your decadent decline, your paltry friends. In memory I restore you to your glowing past, when you were young and strong and brave to me."

Chapter 19
Trotskyism and Poyntzism

WHEN the Commission of Inquiry into the Charges against Leon Trotsky was formed in 1937, Tresca gave his name to it. He had known Trotsky slightly in New York in 1917, and they had had dinner together once or twice before Trotsky returned to Russia. In 1937 James T. Farrell heard Tresca speak at a commission meeting. He had no use for Trotsky's politics, Tresca said, but he had often enough defended people he disagreed with; something had to be done, he said, to challenge the Moscow trials.

Tresca's presence on the commission was galling to the Communist party. The *New Masses* of April 20, 1937, acknowledged that he was the only one of the commissioners to have a legitimate connection to the labor movement, but by December 28 the *New Masses* derided his stance of nonpartisanship.

Stalin's purges were underway in Moscow. One by one the old Bolsheviks "confessed" that in their betrayals of the Soviet Union they had conspired with, among others, Trotsky. Christian Rakovsky added that Max Eastman had introduced him to the British secret service. On March 3, 1937, Stalin told the Central Committee of the Party about a "well-known gang of writers from America headed by the notorious crook Eastman, all these gangsters of the pen who live by slandering the working class of the Soviet Union, are they not a reserve for Trotskyism?"

The *Daily Worker* in New York blazoned the news that Eastman was a British spy. According to Eastman, he immediately received a telephone call from Tresca, who warned: This means open season on you Max. Stalin has killers in every country. Keep off vacant streets at night. Don't walk home without a companion. But more important, your main protection is as a public opponent of Stalin. If I were you I'd sue Earl Browder and the *Daily Worker* for libel. When this gets into the papers they'll be afraid to shoot you.

The Commission of Inquiry, chaired by John Dewey, supported in part by a donation from Margaret De Silver, opened hearings on April 10, 1937, at Diego Rivera's house in Coyoacán, Mexico, where Trotsky lived with his wife and grandson. Tresca was not in Mexico for the hearings, but when they were completed he signed the commission's findings, a four hundred–page volume that found Trotsky innocent of charges by the Moscow defendants and concluded that the trials themselves were "frame-ups."

On the night of May 23, 1940, as Trotsky and his wife slept, more than two hundred machine gun shots were fired into their bedroom. Trotsky's secretary, Sheldon Harte, was killed, although Trotsky and his wife escaped serious harm. A week later Trotsky wrote to the Mexican public prosecutor and a number of other Mexican officials: "During the last few years Stalin has shot hundreds of my friends, real or supposed. He has, in fact, exterminated the whole of my family, with the exception of myself, my wife and one of my grandsons. Abroad he has had Ignace Reiss, one of the chiefs of the GPU, assassinated by his agents because he publicly declared himself to be in favor of the ideas which I uphold. . . . The aim of all the Moscow trials during the years 1936 and 1937 was to obtain my extradition and put me in the hands of the GPU. . . . I do not mean to say by the above that the possibility of participation in the attempt by the Gestapo is excluded. At present the GPU and the Gestapo are to some extent in touch with each other; it is possible and even probable that in certain cases they use the same agents."

Trotsky went on to describe the methods used by the GPU to organize assassinations on foreign soil: the principal organizers were sent from abroad, to make contact with the national GPU representative and to work out plans for implementation of the assassination. "There cannot be the least doubt that the leaders of the Communist Party [in Mexico] know perfectly well who is the representative of the GPU in Mexico. I may also add that David Alfero Siqueiros, who participated in the Spanish Civil War as an active Stalinist, cannot help but know."

Siqueiros, who had helped Vidali and Modotti escape from Spain, went into hiding. He was arrested in October and admitted being present at the attack on Trotsky, but insisted that he had only intended to steal Trotsky's documents. By that time Trotsky was dead. On August 20, Ramon Mercader, traveling on the passport of a missing Canadian member of the International Brigade, had succeeded in killing the old revolutionist.

Carlos Contreras was openly mentioned in connection with the initial attack on Trotsky. Vidali had then been in Mexico for about a year. The Nazi-Soviet Nonaggression Pact had been signed in August 1939, and the United States Office of Naval Intelligence believed Vidali to be a GPU operative in Mexico and a principle contact between Mexican Communists and a German agent named Max Weber. Western intelligence agencies had little doubt that contact between German and Russian espionage networks had been forged and that Vidali, "with many other German and Russian agents was allegedly involved . . . in plans to gain political control of Mexico for the Axis to use as a base of operation against the allies."

The Mexican police, however, found no evidence on which to hold Vidali for Trotsky's murder and, despite persistent rumors, no material evidence has ever come to light. But rumors did persist. Jesus Hernandez, who had fled the Soviet Union after Franco's victory, happened to be in the company of the Italian Communist leader Palmiro Togliatti when the details of the first attempt on Trotsky's life reached Moscow. Hernandez would say that Togliatti was enraged when he heard that Vidali had been involved. Togliatti shouted: He was ordered to have nothing to do with it!

In 1951, Gen. Valentin Gonzales, known as El Campesino during the Spanish war, wrote that in 1939, while in Moscow, he had dispatched a squad of three Spanish Communists to Carlos Contreras in Mexico City. The squad was provided with a list of twenty political personalities slated for assassination: included were Trotsky, Julian Gorkin, and Carlo Tresca.

"Ask your questions," Vidali said to his interviewer in Trieste in 1950. "You want to ask me about Carlo Tresca and Leon Trotsky, don't you?"

Before Trotsky's assassination in 1940, a number of assassinations of dissident communists and leftists were carried out on foreign soil—in Spain, of course; in Switzerland, where Ignace

Reiss was murdered in 1937; in Paris, where Rudolf Clement and Trotsky's son Lev Sedov were killed in 1938. But until the disappearance of Juliet Stuart Poyntz in the spring of 1937, there was no hint that such activity would take place in the United States.

Juliet Stuart Poyntz was a founding member of the American Communist movement and for many years at the center of its internal workings and bitter factional struggles. In 1923 the Comintern issued "binding instructions" for the factions to unite, but despite the appearance of unity, the Party remained divided. William Z. Foster headed one faction, C. E. Ruthenberg the other. Juliet Poyntz was then among the Fosterites, along with James Cannon, Ludwig Lore, and Moissaye Olgin.

In 1924, as they had done before, delegates from each faction traveled to Moscow to have their differences settled. Once there, Olgin, who went as a representative of Ludwig Lore and who, with Lore, supported Trotsky against Stalin in the power struggle then being waged in the Russian party, saw which way the wind was blowing. The Comintern called for "an ideological campaign" against "Loreism," and Olgin returned home to denounce Lore.

Juliet Poyntz remained loyal to both Lore and Trotsky until 1925. Then, once again, U.S. delegates went off to Moscow, where the Comintern insisted on Lore's expulsion from the Party. In July 1925 the *Daily Worker* called for the liquidation of "Poyntzism" as well as "Loreism." Poyntz submitted. "I stand by the Comintern," she declared at a meeting of the Central Executive Committee. "I support it organizationally and ideologically. I support the old guard of the Russian Communist Party against Trotsky."

For the next decade Poyntz was at the forefront of the Party. She stood by the Comintern through the doctrine of the Third Period, which required Communists to denounce all liberal reformists and social democrats as "social fascists." In practice this doctrine meant that in Prussia, in 1931, Communists threw their support to the Nazis in a call for a referendum to oust the Social Democratic leadership; in Germany, to reject an alliance with the Social Democrats against growing Nazi power. In the United States it meant labeling Norman Thomas, and all socialists and trade unionists, "social fascists" and denying the platform of a 1929 antifascist meeting at Madison Square Garden to the "fascist" Fiorello LaGuardia. During those years Juliet Poyntz was director of the Communist Workers School; she ran for Congress, for the state attorney generalship, and for the state assembly on the Communist party ticket. She was intelligent, very well educated, and a loyal and highly visible Party member.

Tresca had known Juliet Poyntz at least since the winter of 1913 when they met at Mary Heaton Vorse's house to plan the unemployed demonstrations. In 1929 both of their names appeared on a list of members of the Reception Committee for Soviet Flyers. Tresca no doubt saw something of Poyntz in the early 1930s in the company of Schachno Epstein. Epstein, who many years earlier had been editor of the Jewish-language organ of the ILGWU (where Poyntz was then educational director), had returned to Russia in 1917 or 1918. When he came back to New York in 1933, he called himself Joseph Berson and was given the job of associate editor of the *Freiheit*, the paper edited by Moissaye Olgin. Epstein's return to the United States occurred shortly after the period when Tresca and Olgin had shared living quarters. According to Tresca, Epstein was an agent of the NKVD (the successor to the GPU). At this time Epstein may have resumed an old love affair with Poyntz.

In 1934, Poyntz dropped out of the Communist party. She no longer appeared at meetings, made speeches, ran for public office, or saw her old comrades. Those who knew how to read the signs concluded that she had been recruited for secret work. At some point she was known to be in China as a Comintern agent. Epstein was recalled to Moscow in 1935. In 1936 Poyntz was reported to be in Moscow and was seen there in the company of George Mink.

Juliet Poyntz returned to the United States sometime during 1936. One of the few people she sought out was Ludwig Lore, whose name remained an anathema to the Party. To Lore she confided that she had been badly shaken by what she had seen in Moscow—Lenin's old comrades confessing to impossible crimes, the imprisonments, the torture. Her own loyalty had been questioned, she said. After she had managed to allay suspicion she had been assigned, with George Mink, to interrogate others. She didn't know what to do: it no longer seemed possible to continue with the underground work she had been assigned. Through the remaining months of 1936 and into 1937, Poyntz saw Lore frequently.

By chance Tresca met Poyntz on the street in May 1937. Later, he told the newspapers, "I knew Miss Poyntz very well. . . . She confided in me that she could no longer approve of things under the Stalin regime in Russia." The last reported sightings of Poyntz occurred on June 4 or 5.

Some six months passed. In early December Poyntz's lawyer, Elias Lieberman, informed the police that she was missing. A detective went to her one-room apartment at the American Women's Association on West Fifty-seventh Street. He found her clothes hanging in the closet, her lingerie in the drawers. Her luggage was empty; her passport was in a desk drawer; unopened packages on the table contained books, sketch pads, and a box of moth balls. A bowl of jello had been left on the kitchen table.

On February 8, 1938, the *New York Times,* in a front page story, reported that

> on the basis of information at his disposal, Mr. Tresca declared that he was convinced that Miss Poyntz . . . was 'lured or kidnapped' to Soviet Russia by a prominent Communist, formerly resident in New York and subsequently connected with the secret police in Moscow, who was sent specially to this country for the purpose of delivering Miss Poyntz to Russia.
>
> Mr. Tresca disclosed that, like Miss Poyntz, the man in question had been a close friend of his in the years when Mr. Tresca had intimate contacts with the Communist Party here.
>
> He said he could name a witness who saw Miss Poyntz in the company of the man at about the time she disappeared. . . . "I knew Miss Poyntz very well . . . she confided in me that she was withdrawing from party activity. Her critical attitude was well known to the Communists here and this made her a marked person, similar to other disillusioned Bolsheviks who have turned upon the party. I need only recall the case of Ignace Reiss, prominent Russian Communist official, who was assassinated near Lausanne last summer after he had threatened to make public documentary material exposing the Zinovieff-Kameneff and Radek-Piatakoff trials as frame-ups. It is also interesting in connection with the Poyntz case, to recall the kidnapping last year in Barcelona of Mark Rein . . . and the assassination in Spain of Andrés Nin. . . . The Poyntz case is, therefore, by no means an isolated one. I repeat: she knew too much for the comfort of the Communists. . . . I know she was in China as a secret agent for the Comintern shortly before she withdrew from the Communist party. . . .
>
> "The time has come when radicals in the United States who dare to speak against the Stalin regime should take some measures of self-defense against the terrorism of the Soviet GPU."

A few days later Tresca had an interview with U.S. Attorney Francis Mahony. Mahony told reporters that Tresca had given him "names, dates and places," including the name and life history of the agent of the Soviet secret police who delivered Poyntz to Russia. "This man," the *New York Times* reported, "for years had been an editor of a Communist foreign-language newspaper published in this city. He then returned to Russia where, according to Mr. Tresca, he entered the services of the secret police . . . made various trips to the United States on confidential missions . . . and came here again in 1937 with the particular mission of 'luring or kidnapping' Miss Poyntz to Russia. . . . [Tresca] also named persons who saw the man in the city at the time of Miss Poyntz' disappearance."

On February 21, Tresca gave Schachno Epstein's name to a grand jury.

If there was no confusion in Tresca's own mind about the radical springs of his anti-Stalinism, he had nevertheless enlisted the aid of the United States government in an accusation of the Soviet state. The Italian National Commission of the Communist Party declared that "Tresca's isolation is a measure of elementary self-defense for all antifascists." Pietro Allegra, in "The Moral Suicide of Carlo Tresca," called him "politically dead" and demanded his "elimination from society. . . . It is a duty to put a stop to his deleterious, disgusting work." The anarchists of *L'Adunata* were confirmed in their estimations of his treachery. Beatrice was upset; her father's actions seemed to her a distinct violation of his principles. But Emma Goldman, despite some reservations, approved. On February 22, although they had not corresponded since her deportation (and she was somewhat testy about that), she wrote Tresca from London:

> Dear Carlo. You will be surprised to hear from me after all these years. I assure you I never could explain why you failed to get in touch with me all these years. I suppose we are both busy people and therefore take it for granted that we both would understand that though we do not correspond we have not ceased to be friendly. I said we are both busy people. I see that you have added a new job to the many, that is to show up the long arm of Stalin. Well, I do not envy you! In the first place it will prove a difficult task because Russia has poisoned all the wells of decent public opinion. . . . In the second place you will become a target for the rotten Communist gang not only to besmirch your character but also endanger your life. For they are capable of murder open and underhand as they have proven for a very considerable number of years. Then too it's a rather disagreeable job to

have to apply to a Capitalist court to expose the Stalin gangsters. All in all I do not envy your job though I think you should go ahead and expose the disappearance of Miss Poyntz.

When the *L'Adunata* group got wind of this letter, Goldman backed off. On June 17 she wrote to a friend, "lo and behold a few weeks ago the L'Adunata group started a new campaign. This time not only attacking Carlo but complaining that I had written a letter wherein I congratulated him on having gone to the District Attorney in the Poyntz case. Of course I never wrote such a letter to Carlo. . . . I wrote [Carlo] this week and told him that I should never have gone to the authorities even against the communists. I don't see what Carlo hoped to gain by it. . . . [But] I cannot get excited or indignant over Carlo having done so."

Referring to the anarchist feud, Sam Dolgoff said, "It had a very bad effect on his reputation. It gave ammunition to his opposition. Not that his opposition was anything to write home about, but you couldn't really blame them."

In the March 7 issue of the *Martello,* Tresca was defiant.

The Italian National Commission of the Communist Party says that if Tresca is still alive, healthy and unwilling to die either physically or morally, he must be put out of the way. In a word what is needed is a George Mink . . . the murderer of our comrades Berneri and Barbieri. One does not have to be very intelligent to understand what . . . the C.P. of A. means when it says that Tresca must not be tolerated any longer.

These are the same words used by Mussolini when he wanted to incite to action the murderers of Matteoti.

I am waiting unflinchingly for the four scoundrels of the Commission to act.

Juliet Poyntz was never seen again, nor was her body found. Despite Tresca's testimony, police agencies were unable to discover anything about the circumstances of her disappearance. Working with Herbert Solow, a journalist and friend of Margaret De Silver, Tresca pieced together information showing to his and Solow's satisfaction that Schachno Epstein, using false papers, had again arrived in New York a few weeks before Poyntz disappeared; they located witnesses who said they had seen Epstein on the street, but, when approached, he had denied his identity; they found that Epstein had left the country on the *Queen Mary*, using yet another false passport. And they concluded that Epstein, drawing on Poyntz's affection, was able to take her somewhere out of the city, perhaps to be killed, perhaps to be shipped to Moscow. In 1944, Poyntz was declared legally dead.

Another curious event was taking place just about the time of Poyntz's disappearance, one that both Tresca and Solow saw as connected to it. On December 2, 1937, "Donald Robinson" was arrested in Moscow and charged with espionage for the Nazis. Robinson and his wife, Ruth, also had in their possession passports in the name of Rubens; the incident became known as the Robinson-Rubens case. As the story unfolded, Rubens was identified by Gen. Walter Krivitsky (a leading agent of Soviet military intelligence who defected in 1938) and Whittaker Chambers as a Soviet operative in charge of producing false passports—"boots"—to facilitate the travel of Communists to the Soviet Union. As soon as Rubens was arrested, his wife, a U.S. citizen, contacted American reporters in Moscow. She herself was soon arrested. The U.S. chargé d'affaires in Moscow, Loy Henderson, visited her in Butkuri prison, where he spoke to her in the presence of Soviet officers. At that time she told Henderson that she wanted no help and was content to remain in jail. She later pled guilty to entering the Soviet Union on a false passport and was released. In June 1940 she became a citizen of the Soviet Union; that year she wrote to a relative in the United States, saying that she expected her husband would be in prison for many more years.

In the context of the purge trials and the Sino-Japanese War in which the Soviets feared Japanese aggression against their maritime provinces, Tresca told a *Mirror* reporter on February 8, 1938, that "the purpose of the 'Robinson' frame-up is to create a spy scare in the U.S. with two objectives in mind. The first is to speed a United States war against Japan thus aiding Stalin's foreign policy. The second is to smear Stalin's enemies in this country." In March, in the *Modern Monthly*, he predicted a "Moscow trial which would aim to demonstrate by means of a confession made by Rubens and other GPU agents that all Stalinist opponents in the United States are Japanese spies. It is the Rubens case which forms the background for the disappearance of Juliet Stuart Pointz [*sic*] . . . if she could be produced in Moscow. . . . She would be in a position to 'confess' that she had often gone to the German consulate (she was suing for her dead husband's estate) and that she had met Rubens [there.]"

Solow, in the *American Mercury* of July 1939, asserted again that Rubens was a Soviet operative working under Gen. Walter Krivitsky and speculated on a possible Moscow trial with an "American angle" designed to discredit anti-Stalinists in the United States.

The *Daily Worker* denounced Tresca as a Japanese-Fascist spy. Eventually three men were convicted as part of Rubens' false passport ring, but there was never a public Rubens trial in Moscow. The issue became significant in another context, however, when copies of telegrams about the Rubens case, sent to the State Department by Loy Henderson in Moscow, turned up, in Alger Hiss's handwriting, among the documents Whittaker Chambers turned over to authorities.

In February 1938, Chambers paid a visit to Herbert Solow, who had been his classmate at Columbia University. He told Solow that he had read about Tresca's testimony to the grand jury; although he himself had not seen Poyntz for many years and had no information about her disappearance, he was concerned that Tresca might have mentioned his name in the course of the testimony.

Solow assured Chambers that Tresca did not know his name. Two months later Chambers broke with the Party. In the fall of 1938 he met Tresca at Solow's house. Not long after, Tresca warned Chambers that George Mink was in the country.

Chapter 20
The Bull of Lawrence No More

IN 1939, as he approached sixty, Carlo Tresca was looking his age. He was much heavier than was good for him, bulky in the middle, hair graying, beard growing sparse to reveal the old scar. One night at a party he pointed to the scar and demanded of the novelist Dawn Powell: Do you know how I got this? Helena Rubinstein? she replied.

Tresca's younger American friends thought him a bit quaint—a leftover Italian anarchist in a time when no one took anarchism very seriously; a teller of improbable tales of bizarre conspiracies with plots too complicated to follow; a womanizer, old enough to know better. "If you just met him at a party he might seem like a vaudeville character," James Farrell said. "Many of his friends were younger people and there was a gap in understanding. I think Carlo understood this and was depressed about it. At times he'd just sit, saying nothing. Carlo was a politically serious man; he was larger than the life he had led for a number of years."

Anna Walling, daughter of the socialist William English Walling and Anna Strunsky, had known Tresca since her childhood. In the late 1930s she was a young married woman. Of herself and her contemporaries she said, "I always thought that Carlo had two worlds. We were his amateurs. We were talkers, not organizers, and he entertained us. But he had his paper and his anarchist life, which I always thought was his real life."

Tresca still spoke with a thick Italian accent, but the people who had known him longest suspected him of putting it on for charm's sake. He must have spoken differently in the presence of FBI informants, for a description in his files in 1941 notes, apart from his height, weight, eye and hair color, that he "speaks English rather well, with a slight Italian accent."

Leon Trotsky sent a telegram to his sixtieth birthday party: "Dear Comrade Tresca, In spite of all the profound differences which neither you nor I have the habitude to deny or attenuate, I hope that you will permit me to express the deepest esteem for you, as for a man who is in every way a fighter. Your sixtieth birthday is being celebrated by your friends and I take the liberty of counting myself among them. I hope that your moral vigor and revolutionary ardor will be conserved for a long time to come."

In that remnant of the anarchist movement not dominated by the *L'Adunata* group, Tresca was still a hero. Sam Dolgoff accompanied him to a meeting in New Haven and, after Tresca spoke, Dolgoff remembered, "One of the members took his youngest son by the ear and brought him over to Carlo: 'This is a big man, Carlo,' he said to the boy. 'Say hello to Carlo. Remember, you *know* Carlo.' Carlo picked the boy up and kissed him on both cheeks, and then a whole line of them came. These were not the sort of people to fall down on their knees, but they loved him. Some of them had worked with him in the mines in Pennsylvania. There were people who had worked with him all over the country. They looked on Carlo as a sort of paterfamilias."

Tresca's influence with the clothing unions was still strong. He called continually on Luigi Antonini, head of the Italian Local 89 of the ILGWU, for donations to "companions that deserve help— The persecuted, those defeated by the storm of fascist and stalinist reaction."

Despite his alliance with Margaret De Silver, Tresca was still short of money to pay the *Martello*'s bills. In July 1938, he once again filed a petition of bankruptcy for *Il Martello* in federal court. The paper's assets were listed at $98.43, liabilities at $4,420.34. The eight outstanding judgments ran from 1918 to 1936. With a printer's bill hanging over him, he telephoned August Bellanca of the Amalgamated Clothing Workers Union: You've got to give me a hundred dollars for the printer. It's very important that this issue come out. I'm attacking you.

Tresca wanted to be relieved of the administrative burden of the newspaper and turn the incessant job of raising money over to the *Martello* group. He was annoyed with Luigi Antonini, who insisted that the *Martello* could not exist without him. That "means you are decided in keeping me nailed to the cross," he wrote Antonini. "For six years now I've been running the paper and maintaining a certain agitation—not useless in our field—without any compensation. I can do it and it is my duty to do it, and I do it with pleasure. But beyond my personal energies I also put my savings into it. . . . I've thrown in 2,040 dollars. . . . One cannot go on in this way indefinitely. . . . I had to resort to energetic measures to relight in the comrades the will to think by themselves on the fate of the newspaper. And these were my conditions: I will not give you a penny . . . but I will give you my work."

In a number of letters exchanged between Tresca and Antonini, undated but probably written in 1938 or 1939, there was some banter about a flirtation, or perhaps a more serious affair, that Tresca was carrying on with Antonini's secretary, "the lady Di Nola" as Tresca referred to her. Antonini told him to "stop it"; but why must I stop it? Tresca answered.

From Truro, on Cape Cod, where Margaret De Silver had rented John Dos Passos' house, Tresca also wrote Antonini that he was working hard to complete his autobiography.

The house in Truro, sunk in a hollow, with a view of a church on a hilltop, was where Carlo and Margaret now spent their summers. Carlo planted a vegetable garden, mostly tomatoes, and spent weekends in his pyjamas. The memoirs that he agonized over for several years and that he tried to entice Jerre Mangione and others to work on with him were never completed. He was a rhetoritician and a polemicist, with little patience or talent for extended narrative or introspection. The unfinished manuscript reads like a boy's adventure story, broken by lectures, anecdotes, and quotes from the *Martello*.

In any case there was too much social life on the Cape for him to concentrate on writing. Mary Heaton Vorse still had her house on Commercial Street in Provincetown, where the Dos Passoses also had a house. Edmund Wilson spent summers on the Cape, as did Ella and Bertram Wolfe, and E. E. Cummings and his wife, who was a good friend of Mary Hunter's. Anna Walling lived in Wellfleet with her husband and children. Several times during the summer

Margaret would send out a large number of postcards announcing that Carlo Tresca was cooking spaghetti. At least one woman, on receiving the invitation, remarked that if she didn't wear her girdle, Carlo would pinch her black and blue.

Tresca was of two minds about the Cape: "If I tell you," he wrote Luigi Antonini, "that in these days of September, the dunes, the bay, and the always majestic sea that surround us, and the green that starts giving way to the red and yellow . . . is simply glorious, if I tell you that here is a strip of paradise, you will respond: 'if you caught the devil from hell you would make him go mad.' . . . I feel as if I am in exile. I enjoy more the crowd."

Carlo and Margaret were on the Cape when the nonaggression pact between the Soviet Union and Germany was signed on August 24, 1939. On September 1 they drove over to Wellfleet to have dinner with Anna Walling and her husband, Norman Matson. After supper, when the Matson children had been put to bed, the two couples turned on the radio and heard the news that Hitler had invaded Poland. Margaret threw herself down on the sofa crying, Not again! Not another war! Carlo, who had been a member of Norman Thomas's Keep America Out of War Congress in 1938, took the news quietly. He had not been surprised at the signing of the Nazi-Soviet pact. On the first day of September 1939, he wondered aloud, What will happen next?

Despite the war the anarchist feud continued unabated. Emma Goldman's good friend Eleanor Fitzgerald wrote to Goldman in Toronto on November 25, 1939, about the case of Arthur Bertolotti. Bertolotti, an antifascist anarchist in Toronto, was threatened with deportation, and Goldman had written Fitzgerald in New York for help, telling her specifically "not to approach Carlo." Fitzgerald responded: "Carlo knows the ropes, has access to all the labor unions, has handled so many of these deportation cases and has succeeded and does have influence enough to get publicity and money for such cases. Just why cannot he be asked to work on this case? I'd like to know."

Goldman herself was feeling bitter about Tresca. She had hoped that he would be able to use his influence to get her into the United States, although Roger Baldwin had assured her it was a hopeless cause. But in addition, she wrote, "One of the saddest aspects of our movement, little as there is of it, is the everlasting recriminations against each other and the feuds which exist. . . . I have not known in all the fifty years of my public activities a group of Anarchists whose members were not at each other's throats. . . . Possibly Arthur would not object to C.T. as far as he, himself, is concerned, but he would not want to do anything to hurt the comrades of L'Adunata."

Fitzgerald replied that Giovannitti, who was crippled with arthritis, and August Bellanca, who had grown old and feeble, had both "suggested that I see Carlo," to which Goldman answered, "nothing doing about Tresca. We simply must leave him out. . . . Since the Italians feel that way about Tresca . . . then it is no use forcing it. . . . It is a dreadful thing for people who want to change the world to be so set, so fanatical and so bitter. But what is one to do. . . . Besides . . . he has failed me completely. He has done nothing, not even the slightest attempt [to get her back into the United States]."

Goldman did write to Tresca on January 14, 1940. He replied that he had been approached about the Bertolotti case and "at first under emotional impulse I promised to them to do what I have ever done, to do all in my power to do to help. After a second tought [*sic*] I decided to do just as much as any comarade [*sic*] do in such circumstances: I contributed to the fund for defense. . . . Very sorry for Bertolotti. I think that he is a swell fellow and comarade. But in the past I have experienced very bad ingratitude from the bunch he is associated. You must know the sordid story. Of course! You don't believe that I am a spy. . . . [But] after all I am human—if you, my dear Emma, call on me to do so with easy feelings, your call is allways [*sic*] a command for me."

In the fall of 1940, Tresca dropped his opposition to Roosevelt. In 1934 he had written of Roosevelt as "an industrial and social dictator" whose attempts at reforms served to preserve the failing capitalist system. But in the November 14, 1940, issue of *Il Martello* he wrote:

> Roosevelt has been re-elected. By a large majority. "It's all the same to us," the distinguished revolutionist will say, guzzling a bottle of good, bad or indifferent wine . . . "it's all the same to us" will say those who delight in dulling their minds by a constant repetition of the sacred principles.
>
> To me it does make a difference.

Willkie's election would have frozen my blood; Roosevelt's warmed it up. I say this in all frankness and sincerity because in these times to hide one's emotions is hypocrisy.

I am not a hypocrite. . . . I immediately thought that Roosevelt's reelection would be regarded by the whole world as a moral and material defeat for the Axis. . . . As it is my belief that in this tragic hour the most important task of the human race is to strike a death blow to Nazism and Fascism I . . . do fervently hope that a crushing defeat will be inflicted on Hitler, Mussolini and Stalin. . . .

Reason tells us that this is an imperialist war.

Sentiment impels us to preference to one of the fighting camps. . . . Come! In this hour so utterly bestial, so somber and threatening, there is no need to confine our emotions in the strait-jacket of dogmas, doctrines and immutable principles.

Still, he urged only economic assistance to Britain, and he remained opposed to active intervention in Europe. He continued to hope that the men under arms would awaken to their class interests and turn on their oppressors.

Elizabeth Gurley Flynn was now writing a column for the *Daily Worker*. One of her pieces appeared in the Sunday *Worker* of June 22, 1941. She addressed herself to Fiorello LaGuardia, reminding him of his radical past and rebuking him for his interventionist stand on the war. She herself, she wrote, "was considerably immersed in Italian affairs due to my long association with Carlo Tresca (who is also a war whoopee today I hear). When he went to jail in 1924 . . . I spent much time on his case. . . . I am against Mussolini too, but we are living here and there's plenty to concern ourselves with as Americans."

But the article appeared just as Hitler launched his attack against the Soviet Union; on December 14, 1941, Tresca commented on the change of the party line:

The Communists have discovered a second fatherland. . . . Until now they had had only one—that ruled by Stalin. And for the sake of that adored fatherland of theirs they only yesterday ridiculed the democracies and accused the plutocracies of having provoked the war; they had looked on themselves as good allies of Hitler. . . .

But today!!

Listen dear readers: "Our country is at war. The United States, our country and the country of our children and of their future has been treacherously attacked. . . ."

Even the Communists are Americans now. . . . Yesterday for thirty pieces of silver—the money stolen from the Loyalist government of Spain—they mocked at liberty and recognized only Stalin's liberty to massacre and to exile all those who fought for freedom.

But suppose Stalin concludes a separate peace with Hitler? Everything is possible . . . among gangsters. In that case they will take off the republican cockade and don once again the livery of abject flunkeys of one of the most bloody despots history has ever recorded.

Chapter 21
1942

THE last full year of Carlo Tresca's life began, quite literally, with blood. He had been hospitalized for nasal hemorrhaging in early 1941, and the episodes of severe bleeding continued as 1942 began. In January while he was still housebound, his brother Ettore died of cancer.

"My dear Beatrice," he wrote his daughter toward the end of February,

> Your very human, kind, understanding letter comes as a caress, a kiss, a flash of light in the darkness.
>
> I suffered immensely, intensely, deeply for the departure of Ettore. Strange thing is life. Just when I felt more at easy with him; more close to him he had to go.
>
> Well!! it is life.
>
> My repetitious troubles are very annoying. Not only for what they do to me, but, more than that, what they do to my dear Margaret to whom blood, the flowing of it makes very miserable. Ge!!! I spilled very generously. I had four very bad attack. I am getting on very well now but I am forced to stay away from the office to rest. And I hate it. I want to work, to fight. . . . You will be surprise how weak I feel.

Carlo and Margaret had moved from the house in Brooklyn Heights to a comfortable, bright six-room apartment at 130 West 12th Street, only a few blocks from the *Martello* office.

Elizabeth also lived on 12th Street, but on the east side of town. Her mother had died and, in March 1940, at the age of twenty-nine, her son Fred died. "My son, my dear, my only son. Was dead.

Is dead! Forever will be dead!" she wrote in her terrible grief. Fred's funeral took place on April 1. Among his belongings was an illustrated book of puppets and wood carvings, inscribed "Greeting to Buster" and signed, "Carlo, 1918."

Little more than a month after Fred's death the American Civil Liberties Union held a "trial" and expelled Flynn from its board of directors on the grounds that she was a member of the Communist party. It was an incident Roger Baldwin later considered shameful, although he favored Flynn's expulsion at the time.

At the same time in 1940, Bina Bobba was sick in San Francisco, suffering the latent effect of the rheumatic fever she had had as a child. On December 10, 1942, Elizabeth wrote in her journal, "Sister Bina died."

Pete Martin was in the army in 1942. He had left home in San Francisco in 1940 to join the Civilian Conservation Corps, and, since he was underage, Bina had to sign permission papers. The question of his legal name and parentage arose at that point. Bina raised the subject hesitantly, not knowing how much Peter remembered. You know, she said finally, Romolo is not your real father. In that instant Peter recovered his memories. If he ever got to New York, he promised his mother, he would look up Carlo. Beatrice was living in Arlington, Massachusetts, with her husband, her son, Carl, and daughter, Sandra. Helga Tresca lived on Long Island. In April 1942 she was notified that papers, filed in Mexico, had divorced her from Carlo Tresca.

By the early spring of 1942, Tresca had put grief and weakness aside. He was heartened by news of internal resistance in Italy and purges within the Fascist party, and he began to form the idea of returning to Italy after the war. He believed, and time proved him right, that the men who would influence the course of postwar Italy would be drawn from the antifascist exiles who were organized into the Mazzini Society. The society, founded in late 1939 by the historian and veteran antifascist Gaetano Salvemini, brought newly arriving antifascists into contact with the existing antifascist movement. The new arrivals who were fleeing the European war were, in large part, intellectuals, professionals, and politicians. They conferred respectability on the movement, and, as the United States was drawn into the war, the Mazzini Society found influential allies in Washington.

The society represented varying shades on the antifascist political spectrum, but, despite potential disagreements, members were initially united in the task of breaking the hold of profascist opinion, on Italian Americans in particular. After 1941, however, the society found itself divided on the question of admitting former profascists who had renounced their views only with the Japanese attack on Pearl Harbor. The highly respected Salvemini was opposed to the admission of these "December 7th patriots," as was Tresca. Tresca was also strongly opposed to the admission of "June 22nd democrats"—the Communists who, since Germany's invasion of the Soviet Union, were pressing for a united front with the broad antifascist movement.

Generoso Pope, the wealthy and influential New York publisher of *Il Progresso,* was an emblem of the profascist element; Vittorio Vidali, still in Mexico, was instrumental in directing the Italian section of the U.S. Communist party in the attempt to gain a foothold in the Mazzini Society. In the *Martello* of May 4, Tresca launched a vitriolic attack on Vidali:

> A band of assassins works in Mexico for Stalin. It is part of that larger band which in Spain . . . killed, imprisoned and tortured the best and most militant antifascists, anarchists, socialists, syndicalists and communists of the opposition. . . . Among the stabbers, the spies, the executors, those who distinguish themselves for "shooting in the back"; among the . . . Moscovite Company that did away with Berneri and many others, there stands out Commander Carlos, the head of spies, thieves, assassins.
>
> Commander Carlos is at the present time in Mexico. . . . There, south of the Rio Grande, he devises new crimes, carries on his criminal career. The latest attributed to him is that of having murdered his own sweetheart, Tina Modotti, because she knew too much. . . . He is none other than . . . Enea Sormenti. And it is Enea Sormenti who sends trumpet appeals . . . invoking that antifascist unity which Sormenti himself stabbed in the heart in Spain. . . .
>
> Commander Carlos now moves Stalin's hordes to the assault of the Mazzini Society.
>
> The watchword is: "Either conquer or break up the Mazzini Society." The method is familiar: if you don't want unity with us, you are agents of Hitler and Mussolini.

Vidali had now been in Mexico for three years, living under his nom de guerre. In his official capacity he was on the staff of the Communist newspaper *El Popular;* he was also attached to the staff of Constantine Oumansky, NKVD chief for North and Latin America, in which position he was concerned with Stalin's policies in the Americas.

A number of refugees from the Spanish Civil War had found a haven in Mexico. Julian Gorkin, the POUM leader, had made his way to Mexico; so had Victor Serge, communist dissident and comrade of Andrés Nin (Tresca published an Italian edition of Serge's book on Stalin in 1941). Gustav Regler, the German writer, once commissar of the Twelfth International Brigade and now among the disillusioned former-Communists, was also in Mexico, along with Marceau Pivert, Socialist and former secretary to French premier Léon Blum. (The Mexican Communist party had recently instigated a campaign to have these men, among other "fifth columnists" in Latin America, deported; a petition from the United States, signed by 160 prominent people, including Tresca, had persuaded Pres. Avila Camacho to allow them to remain.)

It was to Pivert, Gorkin, and Serge that Tresca turned for information about Vidali's activities, and on May 28 the *Martello* published names and details of the Communist plan for penetration of the Mazzini. Tresca wrote that Dr. Francesco Frola, head of the Garibaldi Alliance in Mexico, was

> a docile instrument in the hands of Vittorio Vidali, alias Commander Carlos—a tool of Stalin's international police . . . and it is with such tools that the Communist party organizes . . . united fronts of the "Garibaldi Alliance" type. . . .
>
> There was, oh yes, there was in Spain, during the first months of the epic fight, antifascist unity. It had been spontaneously formed in the trenches. . . . Then came foreign intervention. And from Moscow there swooped down, masquerading as "Commanders," the buck privates of Stalin's police. Henceforth the united front became fratricidal. . . . Commander Pacciardi surely remembers! He surely has not forgotten! . . . but Carlos, the graduate of the Lubianka . . . believes that Pacciardi if he has not forgotten has learned nothing from the terrible lesson.

Randolfo Pacciardi had led the Garibaldi Battalion in Spain and was wounded at the battle of Jarama. He had known Vidali in Spain, but he was not a communist. However, in the summer of 1942 Pacciardi began to insist that the Mazzini present a "united front" against fascism and extend its membership to communists. In a series of meetings held in the office of Adolph Berle, assistant secretary of state, during the summer and into the winter of 1942, discussions were held on whether to permit Pacciardi to recruit Italian exiles for a Garibaldi Legion to fight in Italy. Pacciardi never received official permission from the War Department for his plan, and when he proposed it to a convention of the Mazzini in June 1943 (five months after Tresca's death), it reminded many present of the "united front" in Spain and exacerbated existing tensions in the organization.

In June 1942, Tresca knew nothing of Pacciardi's proposal to Washington. He did, however, have in his possession, a letter from Vittorio Vidali addressed to the Communist newspaper *L'Unita del Popolo*. Vidali suggested that Pacciardi should be persuaded to take a position in the Mazzini Society leading to an agreement of unity with the Communists, as "this would be very useful to the antifascists." At the June convention of the Mazzini, Tresca took the floor and read the letter.

Pacciardi interrupted angrily. Where did you get this letter? he demanded. I will not be a Trojan horse for the Communists!

Tresca responded: The letter is genuine. That is all that matters. Unity is spoken of here, as it was spoken during the Spanish Civil War. If the Communists were sincere, I would extend my hand for common action. But they are not, and they must not enter the Mazzini Society.

Tresca told friends that he got hold of the letter when a comrade picked the pocket of the courier. However he got it, its authenticity is confirmed by the Office of Censorship, which intercepted a July 14 letter from Pietro Allegra in New York to Francisco Frola in Mexico: Allegra complains bitterly about the chaos in the antifascist movement, blaming Tresca among others. "Now," he wrote, "I am leaning toward the communists. I work together with them faithfully and enthusiastically. . . . We have spoken about the possibility of forming a branch of the Garibaldi Alliance in New York, inviting also Natoli and Pacciardi—BUT we must see how our enemies react."

All during 1942, Tresca's attention was divided between Vidali's activities in Mexico and those of Generoso Pope in New York.

Pope had arrived in New York from Italy in 1904. In a relatively short time he achieved financial success and eventually was owner and president of the Colonial Sand and Gravel Company and the

Goodwin and Gallagher Sand and Gravel Corporation. These companies sold material for paving streets and building highways and bridges in the city, a business that required extensive goodwill and influence with the construction unions and with Tammany Hall.

In 1928 Pope bought the Italian-language newspaper, *Il Progresso Italo-Americano*. There was much correspondence about this sale between the Italian ambassador and Rome, but in the end Rome was pleased to have *Il Progresso* in Pope's hands. A few months later *Il Corriere d'America*, owned by Luigi Barzini, was offered for sale. Barzini agreed with the Italian ambassador that the purchaser should be a person "faithful to the Royal Government," but when Pope indicated that he also wanted to buy this paper Barzini wrote to Mussolini, describing Pope as unreliable and an opportunist; he informed Mussolini that Pope was associated with Tammany Hall and the Mafia.

But Pope visited Rome. There he convinced the authorities of his fidelity to the Fascist regime, and by 1931 he owned the most widely read Italian-language newspapers in the United States. His publications remained in Mussolini's service until shortly before Pearl Harbor.

In 1934, in the October 28 issue of the *Martello*, Tresca attacked Pope under the headline: "We Accuse Generoso Pope . . . of Being a Gangster and a Racketeer." The signed article discussed Pope's use of "underworld characters" to settle his disputes and his personal recourse to violence to break an attempt to unionize his newspapers. "There's the man for you: abusive, presumptuous and violent," Tresca wrote,

But that is not enough. Up until now, given his quality as director of Fascist papers . . . his relations with the more presentable parts of Tammany, his intimate friendship with Jimmy Walker . . . [n]obody has ever dreamed of lifting his mask: of presenting him to the public as a gangster and a racketeer. We are forced to do it because . . . he is using against us and all anti-Fascists the same methods of gangster and racketeer that he has been using up to now to impose his monopolistic will on all possible rivals.

. . . In the last few weeks there has developed a political controversy between [the anti-Fascist paper] *La Stampa Libera* and Pope. In this polemic Pope has been worsted. Just about the time when the dispute was assuming a rather harsh aspect, one of the editors of *La Stampa Libera* received repeated visits from the same otherworld characters that on other occasions had visited Giordano and Sisca. These fellows demanded . . . the . . . complete cessation of the attacks against Pope. . . . In the course of the last visit of these above-mentioned fellows they hinted that they would not return again . . . and they added: "And you know what we mean."

Through long experience . . . all those who have had controversies with Pope know the meaning of the phrase: "And you know what we mean."

These are true and indisputable facts that we can prove to any court Pope would care to bring us before. . . . Moreover, if he wants to try other ways known to gangsters and racketeers, the ones he used on Giordano, Bernabei, Gentile and Sisca, then let him know that we are no food for him to sink his teeth into. We are not afraid of him.

And let us say more. We say that this indecency must end. Generoso Pope . . . has to get it into his head that his hired cutthroats cannot ramble around the offices of the anti-Fascist press with impunity. We . . . will not allow such threats to be made to our comrades in the anti-Fascist trenches. If one of our own is struck, the author of the blow is known: it is Generoso Pope.

We have denounced him before public opinion. There isn't a city editor of the New York dailies who does not know today who Generoso Pope is and what gangster methods he employs.

Our attorney Morris L. Ernst . . . is informed of the situation. He knows that if an anti-Fascist is smitten the source of the blow is Generoso Pope.

In any case we are ready, either to face the courts, or Pope's assassins.

After the appearance of the article, Tresca told some friends, including Girolamo Valenti, editor of *La Stampa Libera,* that he had been visited in his office by the underworld characters employed by Pope. He said that one of these men was named Frank Garofalo.

Frank Garofalo had been associated with Pope for a number of years. He handled the distribution of *Il Progresso,* and he also functioned as an "adjuster" for Pope's business difficulties. On the occasion of his visit to Tresca's office in 1934, Garofalo reportedly warned Tresca that Pope had been far too patient with him; should defamation of Pope's character continue, Tresca could expect to pay with his life. To which threat Tresca said he had replied: Get out! If Generoso Pope wants to know how to kill people, tell him to come to me instead of sending cheap hoodlums like you.

There is one indication of a consequence of this confrontation. According to FBI records, in 1934 Francesco Cerbini organized "a group of Italian criminals in this country" to have Tresca "tied up and ready to place in two bags for delivery to an Italian ship." But no further substantiation of the episode itself exists, and nothing in the records connects the incident with Pope or Garofalo.

What can be substantiated, however, are Pope's political sympathies and activities; indeed, during the 1920s and most of the 1930s, given the generally sympathetic climate toward Italian Fascism, he had no need to dissimulate.

In 1935, for example, Pope addressed an audience in New York's Central Opera House on the occasion of Mussolini's invasion of Ethiopia, saying: "We can be sure that Italy will triumph under the guidance of the Duce and will be greater and more feared in the future. . . . Long live Italy, long live the King, long live Mussolini!"

Pope was more than a simple propagandist for the Fascist government. He raised $800,000 for the Ethiopian invasion, proclaiming that "we are proud to be the sons of that Italy led by Benito Mussolini which will produce a glorious page in world history with its African victory, a victory of civilization over barbarism." And because Pope was acknowledged to be one of the four or five men who controlled the Italian vote in New York, he had influence on the conduct of policy in Albany and Washington. For instance, after Pope held a conference in Washington with Sen. Robert Wagner, Harold Ickes, and Roosevelt himself in 1936, Congress refused Roosevelt the authority to ban exports useful to Italy in her African invasion. Pope then wrote to the president, who was facing reelection: "My newspapers will spare no effort to give their readers all information in news and editorial . . . on your behalf. . . . They are at your disposal."

In 1937 Pope visited Rome where he received the title of Grand Officer of the Crown of Italy and was photographed with his arm raised in the Fascist salute. Returning to New York, he organized the Columbus Day celebration, inviting Mayor Fiorello LaGuardia, Gov. Herbert Lehman, and Special Prosecutor Thomas E. Dewey, all of whom, in deference to Pope's proven ability to deliver votes, appeared on the platform by his side.

Pope would later claim that Mussolini's enactment of anti-Semitic laws in 1938 had at last opened his eyes to the true nature of the Fascist regime. He no doubt did become disturbed by the policy, given the ethnic composition of New York, but first, on August 28, 1938, he offered an explanation of Mussolini's new laws in *Il Progresso:*

It is hardly necessary for me to repeat what Mussolini told me last year concerning the Jews in Italy. . . . In substance there has merely been established a proportionate distribution of public offices among Italian Jews who represent one per thousand of the National Italian population. . . .

It is not true that doctors and lawyers and businessmen are hampered or forbidden to continue their work. The proportional system may be applied in the future. . . . It can be stated that there is the fullest respect for those Jews who do not meddle in the politics of international anti-Fascism. . . . In the meantime it would be highly deplorable should divisions and rancors develop between Jews and Italians in the United States.

Hitler invaded France in September 1939, and Pope wrote of Germany's "indisputably just cause." On June 10, 1940, Mussolini declared war on France. "On this tenth day of June 1940, the hand that held the dagger has stuck it into the back of its neighbor," Roosevelt said at a commencement address at the University of Virginia, while Pope wrote that although he regretted that Italy was "against the side with which Americans are in sympathy," Italy was nevertheless defending her vital interests.

Roosevelt, now publicly hostile to Mussolini, was again facing reelection in 1940 and was threatened with loss of the Italian vote. Although Pope assured Democratic party officials that he favored Roosevelt, Count Carlo Sforza of the Mazzini Society told Harold Ickes that no matter what he said, Pope would not work for Roosevelt's reelection; the Italian vote would go to Willkie. This proved the case. In an examination of *Il Progresso*, the Mazzini organ, *Il Mondo*, found that Pope never endorsed Roosevelt: he voiced general support of the Democratic ticket and, without mentioning Roosevelt's name, urged Italians to go to the polls.

In early 1941, Count Sforza again visited Harold Ickes, saying that he thought Pope, who did not have too much courage, could be persuaded to yield his paper to antifascist editorial control. A few days later Ickes had a conversation with Roosevelt; Roosevelt said that he would send for Pope and talk to him "straight from the shoulder."

At about that time Pope learned that the FBI was preparing to investigate his activities. In his meeting with Ickes that April he was apparently persuaded that he was in serious trouble. In August he turned *Il Progresso* over to his son, and in September made a public statement that "the quicker Hitler and the Axis powers are destroyed, the better off the world will be. And when I say Axis powers, that includes Mussolini."

As the antifascist cause, particularly the Mazzini Society, gained influence in Washington, Pope realized that he now had to deal with a powerful adversary. An October 1941 memorandum in the files of the Coordinator of Information (predecessor agency of the Office of Strategic Services) notes that the campaign against Pope was being picked up by the *New York Post* and *PM:* "This is an achievement of the first importance. . . . The Mazzini Society now intends to work for (*a*) the dismissal of six Fascist agents still working for [Pope's] newspapers (*b*) to drive Pope into a positive pro-Allied and Interventionist policy."

Il Mondo, La Stampa Libera, and *Il Martello* continued vigorous attacks on Pope despite his change of tone. When LaGuardia named Pope to the "I Am An American Day" committee, Tresca was furious. In the May 14 issue of the *Martello* he accused La Guardia of doctoring a police memorandum by deleting at least five references to Pope's Fascist activities. Pope's papers, Tresca wrote, were still "the main source of Fascist propaganda in the United States. He's a Fascist to the core and LaGuardia knows it."

If Pope hoped for bygones from the veteran antifascists, he was disappointed and he reacted strongly. He first approached his friend Cong. Samuel Dickstein for help. In the Congressional Record for March 25, 1941, Dickstein stated that Pope "has always condemned fascism and the Mussolini movement." On June 17 he added that the attacks on Pope were instigated by Girolamo Valenti, an "avowed provocateur," and that Valenti and Carlo Tresca were at the same time Communist propagandists and secret Fascists. The Mazzini Society itself, Dickstein declared, was organized by Fascists who had fallen out with the Fascist party and "wish to propogate their own brand of Fascism against that officially adopted by the existing Fascist organization."

But Pope took matters further than official name-calling. According to a report by Casimir Palmer, a former Scotland Yard investigator who, in 1941, worked as an investigator for U.S. agencies, Congressman Dickstein delegated his confidential secretary, a man named Richard Rollins, to take charge of Pope's difficulties. Rollins apparently used two agents: one a Mr. Lee and the other, Palmer. Sometime late in 1941, Rollins told one of these agents, probably Lee, that "Generoso Pope was out to get Max Ascoli [then president of the Mazzini Society], Tresca and several others who had accused him, Pope, of being a Fascist." Lee was instructed to bring back evidence that Ascoli and Tresca and the others were Communists. The agent reported, however, that "every evidence exists that such was not the case, but on the other hand there was abundant proof that Generoso Pope was a Fascist. Time went on and Rollins kept muttering that 'we will get these fellows one of these days' and if I am not mistaken he had the notorious Frank Prince [Garofalo?] working with him in some capacity. Rollins told me that Prince . . . could get anybody killed for a price and that there would be no prosecution due to Washington influence."

In June 1942, Rollins was still active on Pope's behalf. He ordered Lee to offer Max Ascoli the sum of five thousand dollars plus a partnership in Pope's newspapers if the Mazzini would end its attacks on Pope. Lee made the offer to Alberto Tarchiani, Mazzini secretary. Tarchiani threw him out of the office. Rollins next suggested that Lee try to bribe people into giving false affidavits, but Lee was unable to achieve this.

In the mid-1950s, Casimir Palmer made the Tresca Memorial Committee aware of the incident, writing to them that when, at the beginning of the war, he had been asked to investigate the Mazzini Society he had been specifically instructed to ascertain what Tresca was doing. This shows, Palmer said, the importance Pope had attached to Tresca's activities.

By early 1942 when the United States had entered the war, Pope was on firm ground again, despite continuing attacks by the Mazzini Society, the *Martello,* and a few other antifascist papers. For one thing he had become an asset to the Treasury Department, which turned to him to raise money for war bonds, as he had once raised money for Mussolini. Also, by then the attitude of the Office of War Information had changed toward him. The Foreign Language Division of the OWI, which earlier sought to undermine the influence of former Fascist propagandists on Italian-American opinion, now favored a united front of all Italians behind the war effort. Cong. Vito Marcantonio began writing Pope friendly notes.

Luigi Antonini, head of the influential ILGWU Local 89 and Tresca's old friend, was also now eager to welcome Pope into the antifascist fold. In fact, Antonini's friendly relations with Pope went back to 1934, when Pope was sending emissaries to the anti-fascist newspapers. Antonini then apparently agreed to stop the attacks on Pope in *Guistizia*, Local 89's newspaper; in return, Pope's papers began to carry news of Local 89 activities.

Antonini was prominent in the antifascist movement, and his welcoming attitude toward Pope drew the wrath of the most respected of the antifascist exiles, the historian Gaetano Salvemini. "Allow me to be outspoken with you," Salvemini wrote Antonini from Harvard in June 1942:

> I am deeply disturbed by your attitude toward . . . Pope and Corsi. . . . I do not think we have to fight them now that they have changed with the wind. But we have to maintain that people who have been helping Mussolini for the last twenty years should not claim leading positions in the present political set-up. Even less are we allowed to appear in public hand in hand with them, sponsoring them as one hundred per cent Americans and good anti-Fascists. This is what you have been doing recently. I have not protested publicly against your conduct because I think we should avoid . . . public controversies among us. But now the Mazzini Society has put you officially in the forefront. . . . Now, if you again appear in public, sponsoring men like Pope and [Edward] Corsi, I will . . . [make] as great a scandal as possible. I know that the Administration wants us to put ourselves at the service of Pope and Corsi. But . . . the Mazzini Society ought not to act as a transmission belt of the Administration.

Tresca had had many differences with Antonini in the past. Now, in 1942, he told friends: Luigi can do what he likes, but I won't swallow it.

It was with this background and in this atmosphere that, on September 10, 1942, a dinner was held at the Manhattan Club under the auspices of the War Bond Savings Committee of Americans of Italian Origin. The committee had been organized at the suggestion of the Treasury Department and included many former fascists and their sympathizers. With some of these men (Edward Corsi, for example, whose father Tresca had known in Sulmona) Tresca was willing to make peace. But Pope was another matter, and Tresca was determined that he bear the full burden of his twenty years in Mussolini's service.

Tresca received an invitation to the dinner. He was willing to lend his support to the affair, but there had been attempts in the past to make it seem that he, like Antonini, was willing to forgive Pope. He told friends that he would not go to the dinner if Pope was also to be there.

Tresca made some telephone calls and was assured that Pope would not be present. He decided to go to the Manhattan Club. He told friends that he would stay only a little while and join them later at a restaurant on Bedford Street.

Pope may have been present when Tresca arrived; if not, he came in a short time afterward. He was accompanied by Frank Garofalo and a woman named Dolores Facconte. On catching sight of the trio, Tresca rose from his seat. In a voice loud enough to be heard by dozens of people, he called out: Not only a Fascist is here, but also his gangster! This is too much! I'm leaving! He continued to speak loudly as he left the room, calling Garofalo a notorious killer, a *male vita*. There are reports that Garofalo followed him into the lobby where a scene took place and threats were exchanged: Tresca saying that he would expose Garofalo's criminal record, Garofalo replying that before that happened, Tresca would be found dead in the gutter.

On the following morning, September 11, Tresca received a telephone call from City Treasurer Almerindo Portfolio who had also been present at the dinner. Portfolio asked him not to publish anything about the events of the previous evening. Later that morning, Dolores Facconte, Garofalo's companion, telephoned and a little later appeared at Tresca's office. Tresca took her into his private office and closed the door. Facconte, an assistant U.S. attorney, had been Garofalo's lover for some time. There were no witnesses to her conversation with Tresca, but Facconte later told the district attorney's office that she had begged Tresca not to print anything about her relationship with Garofalo. Tresca sat her on his lap and promised that he would not. He added that she ought to have some respect for her position and break with Garofalo.

No report of the events of September 10 appeared in the *Martello*. On September 23, Pope gave a party at the Hotel Biltmore to raise money for war bonds. The list of guests included "Frank Garofalo and friend," Cong. Samuel Dickstein, and City Councilman Samuel DiFalco, Pope's godson and nephew. More than two million dollars was pledged for war bonds.

International events were moving quickly as 1942 drew to an end.

From Switzerland, where Ignazio Silone led the Italian under-ground, hundreds of copies of the *Martello* were smuggled over the mountains into Venice to be distributed in Italy through the underground. Through his connections with the Italian under-ground, Tresca may have been aware of the fact that in November, dissident Fascists in Italy were attempting to contact the Allies and make a deal to oust Mussolini and form their own government. Mussolini's position was now shaky. The Allies had landed in North Africa; planes bombed northern Italy through the autumn. Tresca believed that it was more than possible, for reasons of expediency, that Britain and the United States would accept the deal with the Fascists in Italy, in order to take Italy out of the war.

Early in October the Garibaldi Alliance in Mexico requested *L'Unita* in New York to publish a defense of Vittorio Vidali who had been basely slandered and accused by Carlo Tresca and other Trotskyites, "using a method typical of the agents of Mussolini, Hitler and Franco."

On November 9, the luxury liner *Normandie*, in the process of conversion into a troop carrier, burst into flames at its west side dock. The Office of Naval Intelligence suspected sabotage and took the first steps toward a relationship with the Mafia-controlled International Longshoreman's Association, hoping in this way to gather information about espionage and sabotage activities on the waterfront. There are also excellent reasons to believe that the ONI was seeking Mafia aid for the upcoming invasion of Sicily. Lucky Luciano, imprisoned in upstate New York, received a num-ber of visits from his associates (criminals, normally forbidden to visit prisoners) and also from agents of the New York district at-torney's office with responsibility for coordinating the operation.

On November 9, FBI agent Foxworth, in New York, reported to J. Edgar Hoover on the events at the Manhattan Club of Sep-tember 10. He cited Tresca as the source of his information and mentioned as well that Dolores Facconte had sponsored Frank Garofalo for membership in the Sons of Italy; Foxworth added that Garofalo was a gangster, a bootlegger, and an associate of Luciano's. Garofalo was politically harmless, Foxworth noted, but criminally dangerous.

On the evening of November 14 two banquets were held in New York. The Mazzini Society gave a dinner in honor of Assistant Secretary of State Adolph Berle. The dinner was important to the antifascists, a signal that Washington recognized the authority of the Mazzini to speak in the name of the antifascist community.

Although Antonini had argued for him, Pope did not receive an invitation to the dinner. Tresca was among those who vehemently opposed Pope's inclusion. Therefore, to save face for Pope, Antonini arranged a second dinner to be held on the same night, under the auspices of the ILGWU and the American Labor party, ostensibly to honor Pope for his contributions to an ILGWU sanatorium in Los Angeles.

On November 18, Tresca wrote to Marceau Pivert in Mexico, "I am engaged in a controversy with Carlos or Sormenti or what not," he wrote. "I mean the GPU agent in Mexico and his hirelings. . . . The Stalinists tried to get control of the Mazzini Society here in the U.S. I blocked them there. Then they tried very hard to launch the Garibaldi [Alliance] here, using Frola. They have failed also, and I must get the credit for their failure." Tresca asked Pivert to send him information—addresses and activities of Sormenti. Later that month Pivert answered that Julian Gorkin would forward the information about that "scoundrel Carlos."

Through the spring, summer, and winter of 1942, meetings were periodically held between officials of the Office of War Information and Assistant Secretary of State Berle. In August, Berle mentioned growing opposition to the Mazzini Society on the part of the Garibaldi Alliance, which had organized branches in Italian communities in South America and the United States; in early November, Berle mentioned again the increasing divisions between adherents of the Garibaldi Alliance and the Italian anti-fascists. Lee Falk, of the OWI, answered that his section of the organization had created a new antifascist organization, the Italian-American Victory Council (IAVC), which in several cities had been successful in uniting former Fascist sympathizers, Communists, and liberal antifascists.

Late in the year, Carlo's younger brother, Mario, died. "I am still feeling very, very bad mentally," Carlo wrote to Beatrice's husband in early December. "I get the idea of being a wanderer without a purpose or aim. Will try to get on my feet. I must. It is too much work to do." To Luigi Antonini he wrote, "I am going through a very serious spiritual crisis since the dead of my brother. I feel like a wanderer who have lost his way." Then he added, perhaps referring to their disagreements, "I just wanted to tell you Luigi, that I am still—immutato—your friend and that, as such I love you."

On December 6, Tresca spoke at Irving Plaza Hall, warning of the danger still posed by fascists and of the increasing influence of Generoso Pope in official circles in Washington.

By the middle of December, Carlo was, he wrote to Beatrice, "feeling much, much better. I am sending you—as Xmas present—some dresses. I hope they will be allright." A few days later he wrote again:

> Darling . . . I lighted my pipe, sited back and read comfortably many times your last letter, the best one I ever have gotten from you. It give me . . . a very sweet feeling of wanting to go on. I must.
>
> When I wrote to Tity [her husband] I was in a sense of despair: it seemed to me that I was living in an empty world. I am getting back to the old cheerful and I don't give a dam Carlo. It Is the best way to face this world and the adversity that nature bestow to me now and then. So I am postponing the necessary care to reduce. The only thing a doctor can find for me to do; the most severe prescription any doctor can give to me. After 1942. I want to kick this terrific year in my life with a good old bang. And then, maybe yes, maybe no. I will try to be slim and alert and what not.
>
> Hope to see you in January.

He added a note to his grandson, Carl:

> My dear, very dear grandson. Your lovely letter has brought to me a very great pleasure. You write well and say many good things. Glad to know you are already at 4th grade: you are growing fast and very soon you will have big whiskers like your nono is carrying along. When I come to see you I will try to get on your sled and see if we can go thirty miles an hour.

On December 22 Tresca had not yet heard from Julian Gorkin in Mexico. He wrote again, asking for the information on Vidali.

On December 23, a man calling himself Charles Pappas entered the showroom of Con-Field Motors at 1900 Broadway. He told the salesman, Harry Sommerfield, that he was interested in buying a 1938 or 1939 Ford or Plymouth sedan. It so happened that a 1938 Ford sedan was available. The next morning Pappas returned, took a demonstration drive in the Ford, and left a deposit of $25 on the car. He returned that afternoon to pay the balance of $281 in cash, which included the license plates, IC9272.

Sommerfield, when later asked for a description of the man, said that Pappas was about thirty-three years old, nice looking and well spoken, about five feet seven inches tall, with a straight nose, dark hair, and of Spanish or Italian descent.

At about noon on December 24, Tresca joined Luigi Antonini and a few other friends for lunch at John's Restaurant on Eighth Avenue near Fortieth Street. Antonini later reported that the following conversation took place:

Luigi, the "friend" is here.

Which "friend"?

Enea. Or Carlos.

Are you sure?

Yes, he's been seen. I smell murder in the air.

At home, at about half past ten that night, Tresca received a phone call. He left the house in an agitated state, without telling De Silver where he was going. When he returned at one thirty, he did not say where he had been.

On December 26, Marceau Pivert wrote again to Tresca, asking whether he had received Julian Gorkin's letter. Pivert was afraid that mail was being stolen or intercepted.

On the evening of December 30, Tresca spoke at a Mazzini Society meeting. Once again he said he feared that Pope's connections in Washington and New York might lead Washington to conclude an agreement with the Fascists in Italy. He called on the Mazzini to launch a campaign to nullify Pope's influence. At that meeting a committee was formed with Tresca as chairman, to decide on methods to oppose Pope. Guiseppe Calabi, who was present, was designated one of the members; the others, who apparently were not present that evening, were Vanni Montana, educational director of the ILGWU, Giovanni Sala, of the Amalgamated, Giovanni Profenna, a member of the Mazzini board of directors, and Gian-Mario Lanzillote, a member of the Youth Board of the Mazzini.

On December 31, Tresca had lunch with Errico Parenti, a union organizer from Boston, an old friend Vincenzo Lionetti, and Ezio Taddei, a refugee whom Tresca had made managing editor of the

Martello. Tresca mentioned to Parenti that he planned to go to Boston to see his daughter, and he asked Parenti to arrange for him to address a few meetings while he was there. He added: I will come if they do not kill me first.

Why talk like that? Parenti said. Have you been threatened?

Yes, Tresca said. Sormenti is here and he is preparing a blow.

That same night, New Year's Eve, Tresca had dinner at Giamboni's Restaurant, with his guests Edward Corsi and Dr. Charles Fama. Soon after they had begun their meal, Tresca noticed that Frank Garofalo and Dolores Facconte were in the restaurant. He made some disparaging remarks in his resonant voice that may have been overheard by the couple.

Later on that holiday evening Carlo telephoned Beatrice. Beatrice was depressed at having to stay home with her children on a festive night. She was very pleased by her father's thoughtfulness. Carlo wished her a happy new year. He referred to the painful events of the year just ending and said: Well, I've survived it.

Early in January, Tresca met with Alan Cranston (later senator and presidential candidate) and Lee Falk of the OWI. The Foreign Language Division of the OWI was holding discussions with Italian leaders in the city about the possibility of setting up a branch of the Italian-American Victory Council. One controversial matter was whether the International Workers Order, an auxiliary Communist party organization, was to be included in the Victory Council. It was decided only that the subject would be discussed further at a larger meeting to be held on January 14.

During the first week in January, Vanni Montana telephoned Tresca to tell him that both Cranston and Falk had urged the Mazzini Society to consent to the inclusion of the International Workers Order. According to Montana, Tresca replied that Falk was using a false name; Louis Nelson, a former Communist and now a vice-president of the ILGWU, had told him that he, Nelson, had known Falk in the Party under the name of Feinstein.

On January 6, Inspector Joseph Genco of the FBI had a conversation with Tresca. Genco was assigned to gather information about Fascist activities in New York and had used Tresca before as a source of information. In fact the FBI considered Tresca one of its informants on Fascist activists. Genco was later unable to recall the substance of this particular conversation, but he was sure it did not concern Frank Garofalo or Dolores Facconte; nor did Tresca mention being in any danger from Garofalo or from Vidali. If he had, Genco said he would have immediately notified his superiors.

On Thursday, January 7, Tresca visited the offices of the Amalgamated Clothing Workers Union, where he spoke with August Bellanca and Giovanni Sala. He told Sala that the first meeting of the Mazzini subcommittee, which had been formed on December 30, would be held at his office on January 11. Sala asked to be reminded of the date by mail.

Before leaving Sala's office, Tresca remarked that he felt depressed, a hangover from a dream of the previous night in which someone had died.

It's curious a dream should worry you, Sala said. You're never afraid of anything.

The following day, Friday January 8, Tresca mailed five letters of invitation to members of the newly formed committee: "I hope sincerely to have your presence at the first reunion of the organizing Committee of the Mazzini Society. This reunion will take place Monday evening, January 11, at 8:30 P.M. at the office of Il Martello, 2 West 15 Street, New York. Do not fail to attend."

The January 14 issue of the *Martello,* which would appear posthumously, went to the printer that Friday. Its contents would affirm Tresca's credentials as a revolutionary. The issue criticized Churchill for placing the blame for war and Fascism solely on Mussolini, rather than on capitalism—the landowners, the monarchy, "those who first disarmed the people and then flung against them, armed to the teeth, all the criminals of the country, whereupon they offered the reins of government to the chief of the gangsters."

An editorial, "Reflections on the War," read in part:

> We need not even add that the more advanced section of the American and British working classes will not be in any way satisfied with the victory that the British and American armies are on the way to winning. . . . Such a victory . . . would not be a defeat for fascism; it would not solve the problems of the peoples who have lived under Hitler's oppression, including the German people. It will leave the capitalist regime intact, the same regime that gave birth to fascism and to the present slaughter. . . .
>
> We can be sure . . . that the military defeat of Hitler will let loose great revolutionary forces, not only in Germany but in Italy, France and in all the

occupied countries. . . . We must expect therefore revolutionary upheavals in which the masses shall fight to reaffirm themselves and destroy the capitalist regime that has brought them such misery.

To prove his point, Tresca went on to quote a recent article by Walter Lippmann: "The fact is that we face the tremendous risk that liberation will be followed by Civil War unless we are prepared to choose correctly and swiftly as the territories are liberated, the authority which the great powers will back to restore order and to negotiate peace."

Therefore, Tresca continued (taking Lippmann as a spokesman for the administration), in addition to troops in Europe "the monopoly capitalists expect to use food and clothing as a political weapon. . . . If workers of any country seize power and establish workers' governments, the American capitalists will not allow the distribution of food and clothing to the people of that country. . . . History warns us to be on our guard."

The issue also contained a swipe at Pope, nothing substantive, but a reminder to him that he was not forgotten.

Tresca delivered the pages of the *Martello* to his printer, A. J. Crocce, at 9 Barrow Street in the afternoon. Crocce later said that Tresca seemed "abstracted and grim," unlike his usual cheerful self. He mentioned that he had an important appointment; as he left, he said to the two linotype operators: Well, I'm going. This is good-bye.

On Saturday evening, January 9, Tresca, with Arturo Giovannitti, attended a dinner given by the Knitgood Workers of the AFL at John's Restaurant on East Twelfth Street. The union pledged a donation of six hundred dollars to help the *Martello* meet a deficit of more than a thousand dollars.

After dinner, Tresca together with an old friend, Tony Ribarich, walked toward Tresca's house. As they reached the New School of Social Research, on Twelfth Street, east of Sixth Avenue and less than a block from Tresca's building, a dark sedan suddenly turned on its bright headlights and swerved toward them. Ribarich pulled Tresca out of the way, cursing the drunkards as the car sped away. But a short time later, as he left Tresca's house, Ribarich was sure that he saw the same car parked on the corner of Twelfth Street and Sixth Avenue.

According to a persistent story, Tresca received a visit from Giovanni Manclavita shortly before his murder. Manclavita, described by the FBI as a gangster from Brooklyn, was also an associate of Bruno Bellea, an organizer for the Amalgamated Clothing Workers. Distinguishing union organizers from gangsters was sometimes difficult; Tresca often boasted of the protection afforded him by his friendly relations with some members of the underworld.

Manclavita now warned Tresca that things were going badly for him and that he had better be careful.

January 10 was a Sunday. Tresca met with David Dubinsky, Luigi Antonini, and other ILGWU officials. An informant reported that a heated argument broke out, adding that he believed Tresca and Antonini had been extorting money from the owners of various garment factories.

On January 11, Tresca telephoned his Mazzini colleague, Dr. Umberto Gualtieri, to discuss the meeting scheduled with the OWI for January 14. Both men agreed that if the OWI continued to insist on the inclusion of the Italian section of the International Workers Order, they would walk out of the meeting in protest.

About an hour later, Tresca, with Margaret and Harrison De Silver, met John Dos Passos for lunch. In spite of his promise to lose weight after the new year, Tresca ate a hearty meal of spaghetti, veal scallopine, wine, cheese, and coffee. The conversation at the table concerned the antifascists and their relations with Washington. Whomever Washington backs, Tresca told Dos Passos, will rule Italy. Dos Passos felt his enthusiasm for the struggle.

After lunch, Tresca went to his office, where Guiseppe Calabi found him alone at quarter of nine that night.

At about ten minutes to eight, and about a mile downtown from the *Martello* office, a paroled convict named Carmine Galante entered the lobby of 80 Centre Street to make his weekly report to his parole officer Sidney Gross. He remained with Gross for a few minutes, leaving the office a minute or two before eight o'clock. As Galante passed through the lobby on his way out of the building, another parole officer, Fred Berson, followed him. Berson had been assigned to find out whether Galante was violating the terms of his parole; Gross suspected him of associating with known criminals.

Galante quickly descended the flight of steps at the entrance to 80 Centre Street as Berson followed at a distance of about ten feet. Once on the street, Galante broke into a run, crossing Centre Street toward Worth Street. To Berson's dismay, Galante did not go down into the subway station, but entered the front passenger seat of a waiting car. Before the car drove off, Berson was able to see that it was a four-door black sedan; he made a note of the license plate, IC 9272.

About half past nine, Tresca turned off the lights of his office and left with Calabi. Arm in arm, they crossed Fifteenth Street, stopping for a moment under the dimmed-out streetlight.

Chapter 22
Last Rites

Fᴏʀ the sake of poetry, "for the sake of his name and memory, Carlo had to die a violent death," Max Eastman wrote. "He lived a violent life, he had loved the dangers, he had loved the fight. His last motion was to swing round and confront the long expected enemy."

As the enemy fled, Calabi cried out for help. A passing taxi stopped, a neighborhood clothier called the police, and a few passersby gathered. Calabi reached down to touch Tresca's hand: Let him stay. Don't touch him, a spectator said. In four or five minutes the police arrived.

The news spread quickly. At the nearby Rand School someone told Daniel Bell that a man had been shot. Out of curiosity he went to see, recognized Tresca and telephoned Vanni Montana—who was to have attended the meeting in Tresca's office. Anna Walling was a passenger on the Fifth Avenue bus that passed only moments after the shooting. She had seen the commotion. A few hours later at a Greenwich Village newsstand she saw the headlines announcing the murder. Margaret De Silver heard the news from her son. At the Canzanelli house in Arlington, Massachusetts, the telephone rang. Beatrice's husband answered the phone, listened, and said to her: *quick, turn on the radio!* Beatrice heard only "shot down on Fifth Avenue." She could see from her husband's face that a catastrophe had occurred. Elizabeth Gurley Flynn was on the platform at Madison Square Garden, at a Lenin

Memorial meeting, when a friend said: Elizabeth, something has happened.

Tresca was taken by ambulance to Saint Vincent's Hospital; he was pronounced dead on arrival and his body removed to the Tenth Precinct, where Calabi was questioned.

Calabi gave his description of the killer: "About thirty-five, five feet, five inches, no more. He came up to my nose. . . . He had the hat really drawn down near his ears . . . very pale . . . dark the cloth, dark the hat. . . . He was two feet away when he fired. . . . He was going very fast . . . very quick." The two Norwegian witnesses described the car. Alarm number 416 was transmitted for the occupants of a 1938 or 1939 black Ford sedan.

At the scene of the shooting Patrolman Charles Clark found a .38 Colt police positive revolver hidden behind some trash barrels; the gun held six cartridges.

The following afternoon, after Harrison De Silver had identified Tresca's body at the city mortuary, Assistant Medical Examiner Milton Helpern performed an autopsy. The causes of death: one bullet wound of head and brain; another wound of the left plural cavity and lung; hemorrhage and shock. Carlo Tresca had apparently been shot first in the back, as the bullet perforation of his Burberry coat indicated; then, as he turned toward the shooter, he was shot in the head, leaving blood stains on the brim and crown of his broad-brimmed black hat.

The discovery of the unused .38 showed that two gunmen had been waiting for his appearance, one at each entrance of the building. At least one more man had been in the car, at the wheel, keeping the motor running.

Tresca's body was taken to the Campbell Funeral Parlor on Madison Avenue. Two hundred people tried to crowd in before the doors were closed.

Beatrice came down to New York on January 13. She went to the West Twelfth Street apartment, where she found Margaret De Silver in a living room crowded with men, all of them arguing about the funeral: Who was going to sit on the platform? Who would speak? In what order? Beatrice paced back and forth from living room to bedroom as the hours passed. Finally, late in the afternoon she could bear it no longer. She stamped her foot and called them to attention. Either they settled it—never mind who sat where!—or she would take her father's body to Boston for a private family funeral. She pointed to each man in turn, reminding him what he owed her father. She allowed them one more hour to make their arrangements.

Early on the morning of January 12, Patrolman Saul Greenberg noticed a black 1938 Ford sedan, license IC 9272, parked on West Eighteenth Street, near the entrance to the Seventh Avenue subway station. The car had obviously been abandoned in a hurry: according to various reports the doors were either standing open or simply unlocked; an ignition key remained in place. Police quickly traced the car to Con-Feld Motors, where they learned the name of the buyer, Charles Pappas. Eventually they traced a number of men named Charles Pappas, none of whom was the right man; the address given by "Pappas" proved to be nonexistent.

Later in the day the report filed by Parole Officer Fred Berson, containing the license number and description of the car in which he had seen Carmine Galante drive off, crossed with Patrolman Greenberg's report. Late on the night of January 12, as Galante and a friend, Joseph Di Palermo (also known as Joe Beck), left a candy store—cum gambling club—at 246 Elizabeth Street, they were picked up by police. Di Palermo made a statement and was released. Galante was not told why he was being questioned. He was held as a material witness in a John Doe investigation. Later this was changed to a violation of parole warrant on the grounds that he was keeping company with Di Palermo, a known criminal.

At 7:30 A.M. on January 16, Tresca's body was moved from the Campbell Funeral Parlor to Manhattan Center at Thirty-fourth Street and Eighth Avenue. Four motorcycle police escorted the car. The gray metal casket, placed on the platform of the Promenade Ballroom, was banked with masses of red carnations. Red carnations surrounded the stage. A red carnation decorated the lapel of Carlo's black-suited body. All morning long a line filed past the open coffin, five or six thousand mourners by police estimates, many in tears, some reflexively signing the cross as they passed the coffin.

Speeches began at noon: Norman Thomas, David Dubinsky, Angelica Balabanoff, Arturo Giovannitti, Max Eastman, fifteen speakers, all characterizing the murder as a political assassination.

At 2:30 the cars began to leave for Fresh Pond Cemetery in Queens where the cremation was to take place. Seventy-five cars of friends and relations, fifteen more filled with flowers, ten carrying reporters and police followed the hearse. The cortege of one hundred cars drove west on 34th Street to Ninth Avenue, then south to 16th Street, where it turned east to Fifth Avenue and south again to 15th Street. There, five hundred mourners stood silently around a six-foot square piled deep in red carnations. Then, over the Williamsburg Bridge to the cemetery, where Giovannitti, tears running down his cheeks, spoke the last words: "Goodbye, Carlo. Your friends and your family leave you."

Part Two

Every occurrence which will later acquire significance is constituted by a complex of tiny occurrences . . . which are drawn in a concentric irresistible motion toward an invisible center . . . no tiny occurrence is accidental, incidental, fortuitous—each part, however minute, has its purpose—and thus its justification—in the whole. And the whole in the parts.

—*Leonardo Sciascia,* The Moro Affair

Introductory Note to Part II

Two years after Carlo Tresca's murder, the Tresca Memorial Committee published a booklet asking, "Who Killed Carlo Tresca?" After two years the case was no closer to solution than it had been in the first days; in fact it was further from solution: Carmine Galante was free with no charges pending against him.

In frustration the committee, composed of Tresca's friends and comrades, demanded to know why the investigation was moving so slowly: was District Attorney Frank Hogan at fault? Was Assistant District Attorney Louis Pagnucco protecting someone? In summarizing the evidence it had been able to glean thus far— some of which it had fed to investigators—the committee extracted two major themes from Tresca's life, and asked: "Could the Communists have killed Tresca?" "Was it the Fascists or ex-Fascists?" In an open letter, Aldino Felicani asked Mayor LaGuardia, "Is there some political reason why the Tresca mystery has not been solved? . . . Would it complicate our international relations?"

After so many years—forty-five years as this is written—I thought it unlikely that these questions could be answered. And it is only fair to say that many conclusive details of Tresca's murder have died with the people who knew them. But the passage of time has opened other doors that were previously closed to inquiry.

Following the strands spun from Tresca's death has led into the center of some complicated webs: into the wartime collaboration of the United States government with the Mafia; into the heart of New York and Washington politics; into collaboration between labor leaders, elected officials, and criminals; into the connections between foreign and domestic Communists and criminals; into the narcotics trade, which figures even today as a facet of government policy.

Some of what I have learned was, at least in its grosser aspects, known or suspected by Tresca. (I am thinking particularly of his statement to a friend shortly before he died, in which he said he had evidence of wartime collaboration between Communists and Fascists in Italy; a year later Stalin extended recognition to the government of Marshall Pietro Badoglio, Mussolini's loyal officer and minister.) In any case, nothing in the following pages would have come as a surprise to a man who understood and detested institutionalized power.

Chapter 23
The Man Who Killed Carlo Tresca

THE investigation of Carlo Tresca's murder was undertaken by the New York district attorney's office and the New York Police Department; there was little coordination between the two agencies. The FBI, with informants in both agencies, followed the details of the investigation closely, but Hoover refused to involve the bureau in any official capacity.

The files of the investigations, examined some forty years after the murder, are no longer complete. Some documents refer to others that are nowhere to be found. There is no knowing whether they have been destroyed, removed, or simply misfiled in the labyrinth of the municipal archives. But from the existing files a researcher can fairly conclude two things: that the investigation had a narrow focus and lacked a guiding intelligence willing to piece bits of information together and follow where they led.

But the files of the police and district attorney investigations remain the best entry point to the mélange of facts, rumors, half-truths and lies that made up the investigation into Tresca's murder.

With excellent cause, investigators assumed that in arresting Carmine Galante, they had arrested the murderer. They counted on a confession from him to make their case, and in this they were disappointed.

Carmine Galante was born in East Harlem in 1910. His parents were immigrants from Castellemmare del Golfo, a village in western Sicily that was also the birthplace of Joe Bonanno and Frank Garofalo.

Galante dropped out of school in the seventh grade. He was still a juvenile when he was arrested for the first time in 1924, so the actual charge is not recorded in his police file. But subsequent charges were recorded, ranging from petty larceny to grand larceny, to assault and robbery, and homicide. In 1926 Galante served a prison term for second degree assault and robbery. In early 1930 he was arrested for participating in the murder of a policeman, but the charge was dropped for lack of sufficient evidence.

Then on Christmas Eve 1930, a suspicious detective noticed a green sedan parked at the corner of Driggs Avenue in Brooklyn. Four men were in the car. As the detective approached, one of the men said something like: Stop where you are buddy, or we'll knock you off. All four then ran from the car. The detective fired at them, shots were returned, and a six-year-old girl, passing with her mother, was wounded in the exchange. The men jumped onto a passing truck; three of them managed to escape, but one, Galante as it turned out, missed his footing and was taken into custody.

At police headquarters, Galante was identified as one of four men who, that same night, had held up the Liebman Brewery in Brooklyn. His interrogation was said to have been brutal, but he was brought to trial without having named his accomplices. After serving more than eight years in Sing-Sing, he was paroled in May 1939.

After that, police records show that Galante lived, or said he lived, with his mother and sisters in Brooklyn. He worked for a time for a manufacturer of artificial flowers, then as a longshoreman. On August 15, 1942, he went to work for a trucking company, Knickerbocker Transportation. This was a very small company, with only desk room on lower Broadway as an office and one secondhand truck used to make pickups and deliveries to garment shops. As a truckman's helper, Galante was paid twenty-seven dollars a week.

When police questioned him about his movements on January 11, 1943, Galante told the following story. He had gone to his job at Knickerbocker Transportation that day. After finishing work, he went to United Sportswear, a company owned by a friend— John Dioguardi, commonly known as Johnny Dio—where he did a little work for Dio until it was time to report to his parole officer. After making his report, he said he had taken the IRT uptown, to the Hollywood Theatre on Broadway, where he had seen a new movie, *Casablanca.*

No, Galante maintained, he had certainly not gotten into a car and he had gone to the movies by himself. Later he amended that last statement and said that he had gone with a girlfriend. He refused to give her name, however, because it might get into the newspapers and damage her reputation.

Galante was sent to the Tombs for violation of parole; two days later Calabi identified him in a lineup.

But immediately Calabi expressed doubts. He said to Assistant District Attorney Eleazar Lipsky: maybe I was influenced by seeing this man's picture in the newspaper. I can't take the responsibility.

Lipsky argued with him: If this were a civil case, he said, would you be more certain of your identification? Calabi said he would. Well then, Lipsky said, let your identification stand; cross-examination will bring out your doubts. Calabi then agreed to identify Galante when the case came to trial.

The owner of Knickerbocker Transportation was brought in for questioning. He was accompanied by a lawyer of some note—Samuel DiFalco, city councilman and nephew, godson, and confidant of Generoso Pope. When his client was asked how he had come to hire Galante, DiFalco advised him not to answer.

From other sources, police learned that Galante had gotten his job at Knickerbocker through Johnny Dio, a known garment center racketeer who, in 1937, had been indicted by Thomas Dewey on ten counts, including extortion of garment truckers.

Continuing interrogation by police and district attorneys produced no more information from Galante. In early February he was moved from the Tombs to the Fifth District prison, where it was hoped an informer could gain his confidence. The informer's name was Emilio Funicello—known as Nick. Funicello, serving a life sentence as a four-time loser, had begun to provide information to the police after the death of his wife; he blamed his former associates for failing to provide medical care for her and hoped to win his release so as to care for his children.

Over a period of weeks, Galante, alternating between suspicion and the pleasure of boasting, gave Funicello at least three different versions of the events of January 11, ranging from denial of involvement to admission that he was the killer, and offering different details of the story at each telling.

In one version, Galante identified the driver of the car as "Buster." There was another man in the car, whom he called "Pap" or "Pep." Early on the evening of January 11, according to Funicello's statement, the three men drove to a bar and grill located between Fifteenth and Sixteenth streets on Fifth Avenue, where they had something to eat. While they were eating, an old man walked past and, smacking Buster on the shoulder, said: I'll see you at 8:30. Galante had the impression that the old man had some connection to Tresca's office.

In another version of the evening's events, Galante said that after this meal, he had met his girlfriend, Helen, at the Hollywood Theatre, had left her inside, and had gone to meet Buster and Pap again, to drive with them to Fourteenth Street and Fifth Avenue. At Fourteenth Street, Pap got out of the car and walked to the entrance of 96 Fifth Avenue, while Galante and Buster drove a little farther and parked on Fifteenth Street, a few doors west of Fifth Avenue.

There they waited. Buster kept his eyes on an upper floor of the building, waiting, he said, for a light to go out. There it is now! he said to Galante.

Galante soon saw two men come out of the building and cross Fifteenth Street. He opened the car door. Which one should I get? he asked Buster. Get that son of a bitch with the whiskers, he was told.

Galante walked up to the bearded man. According to Funicello's statement Galante said: "I let him have the first shot in the right side of the head. It looked like I didn't hit him because he kept right on walking. I let him have another. . . . His little friend there . . . he was looking at me but he looked like he was in a daze because he didn't move. . . . I ran after the car and jumped in the car. I saw Pap standing on the corner. . . . I got out on Sixteenth Street . . . went uptown." Uptown Galante picked up his girlfriend at the Hollywood Theatre and went with her to a hotel, where they spent the night. Galante also mentioned that "this fellow was supposed to be killed" earlier, but "something came up."

Funicello was prepared to testify in court that "Galante himself told me that he was the one that did the killing but they can't prove it."

Galante's girlfriend (he warily called her "Dottie" when talking to Funicello) turned out to be a Helen Marulli, but the police were unable to locate her. They spoke to her friends and coworkers at the Emerson Radio Company on lower Eighth Avenue. One of those friends, Mamie Martello, said that Marulli had told her she had a date with Lilo (Galante's lifelong nickname) on the night of January 11. On the 12th and 13th, Marulli did not show up for work. Mamie Martello met her by appointment on the evening of the 13th. Marulli then said: "Didn't you read about the Tresca killing? . . . That's my boyfriend." Marulli told Martello that she and Lilo had gone to a hotel that night, and she was afraid that if the police found her it would come out that she was sleeping with Lilo and her family would disown her. She said she was going away.

On April 7, police found Helen Marulli in Westfield, Massachusetts, where she had gone together with Joseph Di Palermo's girlfriend, Anna Scaglione, whose child (by Di Palermo) was boarded with a family in that town. Brought back to New York, Helen Marulli presumably made a statement, but there is no record of it in police files. She may have told the story Galante told Funicello she would stick to: that she and Lilo had been to the movies together, that he had excused himself to go to the men's room and she had no idea how long he had been gone. When the movie was over, they had gone to a hotel for the night.

Through the late winter and early spring the police and district attorney's office gathered more information on Galante. He was said to be a bootlegger; he was a member of a gang headed by Frank Garofalo; Garofalo was said to be his cousin. Galante was also associated with Frank Citrano, who was said to be leader of a gang on the Lower East Side.

The driver of the murder car was believed to be Sebastian Domingo, known as Buster, a close associate of Joe Bonanno. Buster, Galante, Di Palermo, and Garofalo were all said to be members of the Castellemmare gang, or La Marese, headed by Joe Bonanno.

Galante was questioned often during this period. At one point he inadvertently admitted that he had gotten into a car on the night of the 11th. After that admission, he lost his temper and became "very abusive," refusing to answer any more questions.

In May, several newspapers reported that District Attorney Frank Hogan was about to present his case to the grand jury. This did not happen. In September there seemed to be a break in the case when police arrested one Frank Nuccio, a small-time bootlegger who leased a garage on Mulberry Street, where it was believed the murder car had been kept from the time of its purchase. Nuccio was released after two months with no further developments.

Galante remained in custody for almost a year on the violation of parole warrant. In late December 1944, with no further charges against him, he was released. Six weeks later he married Helen Marulli in the Church of Our Lady of Sorrows, on Pitt Street.

There was strong, if circumstantial, evidence to connect Galante to Tresca's murder, yet District Attorney Hogan did not proceed against him. There was some justification for this. For one thing, Nick Funicello's credibility as a witness: Funicello had become a too-regular informant for the district attorney's office and a court might reject his testimony, as in fact one judge did when he testified in another case in 1944. But the district attorney's office believed in Funicello's basic honesty. So strongly did Assistant District Attorney Eleazar Lipsky believe in him that when Lipsky later wrote his novel *Kiss of Death*, he used Funicello as the model for his informant-hero.

There was also the matter of Guiseppe Calabi's identification of Galante, which would have been shaken by a competent cross-examination. But taken all together—the evidence of the parole officer who had seen Galante get into a car, the identification of the car by the Norwegian witnesses, the discovery of the abandoned car, the evidence of Mamie Martello and Helen Marulli (before she became Galante's wife and unable to testify against him)—all of this made for a good circumstantial case. It would seem that a district attorney, under strong public pressure, as District Attorney Hogan was, would bring such a case to trial. That Hogan did not do so may indicate that other considerations were involved.

The assistant district attorney placed in charge of the case was Louis Pagnucco. Tresca's friends perceived Pagnucco as a problem from the beginning: he had a history of fascist sympathies. Pagnucco's college thesis had praised the "courageous leadership of Mussolini"; he had received a scholarship from a fund collected by Generoso Pope; in 1941 and 1942, Pagnucco had joined Pope and Samuel DiFalco on the platform of Columbus Day celebrations. Tresca's friends thought that Pagnucco was not the proper person to follow through on evidence that might lead to Pope.

Frank Hogan was said to have political ambitions; there were rumors that he planned to run for mayor in 1945. The Tresca case involved politically sensitive areas, a fact noticed by the FBI agent in New York who followed the investigation closely. In 1944 the agent sent a memo to Hoover expressing surprise that fourteen months after the murder, Pagnucco was still emphasizing the tracing of the murder car—a lead that had been long exhausted—over all other aspects of the investigation. In another memorandum the FBI agent reported that, although the New York authorities seemed to have prima facie evidence of Galante's guilt, they had not proceeded against him. He speculated that this might be because the case had political ramifications and involved the names of Generoso Pope, Sidney Hillman, and Luigi Antonini, among others. For these reasons, he reported to Washington, the New York authorities may have considered it advisable to "soft pedal" the investigation and give it the "brush-off."

Chapter 24
For All Know

"Go down, you who study the conditions of the organized mass in the United States of America. Go down among the tailors, mingle with the cutters . . . ask the officers of the Amalgamated and you will hear from all of them, for all know . . . that the gang which formerly had been taking orders from nobody but Orlofsky, was paid $50,000 by Hillman."

When Carlo Tresca made this accusation in the *Martello* in 1931, Sidney Hillman, head of the Amalgamated Clothing Workers Union, was in the midst of a well-publicized attempt to cleanse the Amalgamated of gangsters. Some subsequent historians of labor union racketeering have put the amount of the payoff—intended to rid the Amalgamated of Lepke Buchalter's man in the union, Philip Orlofsky—at twenty-five thousand dollars; others deny that any such deal occurred. But if he was wrong about the actual money, Tresca was right in that everyone knew that many locals of the garment unions were controlled by well-organized criminals.

By 1930 Lepke Buchalter was in control of trucking—a key element in the garment industry—and of several locals of both the Amalgamated and the ILGWU. Lucky Luciano was also on the Amalgamated payroll and well enough entrenched to offer Joe Bonanno a piece of the action when Bonanno took over his own "family" in 1931.

"Well, there is some times," said David Dubinsky in later years, admitting to knowing Johnny Dio, when "we hire people to do certain jobs for us." But Dubinsky insisted that "we don't let them get on the inside of the organization."

Early on in the investigation of Tresca's murder, investigators were given information that pointed to a clubhouse of the American Labor party as a locus of planning for the murder. The ALP, created in 1936 by the Amalgamated, the ILGWU, and independent Republicans, was organized to support Roosevelt in that year's election, while also functioning to funnel the left-liberal vote away from the Democratic party so as to create a third force in New York State politics.

After Galante's arrest, various informants told investigators that a collection had been taken up to pay his legal expenses. Shopkeepers in the neighborhood of Prince and Mulberry streets, where Galante operated, were asked to contribute, and they naturally did so. The man said to be in charge of the collection was Frank Citrano (also known as Chick Wilson), whose headquarters were the clubhouse of the American Labor party at 280 Lafayette Street. Citrano's name appeared on the ALP's letterhead as a member of the board of governors of the Second Assembly District.

Citrano-Wilson was a known criminal, a bootlegger, and a suspect in a bank robbery. He was also a force in the Second Assembly District, where, according to an anonymous letter written to the FBI, he had "a powerful pull with New York leaders and judges" and kept a supply of guns in his cellar. His son was known as "Buster." Other informants reported that Galante was a member of Wilson's gang and that Wilson was the strong-arm man for the Amalgamated and the ALP.

More reports on Wilson came to investigators: shortly before Tresca's murder a union delegate was said to have delivered nine thousand dollars to Wilson as a payoff for the murder. Another informant named that delegate as Joseph Parisi—a man who had, in fact, stood trial with Lucky Luciano and Lepke Buchalter on a charge of extortion and conspiracy. An inmate in Sing-Sing wrote to the district attorney that Parisi was a logical choice for the Tresca job, as he was known as a gunman who worked under Vito Genovese's right-hand man, Tony Bender, also known as Tony Strollo. (In later years, as secretary-treasurer of a Teamsters' local, Parisi piled up a record of eleven arrests and indictments including armed robbery, homicide, and rape.)

Almost a year after Tresca's murder, in December 1943, the district attorney's office was informed that on a recent night, while playing cards at the ALP clubhouse, Wilson had gotten drunk and said: I wish I'd never met Antonini here. Since I met him all this trouble has started. Wilson then denounced Antonini, saying Antonini had double-crossed him.

In response to the above information, authorities tapped Joseph Parisi's telephone, although apparently they learned nothing from it. Beyond that, little action seems to have been taken. The FBI's informant in the police department reported to Washington that nothing was moving in the Tresca investigation. The informant believed that District Attorney Hogan did not want to antagonize the Amalgamated, "certain members or henchmen of which appear to be connected with the investigation of the Tresca case."

Much of the information received by investigators may have been misleading or inaccurate. (The district attorney's office was told, for instance, that Carlo Tresca had been "shaking down" members of the Amalgamated, which probably means that he was asking for contributions for the *Martello*.) But in sum, investigating authorities had a great deal of information that linked Galante to Garofalo, and connected both those men to Citrano-Wilson, who had a base in the American Labor party which was the creation of the two great garment unions.

It was an inescapable conclusion that Galante was involved in Tresca's murder. But as he had no apparent motive, it was reasonable to consider that he had acted on someone else's orders. The logical person to consider in that role was Frank Garofalo.

Certain things were known about Garofalo. He was fifty years old, single, lived at 339 East 58th Street, had arrived in the United States in April 1910, had never been arrested, had been naturalized in 1930, had a pistol permit, was a wholesale distributor of Italian cheeses.

Indications are that investigators interviewed Garofalo about the Tresca killing, but there is no record of the interview itself, only a memo stating that Dolores Facconte insisted on being present.

The FBI also had information about Garofalo. In November 1942, J. Edgar Hoover had received a memorandum from the bureau's New York office, which advised that "Miss Dolores Faconti, Assistant United States Attorney, Southern District of New York, had brought one Frank Garofalo as a member into the Greater New York Lodge of the Sons of Italy in February, 1942. . . . Garofalo is alleged to be an ex-gangster and bootlegger who was at one time an associate of Charles (Lucky) Luciano. Garofalo's past associations are reputedly of an unsavory character and are said to be well known even to Miss Faconti. He is a friend of the Giordano brothers of *Il Progresso*. Garofalo is not dangerous politically as he does not dabble in politics, but he is said to be criminally dangerous and for this reason the members of the Lodge have been afraid to object to his presence there."

The informant enclosed two photographs that had appeared in *Il Progresso*, depicting members of the New York Lodge of the Sons of Italy; Garofalo and Facconte were identified by arrows. The informant, requesting that his name be kept secret "in view of the dangerous character of Garofalo," added the information that at a dinner given at the Manhattan Club in September 1942, "Carlo Tresca, the anarchist editor of Il Martello [deletion] was commenting on the fact that a number of former pro-Fascist sympathizers were at the dinner. When Frank Garofalo, who had threatened Tresca's life in 1931, entered the dining room, Tresca's indignation knew no bounds and he exclaimed, 'Even that gunman is here.' He immediately rose and left the room."

Because of Dolores Facconte's connection with Garofalo, the attorney general's office opened an investigation on her in November 1942. (The files of that investigation, which were released under the Freedom of Information Act, are so heavy with deletions that almost nothing can be gleaned from them. Facconte, however, did not resign from the U.S. attorney's office until 1947.)

In April 1943 the FBI received further information on Garofalo. Hoover was informed that in 1934, "Garofalo had been charged by Generoso Pope to suppress a competing newspaper. Garofalo went to the offices of this newspaper and compelled it to suspend publication by threatening to kill one of its employees . . . he also had an individual by the name of Sisca beaten up. . . . Tresca denounced the affair in an article which he published in his newspaper." Another memo advised that "although Garofalo had never been active in sponsoring Fascist activities, he was very close to the Fascist group in New York headed by Gene Pope and the Giordano Brothers. . . . Garofalo was a sort of 'strong-arm' man for Pope. . . . Garofalo was described by [name deleted] as a cool suave little spoken individual. . . . Pope has had his hands in many questionable affairs."

In May 1943, Mathias Correa, U.S. attorney for the southern
district of New York, requested that the FBI interview Almerindo
Portfolio, city treasurer of New York. It was Portfolio who was said
to have telephoned Tresca on the day after the Manhattan Club
dinner to ask him not to print anything about the previous night's
events involving Garofalo.

The interview with Portfolio was scheduled to take place on May
12, but on the copy of the telegram informing Hoover of the date
of the interview, there is a penciled notation: "This interview will
not be conducted."

Portfolio was, apparently, unwilling to talk about Frank Garofalo, not surprising in view of the fact that Garofalo was univer-
sally considered dangerous. It was only suspected by authorities at
the time, but it has since been confirmed by Joe Bonanno himself
that Garofalo was his "right-hand man."

Garofalo left New York not long after the murder. He was
thought to have gone first to Arizona, where Joe Bonanno was at
the time; he was later traced to Florida, where he remained for
some time, quite at leisure, according to reports sent to New York.
He did not return to New York until the Tresca investigation had
cooled down.

There is no record in the files of investigating agencies that
Generoso Pope was questioned, but he may have been: among the
papers of John Beffel, who had charge of the Tresca Memorial
Committee, a memo notes that when Louis Pagnucco conducted
an interview with Pope, the stenographer whom he had brought
with him was asked to leave the room. If Pagnucco made his own
notes of the interview, they are no longer in the district attorney's files.

If Garofalo had a motive for the murder based on his quarrels
with Tresca, so did Pope. Pope's fortunes were dependent on his
continuing good relations and influence with public officials. In
1941 these relations had been eroding, but Pope, with the help of
influential friends and with public statements of contrition, had
reestablished himself. But apart from a public relations presenta-
tion of himself as a patriot, Pope made no substantive changes in
his life. In 1941, the COI—Coordinator of Information, the agency
that preceded the OSS—noted that Pope had six fascist agents
working on his newspapers. All may have still been there in 1943,

and at least one was: Vincenzo Martinez, who had been a member of the central council of the Fascist League of North America. Martinez was not only a fascist but, as was often the case, also associated with organized crime. As secretary of the Macaroni Employees Association, he had been indicted in December 1940 on a charge of extortion. The building where he conducted the business of the association—225 Lafayette Street—was called, by Gaetano Salvemini, a "beehive" of fascist activity. It was also a beehive of criminal activity. It was the location of Johnny Dio's Five Borough Truckman's Association, an operation based on extortion, and in the mid-1930s, of County Clerk Albert Marinelli's office, who was, Thomas Dewey charged, Lucky Luciano's man at city hall and a partner of Johnny Dio.

Martinez was known to the police as an associate of both Galante and Garofalo, and he was only one of Pope's connections in the world where former fascists, criminals, and politicians mingled in relationships of mutual interest. These relationships were damaging to Pope only if public attention was persistently called to them. Tresca was always promising to make an issue of whatever he managed to discover about Pope.

Again and again in the years that followed Tresca's murder, his friends pressured District Attorney Hogan to bring the investigation to bear on Pope. But Pope continued to prosper undisturbed until his own death, of natural causes, in 1950.

Chapter 25
Mussolini Told Vito

As anti-Fascists fled Italy in the 1920s and 1930s, others traveled there to sightsee or to do business. Frank Garofalo visited Italy in 1929, 1932, 1937, and 1938. Joe Bonanno also visited at various times. Vito Genovese spent his honeymoon in Italy in 1933 and returned in 1936 to remain for the duration of the war. By the time Tresca was murdered, Genovese had been in Italy for seven years, in good odor with Fascist authorities who were apparently not fully acquainted with the details of his life in America. (Mussolini after all had made a distinct effort to control the excesses of the Sicilian Mafia.)

A story that surfaced early among those who believed that Tresca's death was rooted in his years of antifascist activity had it that his murder had been instigated by Mussolini and carried out through the aegis of Genovese. In 1957 an anonymous letter arrived at FBI headquarters in Washington, repeating the story already in the files of the New York investigating agencies: "I come from Bleecker and MacDougal Streets . . . and I hear many things." The writer went on to mention the names of a number of mafiosi, the murders in which they had been involved, and their sources of income. Then, "when Vito Genovese was in Italy he was very close to Mussolini. . . . Mussolini told Vito that Carlo Tresca was his arch enemy, that if he Vito could get rid of Carlo Tresca he would do anything in the world for him . . . in two weeks Carlo Tresca was dead."

Vito Genovese was a fifteen-year-old boy when he arrived in the United States in 1913. His first arrest came four years later, and by the early 1920s he was closely associated with Lucky Luciano. All existing accounts make him an active principle in the murders of Luciano's rivals during the underworld wars of 1930–1931; he may have been dealing in narcotics as early as 1923.

Genovese married for the second time in 1933. With his bride, Anna (there is also general agreement that he had had her husband killed), he took a honeymoon trip to Italy. There, combining business with pleasure, he laid the groundwork for an enduring operation to smuggle narcotics into the United States.

When Genovese left for Italy in 1933, his close associate Mike Miranda, an importer of Ferrarella Mineral Water, gave him a letter of introduction to the Italian owner of Ferrarella, Achille Pisani. Pisani was also secretary of the Fascist party in San Guiseppe Ottaiano, and the two men became friendly. Genovese also became friendly with Nino Mirabini, who was hired as his chauffeur during that trip. They got along so well that Genovese invited Mirabini to come to the United States; Mirabini sold his garage in Naples and arrived in the United States in September 1933, later to become a source of information about Genovese.

In 1934, Genovese and Mike Miranda decided to murder Ferdinand Boccia, known as "The Shadow," and also a man named Willie Gallo. Their reasons had to do with a card game involving a substantial amount of money, of which Boccia had demanded too large a share of the winnings. Particulars aside, Boccia was shot to death at his uncle's restaurant on Metropolitan Avenue in Brooklyn. But the Gallo killing assigned to Ernest "The Hawk" Rupolo was bungled; Gallo was only wounded and Rupolo went to jail for nine years. Genovese and Miranda were both arrested for the Boccia murder, but not indicted.

During the next two years Genovese went about his business. According to Nino Mirabini he operated out of an office on Thompson Street, where he was often visited by his associates Luciano and Tony Bender. In 1935, Mirabini stated, two of Genovese's associates, Carlo and Santino Pandolfi, who were members of the Fascist party, discussed with Genovese a plan to open a maritime club for Italian sailors. Genovese agreed to the plan. Soon, however, Genovese received word that Carlo Tresca would not tolerate the opening of a Fascist club. Genovese then told the Pandolfi brothers to give up the idea because he did not want trouble with Tresca.

In 1936 Genovese began to worry about the activities of Special Prosecutor Thomas E. Dewey. Dewey had arrested Luciano that year and would soon obtain his conviction on charges of compulsory prostitution. There was much in Genovese's record that Dewey could use to indict him, including the Boccia killing. Genovese applied for a passport. With Luciano's permission he left for Italy, taking with him a large amount of money. Once in Italy, according to a number of sources, Genovese activated and took charge of the drug smuggling operation he had organized three years earlier. He developed a close relationship with Mussolini's son-in-law, Count Ciano, and good relations with the Fascist regime in general. He donated the money that built a headquarters for the Fascist party in the town of Nola.

Genovese may not have remained continuously in Italy. An anonymous letter to Dewey in 1940 claimed that he had been seen in Philadelphia. But even if he did not return he was not cut off from his friends in the United States. Both Garofalo and Bonanno traveled between Italy and the United States during the 1930s, and Genovese's wife visited him four or five times between 1936 and 1940.

Anna Genovese reported news of her husband to Nino Mirabini. He was doing very well, she said. He was friendly with high officials in Naples and had bought several factories, as well as the Castle of Mercogliano near Nola.

But in 1940, Mirabini was talking with Mike Miranda when Miranda remarked that Genovese was having some trouble in Italy: Carlo Tresca had written letters to Fascist officials giving details of Genovese's murderous career in the United States. Achille Pisani was trying to straighten things out, Miranda said, but Genovese was quite upset. Shortly afterward, Anna Genovese, who also knew the story, told Mirabini that everything was all right again; her husband had managed to regain favor with officials despite Tresca's efforts to ruin him.

Then the war broke out. No news of Genovese was reported in the United States until 1944, when Ernest Rupolo was released from jail and began to talk about Genovese's part in the Boccia murder. At the same time, Rupolo mentioned that he had heard that Genovese had arranged the murder of Carlo Tresca.

The Brooklyn district attorney to whom Rupolo made his statement learned that Genovese was under investigation in Italy by an agent of the army's Criminal Investigation Division. This agent, O. C. Dickey, had discovered that Genovese was directing an organized large-scale black market operation—stealing army trucks from the docks in Naples, loading them with supplies from a U.S. depot, and selling the food and supplies to starving Italians at exorbitant prices. Dickey was astonished to discover that Genovese, at the same time, was an employee of the Allied Military Government at Nola, serving as an interpreter. When he caught up with Genovese and arrested him, Dickey found letters, signed by U.S. officers, in Genovese's wallet, recommending him as a "trustworthy, loyal and dependable" U.S. citizen who had rendered valuable assistance to the AMG.

In mid-August 1944, Genovese was indicted in absentia in Brooklyn for his role in the Boccia murder. Agent Dickey, who had caught up with him two weeks later in the town of Nola, had had him held in a military prison. But Dickey soon found that no one in the AMG had any interest in proceeding against Genovese. In fact, Dickey was ordered to remove his prisoner from the military prison. He then had Genovese locked up in a civilian jail, but he was at a loss to know what to do with him until he discovered that Genovese was under indictment in Brooklyn.

Dickey tried to arrange for Genovese's extradition. Once again he had difficulty. The State Department, replying to a request for extradition, refused, stating that "in the circumstances it is thought that no useful purpose would be served by taking any action at this time." Finally nine months later, due only to his own persistence, Dickey managed to get Genovese to New York, where he turned him over to Brooklyn district attorney Edward Heffernan.

Genovese was never convicted for the eleven-year-old Boccia murder. The key witness against him, Pete La Tempa (Rupolo, as an accomplice, could not testify), who had been held in jail as a material witness, was mysteriously poisoned in his cell before Genovese was returned to the United States: enough poison was found in his system to kill eight horses, according to the medical examiner. Judge Samuel Liebowitz, before whom Genovese appeared, said that he had no choice but to direct the jury to acquit. "I cannot speak for the jury," Liebowitz said to Genovese in the courtroom, "but I believe if there were even a shred of corroborating evidence you would have been condemned to the chair. By devious means, among which were terrorizing witnesses, kidnapping them, yes, even murdering those who could give evidence against you, you have thwarted justice time and again."

Things had worked out very well for Genovese. He was back in the United States with no concern about further charges against him, either here or in Italy, where authorities seemed almost afraid to move against him. Brig. Gen. Carter W. Clarke, of military intelligence, noted in a memorandum of June 30, 1945, that the "file" on Genovese was so "hot" that, were it not for the fact that "at some later date someone would talk," he would "recommend that it be filed and no action taken."

In 1944 Ernest Rupolo had mentioned that Genovese was implicated in the Tresca murder. In 1946, Louis Pagnucco finally got around to interviewing Rupolo, and Rupolo told him the following story:

Sometime in February 1943, he, Rupolo, recently released from prison for the Gallo shooting, had met two old friends at the Mapleton luncheonette in Brooklyn. His friends, Gus Frasca and George Smurra, filled him in on the latest news. They said that they, together with "Lilo," had "knocked dead Carlo Tresca and had gotten a good chunk of money for this." Shortly afterward, on another occasion, Frasca mentioned to Rupolo that Genovese ordered the murder because he was worried about Tresca disclosing his activities. Rupolo then speculated to Pagnucco that if Genovese was involved in the Tresca killing, his instructions would have been sent through Mike Miranda or Tony Bender, both of whom were Genovese's closest associates. Shown some photographs by Pagnucco, Rupolo picked out a picture of Frank Garofalo, whose name he did not know, but whom he had seen a few times at the Mapleton luncheonette.

In 1953, questioned again after Pagnucco had left the district attorney's office to become a judge, Rupolo changed his story slightly. "The story I gave [in 1946] . . . was not true. The only truth was that Carmine Galante killed Carlo Tresca and I heard that by hearsay from the underworld and that Vito Genovese gave the order to have Carlo Tresca killed because he was going to expose him." The only difference between the two stories was that in the later one, Rupolo refused to name Gus Frasca and George Smurra as his sources and as participants in Tresca's death.

Corroboration of Rupolo's story is also hearsay. For instance, in 1946, Nino Mirabini told Pagnucco that he had first met Carmine Galante in 1942 at the wedding of one Anthony Florio. Florio, who was one of Tony Bender-Strollo's men, later told Mirabini that Galante was a very good man and must have gotten a lot of money for the Tresca killing. Still later, Joseph Valachi told a writer that whenever Genovese had any trouble, "he depended on Tony Bender." And Lucky Luciano, from his exile in Italy, told his biographer in 1961: "What does this prick Genovese do? He tells Mussolini not to worry about it, that he, Don Vitone, would take care of it. And goddamn it if Vito don't put out a contract from Italy on Tresca, with Tony Bender to do the job."

Chapter 26
Ghoulish Red-Baiting

IN 1945 when the Tresca Memorial Committee issued "Who Killed Carlo Tresca?" someone marked a copy of the pamphlet "Personal" and sent it to Elizabeth Gurley Flynn at the *Daily Worker*. Although the pamphlet was fairly evenhanded in its consideration of evidence from both points on the political spectrum, Flynn, now a member of the Party's Political Committee, concerned herself with the section headed "Could the Communists Have Killed Tresca?" This section recounted Tresca's role in publicizing the Poyntz disappearance, his efforts to keep both Communists and Fascists out of the Mazzini Society, and his relations with Vidali. There was also a reference to an incident that had become known in early 1943—Stalin's execution of the Polish-Jewish Socialists Victor Alter and Heinryk Erlich on charges of wartime treason: "And anyone who has studied the circumstances of the case," the pamphlet read, "is not likely to have any doubts about the Stalinist attitude toward the violent extinction of individuals."

Flynn responded in the *Daily Worker* to the "ghoulish red-baiting 'report.'" "Everyone who knew him, said instinctively—'The Fascists got Carlo.' . . . I knew Carlo Tresca better than anyone who signs this document. I knew his friends and his enemies. . . . It was a dastardly crime and regardless of our political differences with Carlo Tresca we Communists are particularly anxious to see the case cleared up. . . . It is ghoulish to use the dead for such ulterior motives."

"My heart has always loved you Carlo," Elizabeth had written early that year.

> Even to see your name in today's papers
> Evokes the memory of your smile
> The violence of your tragic end—alone.
> The awareness that you are no more
> Creates a somber void within my heart.
> There like a battered ikon you remain.
> Memories, like candles, light the backward years
> That twist the long road to our glorious youth. . . .
> Farewell dear love of yesterday. Farewell.

But despite Flynn's public protestations, the question hung in the air: Could the Communists have killed Tresca?

So far as the conduct of the war was concerned, the opening of a second front was of vital importance to the Soviet Union. Stalin was fearful that Britain and the United States would abandon the Soviets to fight the Germans alone; "the Kremlin is prepared to go a long way to meet the requirements and prejudices of the western world," George Kennan wrote from Moscow in 1944.

As the opening of the second front was postponed in 1942, and again in 1943, Stalin was eager to show that the Soviet Union and the West had more interests in common than not. When, for instance, the agreement with French admiral Darlan was met by bitter public opposition in the United States and Britain as a sellout to a Nazi collaborator, Stalin wrote to Roosevelt in December 1942: "I consider it an important achievement that you have succeeded in winning Darlan and others to the Allied side against Hitler."

The Darlan agreement had the strategic advantage of opening North Africa to the Allies, thus providing a base for the July 1943 invasion of Sicily. But just as significant to those who were concerned about postwar Europe, the agreement indicated that the Allies had no interest in taking a stand against Fascists simply for the sake of principle. So when on the night of July 24, 1943, Mussolini was deposed by the Grand Council of the Fascist party and King Victor Emmanuel appointed Pietro Badoglio in Mussolini's place, anti-Fascists in Italy and the United States concluded that acceptance of the Badoglio government also meant the Allies were willing to accept a continuation of Fascism in Italy.

The internal Italian resistance to Fascism, which poked a cautious head above ground in the spring of 1942, grew, primarily under Communist leadership, into a full-fledged guerrilla resistance against the Germans by September 1943. But although the Allies depended on Italian guerilla resistance to the Nazis now occupying central and northern Italy, Churchill in particular feared that a revolutionary army would form from the bands of Communist-led partisans. And Roosevelt, who generally felt that "American public opinion would never understand our continued tolerance and support for Victor Emmanuel," wrote to Churchill on March 7, 1944, "I fear . . . the Allied authorities will have to use force against the anti-Fascist leaders and groups." The flow of arms to Italian partisans was deliberately restricted.

Stalin, however, was extremely sensitive to the situation. While Communists, Socialists, and other left and center parties in Italy were united in calling for a dismissal of the king and of Marshall Badoglio, both of whom had served Mussolini for more than twenty years, in March 1944 Stalin unilaterally extended full recognition to the Badoglio government. Two weeks later, Palmiro Togliatti, leader of the Italian Communist party, ended his eighteen-year exile in Moscow and arrived in Naples to declare that the Communists were prepared to enter the royal government and form a popular front against the Germans. This action broke the Committee of National Liberation, a coalition of left and liberal parties opposing the Badoglio government. In the north, partisan leaders signed an agreement to subordinate their forces to the Supreme Allied Commander. "Soviet recognition of Badoglio came as a complete surprise and State Department found it difficult to conceal their astonishment from the press," Isaiah Berlin reported to London on March 18 in his weekly summary from Washington. A week later he mentioned the general confusion in the American press, except for the *Daily Worker,* which had labeled all those opposed to recognition "irresponsible liberals." When the war ended and the Italian Communist party claimed a membership of almost two million, Togliatti praised the virtues of private enterprise; two years later the Italian Communist party would ratify an agreement supporting the Catholic church.

As a matter of larger design, Soviet policy in Italy resembled its policy in Spain a decade earlier. For multiple ends—not to endanger the opening of a second front, to keep Italy in the war against the Germans, to insure the policy of Western and Soviet spheres of influence in postwar Europe—Stalin was determined to prevent an uprising on the Left.

The day after Mussolini had been deposed, a letter from Margaret De Silver appeared in the *Militant:*

> Everybody can imagine Carlo whooping and burbling and perhaps getting agreeably drunk at the downfall of his oldest enemy. As to the Badoglio item I think he would be extremely skeptical and might conclude that not Hitler, but Roosevelt-Churchill-State Department had engineered the move. It is sad for Carlo that he did not live to see these beginnings of the collapse of fascism in Italy. But it is tragic for the people of Italy that he is not here to do a lot of necessary debunking. . . . Carlo knew an awful lot about what was going on inside Italy but he frequently remarked that it was nonsense for people here to plan who was to do what in case an allied invasion of Italy should develop a revolutionary situation there because the people inside Italy would have to take care of that. . . . This does not mean that Carlo was unaware of what the allies would be up to in the manner of suppressing any real revolution. And he would have fought against these pressures. Maybe that is why he is not here.

De Silver's natural impulse was to enlarge Tresca. But if world war and international politics seem on a scale beyond his influence, it is still true that several times during the last months of 1942 he spoke to a comrade about documented information reaching him from Italy about a Communist-Fascist collaboration. No such documents have ever come to light among his papers; as events turned out, however, a collaboration of sorts did indeed occur.

With the advent of war the U.S. government entered the anti-Fascist business in an official way. Wartime bureaucracies, hastily formed, began to mobilize public opinion on behalf of government war policies. The Office of War Information (originally the Office of Facts and Figures) took charge of the effort, with a sub-agency, the Foreign Language Division, to mobilize the ethnic groups. The FLD was headed by Alan Cranston, a former journalist, with two associates, Lee Falk and David Karr.

The initial thrust of the FLD was to undermine the influence of former profascist *prominenti.* But that policy proved unsuccessful. In the case of Generoso Pope, it failed, at least in part, because the Treasury Department wanted Pope to sell war bonds; also, Pope had the support of Luigi Antonini. The FLD then embarked on a united front policy to bring all shades of political opinion under the umbrella of the Italian-American Victory Council.

In Chicago, a branch of the IAVC included an uneasy alliance of former fascists, communists, socialists, and liberals. Organization of a branch in New York was informally discussed in early January 1943, with Luigi Antonini, August Bellanca, Tresca, and some others. At that meeting a larger more official meeting was scheduled for January 14.

The IAVC was a significant organization for the antifascists. It was to be the government's instrument of propaganda for policies toward Italy; as such, IAVC members would have influence in formulating that policy. The major subject for discussion at the January 14 meeting was to be the composition of the organization: Antonini, representing the large Italian constituency of the ILGWU, would of course be present; Bellanca of the Amalgamated Clothing Workers; Tresca, without an official constituency, but as a popular emblem of antifascism. It was already clear that controversy would center around both the inclusion of Generoso Pope and the inclusion of a representative of the Italian section of the International Workers Order, an organization with undisputed ties to the Communist party.

Tresca's attitude toward the inclusion of Pope was clear: he would not countenance it. As for the International Workers Order, it was most unlikely that Tresca would not ignore history: Communists had welcomed the advent of Fascism in 1922 as the beginning of the end of capitalism; congratulated Mussolini on his recognition of the Soviet Union in 1924; had attempted, by setting up fictitious branches, to take control of the Anti-Fascist Alliance of North America in 1926. Stalin had compromised the economic boycott of Italy during Mussolini's invasion of Ethiopia. If these events were far in the past, there were the more recent examples of the Spanish Civil War and the Nazi-Soviet Pact. "If the communists were sincere," Tresca had said on the floor of the Mazzini Society convention in June 1942, "I would extend my hand for common action. But they are not and they must not enter the Mazzini Society." By extension, his widely known attitude should have also applied to the composition of IAVC, but his views became a matter of bitter dispute after his murder.

To go over this ground once more: On January 11, 1943, Tresca spoke to his Mazzini colleague, Dr. Umberto Gualtieri, and both men agreed that if the OWI continued to insist on the inclusion of both Pope and the International Workers Order, they would walk out of the January 14 meeting in protest, hoping that others would follow them. Later that day, at lunch with John Dos Passos, Tresca spoke about the schisms in the antifascist organizations and the moves that the Communists were making in the United States and in Europe to gain control of the postwar Italian government. Dos Passos would remember that Tresca spoke with "glee" of the anticipated fight to prevent this from happening.

Before the day was over, Tresca was dead, and almost at once conflicting public statements were made regarding his intentions to accept Pope and the IWO into the Victory Council.

On January 18, under the headline "International Political Background of Fascist Murder of Tresca," the *New York Post,* using Lee Falk of the OWI as its source, stressed that "the stakes for control were of the highest. The prize would have been a big share, perhaps domination of any new provisional Italian government." Less than a week before his death, Carlo Tresca "told [Falk] the plan for the formation of an Italian-American Victory Council . . . had his wholehearted approval . . . that he would not only join in the plan, but that he would help spearhead it." The problem of admission of the Communists had been "adjusted," Falk said, when Tresca agreed to go on record opposing the IWO, but to make no further issue of it.

The following day, Alan Cranston, in stories carried in the *New York Times* and in *PM,* agreed that this was so, downplaying the role of the IAVC as merely concerned with domestic matters such as "the sale of war bonds, participation in the USO and Red Cross activities," and saying that Tresca "was in no sense considered as leader of the proposed council" and that in any case Tresca believed that all antifascists should unite to defeat fascism.

Reaction to these stories was immediate. On January 21, in the *World Telegram,* Norman Thomas "termed the statement as 'preposterous. The OWI' he said, 'is attributing to Tresca the very point of view it tried to force on him. . . . All along it has been trying to include both Communists and Fascists in the Council.'" The *Telegram* story quoted Max Eastman and Girolamo Valenti to the same effect; Margaret De Silver stated, "Carlo was all for fighting the war but not willing for one minute to make concessions to the Communists. I'd swear to that."

Luigi Antonini entered the fray: "Up to this moment I was reluctant to put any statement out," he told the *New York Times* on January 22. "Falk of the OWI came to see me to try and build up a section in New York of this Victory Council. I spoke to Tresca of it many times and he was of my view. Tresca was not 100% against admission of communists, he was 1,000% against it. . . . It is a shame to put in his mouth that he was ready to accept the communists in that body." Antonini added that he was 95 percent sure that the Communists had killed Carlo.

Confusion reigned until the end of the month, when Elmer Davis, OWI director, tried to smooth the waters: "There has been no attempt by the OWI to select or choose the persons or organizations which were to be included in any unity movement. No one in the OWI has stated that the late Carlo Tresca favored collaboration with Communists. . . . The fact that Cranston and Falk are being variously accused of actions favorable to both Fascist and Communist should be a clear indication that they have consistently attempted to steer a democratic middle course." Antonini called this statement "unintelligible" and "a whitewash."

As this issue was being played out in the press, a private correspondence, to which the OWI was privy, was being conducted between Luigi Antonini and August Bellanca, longtime rivals.

Bellanca insisted that Antonini *knew* Tresca had agreed to IWO representation; not only that, but Antonini himself had invited the IWO to participate: "The only issue in disagreement . . . was the question of inviting the publisher Generoso Pope to participate. . . . I advised against . . . and you know that the late Carlo Tresca supported my position." Bellanca stated that Antonini's charges against the OWI were "completely false" and played "into the hands of the fascists themselves."

Antonini responded, charging that Lee Falk had told him it was *Bellanca* who had requested that the IWO be given a place on the steering committee of the Victory Council, and that both Bellanca and the OWI were following the Communist party line, which, "until a few months ago was . . . a united front with everybody, mainly with Generoso Pope," until "the communists realized they could not take control of Pope's newspapers [when] they changed their political line which today is a united front with everybody but with Pope. . . . The disservice to the cause of justice, my dear Bellanca, was rendered by those who, like you, hurriedly organized

. . . a full campaign to show that only the fascists were responsible for the murder of Carlo Tresca."

Antonini's letter held "such little consideration for the truth that I deem it below my dignity to make any extended response," Bellanca replied. On January 29, the *New York Times* reported that Bellanca and his faction had walked out of the Third Congress of the Mazzini Society, after trading charges of fascism-communism with Antonini.

The pressure on Antonini was too great. On February 1, he told the newspapers that he had been "misquoted": "In view of the denial of [Falk, Cranston] and of Elmer Davis I have no reason whatsoever not to believe them."

The Mazzini Society, which had supported Antonini in his charges against the OWI, backed down on February 3 after a "frank and open conversation" with Alan Cranston and Lee Falk.

Cranston thanked Antonini for his "cooperativeness" and to Bellanca wrote, "Lee and I greatly appreciate all your help. . . . If you hadn't stuck to your guns we might have really found ourselves in serious trouble."

Finally on February 4 Antonini wrote to Elmer Davis. Referring to himself as a "scapegoat," he said that he had accepted this role because "some of my friends impressed on me the idea that any fight against the Office of War Information would result in embarrassment to the Roosevelt administration. . . . My devotion to President Roosevelt is exceeded only by the devotion I have for my wife. . . . But, strictly entre nous, the facts still remain."

No branch of the Italian-American Victory Council was ever formed in New York. The intra-Italian quarrels intensified after Tresca's death, with various groups forming, reforming, and splitting. In describing the antifascist movement in the United States in 1940, Gaetano Salvemini had noted that the various groups were "at loggerheads with one another [making] as much noise as possible," except for "the Communists who, for the present and while awaiting fresh orders walk hand in hand with the Nazis."

The new Party line, which derived from the June 22, 1941, invasion of the Soviet Union, was to form a united front, with every group now calling itself antifascist. In the controversy over the IAVC that developed after Tresca's murder, the Party allied itself with the OWI. On January 19, *L'Unita del Popolo* denounced "attempts to use the murder of Carlo Tresca . . . for the purpose of splitting Italian American unity against fascism. . . . The purpose of these accusations . . . is to disrupt the unity movement which is expressed in the formation of the Italian-American Victory Council of New York." *L'Unita* also denounced the vicious smears against "the famous Spanish war veteran Carlos Contreras."

On January 20, the *Daily Worker* reported that "the veterans of the Garibaldi Brigade who have spilled their blood in Spain in the struggle against fascism, indignantly protest the infamous press campaign against the Commandant Carlos. . . . His imaginary presence here in New York has been thought up and communicated to the press by persons interested in covering up the real instigators of the assassination of Carlo Tresca." Two days later, Peter Cacchione, a state councilman on the Communist ticket, charged Antonini with "obscene attempts to drag the corpse of Carlo Tresca across the front pages of our newspapers" and added that charges against the Communists were minor compared with the "irresponsible attack on the Office of War Information which has been the consistent target of the Axis abroad and the pro-Axis elements here." And Joseph Starobin, unable to anticipate Stalin's endorsement of the Badoglio government, wrote that Antonini was out to wreck Italian-American unity, which "will greatly facilitate those circles who insist upon supporting . . . the Italian Darlans."

"The assassination of Tresca," Mike Gold wrote on January 31, "is being used to defame the Soviet people and the American Communist Party, hence the united front. Who can benefit by the current campaign but the Nazis, the Hearsts, the Mussolinis. . . . To repeat, the pattern for all such diversionary frameup was set in the Reichstag fire in 1933."

Tresca's murder and the problem of the united front were frequently mentioned topics in letters exchanged between Communists in Mexico and the United States during January and February 1943. Ambrogio Donini, then an editor of *L'Unita* in New York, later a leading member of the Italian Communist party, wrote to Mario Montagnana in Mexico that "those really responsible for the murder have gone to the length of involving Vidali in the Tresca murder in order to cover themselves and with a view to destroying whatever degree of unity had been achieved."

In Mexico itself no disruption of the "united front" was tolerated. On April 1 the small group of anti-Stalinist refugees—

socialists, anarchists, POUMists—held a memorial meeting for Tresca and Victor Alter and Heinryk Erlich. In a telegram from Mexico City, *Time* magazine's correspondent described the following scene:

> Meeting announced for April first protesting assassination Tresca, Erlich, Alter. . . . Half hour before meeting scheduled begin when only thirty people in hall one hundred Mex Communists some dressed in shock troop uniforms assaulted with sticks crowbars, knives. . . . Assault troops crashed through hastily shut door fought way up stairway. Chairs tables rubber truncheons swung. . . . Blood pools covered floor. Revolvers drawn. Red Cross ambulances police arrived . . . took hundred Communists Police Stationward. . . . Questioned by police detained Communists adopted pose honest workers who roused actionward when "Trotskyist Speakers cheered Franco Hitler." Flaw was attack occurred half hour before meeting scheduled begin. Not a single Trotskyite participated. Speaker Paul Chevalier Italian Socialist who spent seven years Mussolini prisons, Jacobo Abrams Editor Voz Isaelita De Mexico, Victor Serge Russo Belgian Socialist.

Julian Gorkin was among those wounded in the attack. A few days later he charged Carlos Contreras with responsibility for planning the attack on the meeting. *L'Unita* in New York carried the response of Mario Montagnana, who denounced Gorkin as a liar and expressed "complete solidarity with Comrade Carlos Contreras, founder and organizer of the glorious Fifth Regiment in Spain." The Garibaldi Alliance, of which Contreras was a member of the executive committee, "stands ready to prove the falseness of the attacks and . . . denounces the wicked work of the Trotskyite in obeying Hitler's and Mussolini's orders to break up the Anti-Fascist Bloc."

Verbal overkill was the normal means of public and even private expression when Communists spoke of their opponents. But it was certainly not routinely translated into actual assassination. Alexander Orlov, who had been with the Soviet secret police from the beginning of Bolshevik rule and who acted in that capacity in Spain, defected in 1938 and later wrote: "The decision to perform an 'execution' abroad, a rather risky affair, was up to Stalin personally; if he ordered it, a so-called 'mobile brigade' was dispatched to carry it out. It was too dangerous to operate through local agents who might 'deviate' later and start to talk."

The building of an anti-Fascist united front was the main task of

Communists outside the Soviet Union at this time. At stake was the decision to open a second front in the war. The Soviet Union was suffering terribly as it bore the brunt of the war against Germany. Vidali was a prime source of Stalin's information about the status of the united front in North and South America. And if Vidali had been convinced—whether or not his perception was distorted— that Tresca was a substantial obstacle to that united front, there is a possibility that his "execution" would have been in order.

But those who charged that Vittorio Vidali was the instigator of Tresca's murder—whether the charge was sincere or self-serving— faced a problem that was never addressed: What was the connection between Vidali, the Soviet functionary in Mexico City, and Carmine Galante, the small-time hoodlum in New York?

Chapter 27
Two Thousand Miles Away

Norman Thomas wondered about the rumors that Vidali had been seen in New York. Luigi Antonini had been saying so and Thomas, perhaps skeptical of Antonini's devotion to truth where an anti-Communist point could be scored, wrote asking him the source of his information. Antonini replied that Carlo had told him so personally, and had told others, including his close friend Tony Ribarich. Ribarich had further told Antonini that Enea Sormenti had been seen with a "new *mularia*" (a gang of boys). On repeated questioning by Antonini, Tresca had said yes, he himself had seen Sormenti, and Sormenti had been seen by others in Pennsylvania.

In January 1943 a New York City detective went to Landisville, New Jersey, and to Philadelphia where he interviewed several men who told him they knew Sormenti but had not seen him since his deportation in 1927. As far as Assistant District Attorney Pagnucco was concerned that was the extent of his interest in Vidali. Pressed by an FBI agent, in 1944, to give his reasons for abandoning Vidali as a suspect, Pagnucco said that his associate Eleazar Lipsky had looked into the matter and assured him there was nothing to it. The same FBI agent spoke to Lipsky, who said his information was derived from books, such as Ben Gitlow's *I Confess*.

J. Edgar Hoover had been pressed by the Department of Justice to enter the investigation of Tresca's murder: "An FBI case if I ever saw one!" the assistant attorney general wrote. The director of alien enemy control also urged Hoover to enter the investigation, but Hoover remained officially passive. He insisted that the bureau had no jurisdiction in the case and could not override the New York authorities. He continued to insist he had no jurisdiction even after the New York authorities came to him for help.

By 1946, New York investigators admitted that they were at a dead end. Thomas Faye of the district attorney's office went to Washington where he told a bureau agent that he believed Galante was one of the three men involved in the murder; as for the others, Faye said, it "looked almost as if three gunmen from three different parts of the country had been brought together for the purpose of murdering Tresca without being aware of each other's identities, except perhaps by use of first names only."

At that time, in 1946, the FBI agreed to send a summary of information from their files to New York, though they refused to permit a search of their files by the New York investigators. Had such a search been made, it would have revealed that while Hoover refused to use bureau resources to investigate the connections of organized crime to the murder, he had been eager to find a Communist conspiracy and had carried out an unofficial investigation of Vidali. A look through bureau files would have also shown just how scattershot, inept even, Hoover's investigation of Vidali had been.

A week after the murder, Hoover directed his assistant to order "an immediate check . . . on the activities of Vidal [*sic*] alias Contreras, for the purpose of determining his whereabouts at the time of the murder." When no answer had been received from Mexico by March 17, Hoover became irritated and assailed the agent for having "failed to comply with the instructions." Still no answer was received. Hoover telegraphed, demanding a report within three days. The three days passed without response. "Astounded and amazed" at this delinquency, Hoover threatened administrative action, and on April 10 information that seemed almost designed to please Hoover flooded in: Carlos Contreras, "known as the killer type," had been in the State of Chihuahua during the months of January and February; he was said to have killed a man in Chihuahua; he was alleged to have killed another man in the state of Guanajuato; he was at present incarcerated in Mexico City, accused of both murders.

If Hoover hoped to interview Vidali in a Mexico City jail, he was disappointed. Vidali was not in jail, and probably none of the information sent by Hoover's representatives in Mexico was accurate. Hoover then began to check on whether Vidali had been in the United States since 1939. His photograph was sent out to all border crossings, but no immigration agents were able to identify him.

In fact, Vidali had an alibi. On January 11 he had attended a banquet at El Lido restaurant in Mexico City in honor of Luis Quintanilla, Mexico's minister to the Soviet Union. On January 12 *El Popular,* the paper with which he was associated, included his name in the list of guests present. But even if the source is suspect, Vidali would have had no need to be in the United States at the moment of Tresca's death to have been involved in it.

As soon as he learned that the district attorney in New York wanted to interview him, Vidali wrote to *L'Unita* in New York. He said that the campaign launched against him was scandalous and base; the calumny so fantastic that even his enemies in Mexico, even the Trotskyites—those political degenerates, spies, and hirelings, had not dared to take it up. In fact, he said, the assassins of Tresca might well be the very ones who instigated the campaign against him. I hope, Vidali wrote, that the Italo-Americans, among whom I have lived many of the best years of my life as a revolutionary, will awake and cast out those who subordinate the interests and aspirations of the Italian people to their personal interests and their own reactionary and antisocial aims. "As for the charge against me in relation to Carlo Tresca's murder, I do not answer and spit into the faces of the ignoble calumniators." Apart from all this, Vidali asked in conclusion, how could he have been connected with an assassination that took place more than two thousand miles away?

By the early 1940s the American Labor party had split into right and left wings; David Dubinsky, Alex Rose, and Luigi Antonini on the right, Congressman Vito Marcantonio, Mike Quill, and Joseph Curran on the left. Curran was the president of the National Maritime Union.

The National Maritime Union, born the Marine Workers Industrial Union, originated in 1930 as the American section of the

International of Seamen and Harborworkers under the auspices of the Profintern. George Mink was present at its first organizational meeting in New York, and for the next three years Mink received subsidies from the International to support the union.

Information about Mink is scattered. Jan Valtin, who worked with him in Europe, reported that he was "despised" by other Comintern agents, who referred to him as "a cutthroat from the Bowery." Liston Oak, who knew Mink in Moscow and had seen him in Spain, believed that Mink was involved in organizing the assassinations of dissidents in Spain. Oak also testified that in earlier days Mink had been involved in industrial espionage in the United States. According to all sources, in 1935 Mink had been arrested and jailed in Copenhagen as a Soviet espionage agent. After his release from jail, he was assigned to Spain. In 1936 there were reports he had been seen with Juliet Poyntz in Moscow.

In 1943 the FBI's agent in Mexico was given Mink's name as a suspect in Tresca's assassination. Mink was said to be living in Mexico at the time, although "he has been missing from here on alleged secret mission for several months." Other reports on Mink indicate that he disappeared in the late 1930s, probably a victim of the purges.

But with or without Mink, during the years of the Nazi-Soviet Pact the National Maritime Union was a source of concern to military intelligence. In a "confidential report" issued in November 1940, military intelligence noted that "it would be difficult to over-emphasize the importance of the NMU. It is prepared to tie up shipping through strike and sabotage under the guise of a Communist-directed Peace-for-America program. Their real intention is to cut off supplies to England for the benefit of Germany and Russia." A month later Frederick "Blackie" Myers, vice-president of the NMU and a member of the Communist party's National Committee, addressed a meeting of the American Peace Mobilization which was organizing an antiwar march on Washington. Myers said, "The time may come when nothing less than a nation-wide strike against war will be effective. But we've got to hurry."

On January 11, 1943, a remarkable coincidence occurred. On the night Carmine Galante reported to his parole officer at 80 Centre Street, Blackie Myers and Louis Goldblatt (a field representative of the International Longshoreman's and Warehouse-man's Union) accompanied one Ernest Ramsey to 80 Centre Street while Ramsey reported to his parole officer. Ramsey was a transferred parolee from San Francisco, where in January 1937 he had been sentenced to five years to life for ordering the murder of one George Alberts because, as the prosecutor charged at Ramsey's trial, Alberts was anticommunist.

On February 1, police questioned Blackie Myers and Louis Goldblatt. Both men told the police that after their visit to Centre Street, they and Ernest Ramsey had attended a boxing match at the St. Nicholas Arena. Questioned again by Lipsky and Pagnucco, they repeated their story. Lipsky felt that "that ended that trail." He apparently saw no significance in a confluence of names: as Galante had told versions of his story to Nick Funicello, the name Blackie appeared, along with the names Buster and Pap. One more name is necessary to construct this scenario—Frank Citrano, alias Chick Wilson, Galante's associate and a member of the board of governors of the American Labor party's Second Assembly District.

Thus, in late 1942 Vidali is in Mexico, working toward the Soviet Union's policy of a united front. George Mink may be in Mexico, but even if he is dead Vidali has other connections with the NMU. Blackie Myers is in New York, a member of the Communist party's National Committee, a vice-president of the NMU, and the associate of a man convicted of complicity in a political murder. Finally there is Frank Citrano, member of an organized criminal gang of which Galante is also a member, and an official of the American Labor party, which has connections to the NMU. Then, coincidentally or not, Blackie Myers with his convict friend and Carmine Galante are all located at 80 Centre Street on the fatal night.

These links have no force as far as the murder is concerned except as a rhetorical answer to Vidali's rhetorical question: How could he have been involved in a murder that took place almost two thousand miles distant?

In the district attorney's files of the investigation there is a note of a memorandum from a federal officer: an informant reported being present at a meeting of several prominent Communists in New York who were discussing the Tresca murder. All scoffed at the idea that Communists had been involved in it, but they referred to Tresca as a "Trotskyite" and "a dirty renegade." The informant added that if "reds" were involved, however, the "NMU is the organization that could carry out the murder."

In furtherance of official government policy, the OWI took the position that Carlo Tresca had agreed to participate in a united front of all Italian groups. By making public statements to this effect, OWI spokesmen were aware that they were misrepresenting the fact. Memorandums in OWI and OSS files confirm this. One document titled "Memorandum on Assassination of Carlo Tresca and the Italian Situation" notes:

> Tresca himself, a loveable, jovial personality, had through many years made a long list of political enemies. . . . He was engaged at the time of his death in bitter controversy with Italian fascist or fascist sympathizers and also with Communists. . . . He was therefore impartially denounced by Italian fascists and by Communists. Indeed, the day that his death was reported, a reliable witness says he overheard a conversation between Communists and Communist fellow-travelers who were arguing that really Tresca had been fascist in his sympathies since he was a critic of Stalin. . . .
>
> According to apparently reliable and detailed report, the general situation is this: the government and for the present, the Communist Party, each for its own reasons, wants the broadest possible unity of Italians in America. . . . This unity can better be reached on anti-Mussolini than on an anti-fascist basis. . . . One understands the desire of the government for the maximum unity of Italians, but for the government to put pressure on anti-fascists in the direction of the unsound theory that one man only is responsible for Italy's woe, is very dangerous business and cannot possibly further the cause of democracy.

Another report, marked "Secret" and written during the week following the murder, discusses "Political Aspects of the Tresca Murder." This memorandum concentrates on the divisions within the antifascist movement:

> The murder of Carlo Tresca . . . came at a time when Italian factions in the United States were already deep in acrimonious political controversy. Reactions which have been expressed for public consumption follow the ideological cleavages of the moment . . in fact no one cooperated with anyone else across factional lines. Quite the reverse: each faction charged all others with engaging in cutthroat competition in the race to . . . a hoped-for preferred position, eventually, in Italy proper. . . .

The foregoing makes up the political background to the Tresca murder. The victim was virulently anti-Fascist. . . . In the factional fighting . . . he was violently anti-Communist.

In the spring of 1943, Margaret De Silver visited Washington hoping to see the attorney general but settling for an interview with the FBI. She told them of her suspicions of Vidali and left two photographs of Vidali with them. At the end of 1943 she went to Mexico, perhaps to see what she could find out on her own. She stayed in Coyoacán, at the home of Gustav Regler, the German writer and former Communist who had known Vidali in Spain and was now himself the object of attack by Communists in Mexico.

From Mexico De Silver wrote to Ignazio Silone, who was directing the Italian Socialist underground from Switzerland (while being denounced by the Communists as a "second-rate Trotskyist novelist"). In her letter, which Regler routed through Arthur Koestler in London, Margaret expressed her appreciation of Silone's novels, in particular *Bread and Wine* which had moved her deeply. She wrote further:

Carlo loved it too. Carlo shared with you that rare and beautiful gift—he loved people as people and not merely as systems. . . . I wonder if you or your close friends understand clearly . . . that Carlo was killed on account of the developing Italian situation, either by the GPU or by ex-fascists [who want to control] the potential developments in Italy. I believe his death was as disastrous for what all of us desire as was Rosa Luxemberg's and Karl Liebnecht's. . . . If you can possibly get a letter to me through the same sources as this one . . . I would appreciate it deeply—just to let me know that you understand the significance of Carlos' life and death and will use his name for the ends he wished for so passionately.

Chapter 28
The Project

Between the declaration of war on December 7, 1941, and early February 1942, the United States lost a total of seventy-one merchant ships at sea; the SS *Normandie* was tied up at a Hudson River dock while being converted to a troop ship when it was destroyed by fire. It was the business of military intelligence to think in terms of spies and saboteurs, and it occurred to that department that the men working on the East Coast waterfront were in a position to feed information to enemy vessels and also to inflict damage on ships in the harbor.

Sometime during the spring of 1943, a gangster and known heroin smuggler named August Del Grazio paid a visit to George H. White, a former agent of the Federal Narcotics Bureau who was currently in the army and would later serve with the OSS. Del Grazio passed along an offer to White: if Lucky Luciano were promised parole, he would arrange contacts for undercover U.S. agents in Sicily when the invasion took place.

White refused Luciano's offer. He told Del Grazio that although he would be glad to get information, parole for Luciano was out of the question. White then reported the incident to Harry Anslinger, chief of the Narcotics Bureau, and never again heard from Del Grazio.

But the Office of Naval Intelligence was already involved with the Mafia. In the spring of 1942, Capt. Roscoe McFall, who later characterized it a "calculated risk," organized a project involving the cooperation of the criminal underworld. Some details of this project have been established. For instance, on the night of March 26, 1942, Murray Gurfein of the district attorney's office met with Joe "Socks" Lanza in Riverside Park. Lanza, who controlled the Fulton Fish Market for the Mafia, told Gurfein that for certain considerations Luciano would pass the word to waterfront workers to cooperate with the Office of Naval Intelligence.

Less than a month later, Luciano was transferred from Clinton Prison to Great Meadow Prison, an institution more convenient to the city and considered a great deal more comfortable. During 1942 and 1943, Luciano was permitted to receive visitors who would not normally be approved for prison visiting: Meyer Lansky, Mike Miranda (Genovese's close associate), Frank Costello, Willie Moretti, and Joe Lanza. These visits lasted several hours and were conducted out of the hearing of prison authorities. From 1942 on, the Mafia collaborated with the ONI, although the full substance of that arrangement can never be completely documented. In 1944, in an "instance of wholesale destruction" in the words of the commander in charge, all files relating to the Luciano project were burned. When rumors about the project persisted long after the war, the ONI officially continued to deny that anything of significance had taken place. And when the Herlands Investigating Commission persisted in the matter, it was persuaded not to publish its report.

Despite this secrecy, however, traces remain of the uses that the ONI made of Luciano and his friends.

The least controversial aspect of the project was more or less acknowledged by the ONI: Luciano's name was invoked to persuade hundreds of Italian refugees, who otherwise would be reluctant to cooperate with authorities, to give information about their towns and villages—the terrain, the load-bearing capacity of roads and bridges, locations of factories.

The navy was also concerned that work on the waterfront proceed without interruption. In December 1942, a waterfront strike was threatened. Comdr. Charles Haffenden of the ONI got in touch with Luciano's lawyer, Moses Polakoff; Polakoff spoke with another of his clients, Meyer Lansky. With the intervention of Lansky and Joe Lanza, the strike was averted.

But the ONI project went beyond maintaining labor peace and gathering information from refugees. In January 1943, Roosevelt and Churchill met at Casablanca and agreed on the invasion of Sicily. From that time the ONI-Mafia project assumed new urgency. As one historian put it, the ONI made "a mysterious agreement with the American Mafia . . . [which] had agreed to direct clandestine operations on the island of Sicily" in return for Luciano's parole.

Michele Pantaleone, a Sicilian who served as a Socialist deputy in Palermo, has noted that "even while the war was still being fought, the reconstitution of old [Mafia] groups was inaugurated by American gangster leaders . . . who got in touch with their old friends on the island before the Allied landings in order to induce them to help the Allies. . . . It is a historical fact that the Mafia, in agreement with American gangsterism, did its best to clear the way right across the island and so enable the invading troops to advance into central Italy with remarkable safety. . . . Clandestine landings of Sicilo-Americans also took place in the small Mafia-controlled fishing ports between Balestrate and Castellammare . . . these are ports which years later would play an important part in the drug traffic between American gangsters and the Sicilian Mafia."

There is no official documentation of this collaboration. Pantaleone's sources are the stories repeated by inhabitants of his native village of Villalba, which was also the home of Sicilian Mafia chief Don Calogero. Other historians were told about the Allied tanks that brought Mafia chiefs to meetings with Allied officers. Lt. Joachim Titolo, who was with the ONI and later with the New York district attorney's office, said of his own landing at Salerno that "I did seek out members of the criminal element."

Almost at once after the Allied landings in Italy, Mussolini's political prisoners were released. In Sicily, many of those prisoners were mafiosi; as Pantaleone writes, in return for their help, their chiefs were appointed by the Allies to key political and administrative posts on the island. As quickly as the Mafia resumed control in Sicily, they became involved with the theft of Allied supplies and the creation of a black market.

In February 1943, before the invasion of Sicily, but after the ONI-Mafia project had been established for almost a year, Moses Polakoff filed a motion to reduce Luciano's sentence. Polakoff made no mention of Luciano's service to naval intelligence; the navy would have denied it, and Luciano himself was fearful that in the event of deportation, such knowledge would lead to unpleasant consequences for him in Italy. In any case the motion was denied; but Judge McCook, who heard the appeal, was given private information that led him to hold out hope of executive clemency for Luciano at a later date.

But Luciano was impatient. He looked around for another bargaining chip. A month after Carlo Tresca's murder he offered the names of Tresca's killers to Governor Dewey. In 1950, Luciano told journalist Michael Stern in Rome that Dewey had refused to deal.

On VE Day in 1945, Moses Polakoff again appealed on behalf of his client. He asked for executive clemency, and in support of his plea he offered a letter from Comdr. Charles Haffenden that testified to Luciano's great value to the ONI in supplying informants who advised about Sicily. Haffenden added: "Additional assistance . . . came from this same informant which can be explained to you at a later date."

Murray Gurfein, who had made the first contact with Joe "Socks" Lanza, also wrote an affidavit testifying to Luciano's value to the ONI, but first submitted his deposition to the navy for clearance. The navy denied clearance, permitting only parts of Gurfein's statement to be read to the parole board and then only under pledge of secrecy. The parole board unanimously recommended clemency; Dewey commuted Luciano's sentence on January 4, 1946, specifying that Luciano was to be deported and explaining: "Upon entry of the United States into the war, Luciano's aid was sought. . . . It appears that he cooperated in such effort, though the actual value of the information procured is not clear."

On January 9, 1946, shortly before Luciano was to be moved to Ellis Island, Louis Pagnucco visited him in prison. He wanted to know what Luciano could tell him about the Tresca murder. Luciano had already received his pardon; now he wanted to bargain for a stay of the deportation order. He told Pagnucco that if that could be guaranteed, he would try to find out what Pagnucco wanted to know. Pagnucco returned to the prison on January 16, and told Luciano that he had been unable to secure a promise. Later he testified that Luciano had said, "No soap."

On February 9, on the *Laura Keene*, Luciano spent the night celebrating his freedom with his old friends; the next day he sailed for Italy where, with the exception of a brief excursion to Cuba, he remained the rest of his life.

With the destruction of all files relating to it, the ONI-Mafia project remained secret for ten years. In 1954 Dewey, disturbed by persistent rumors that he had been paid off by organized crime with large campaign contributions in return for Luciano's pardon, convened the Herlands Commission to clear himself. The Commission had a difficult time because the navy forbade the testimony of naval witnesses and continued to deny—with some truth— that Luciano's name was contained in its files. The navy also flatly contradicted Commander Haffenden's statements that the ONI had worked with Luciano or any of his associates. William Donovan of the OSS said that "the convicted panderer's alleged aid [is] nothing but cheap talk . . . and completely without foundation."

Despite these obstructions the commission gathered enough testimony to compile a twenty-six hundred–page report. Rear Adm. Carl F. Espe admitted, "We are advised that contacts were made with Luciano . . . and that his influence on other criminal sources resulted in their cooperation." But Espe feared that if Herlands published the report, "a rash of thriller stories" would jeopardize future naval operations; the report remained among Dewey's private papers until a journalist discovered it more than twenty years later.

While the details of the ONI-Mafia project are still shrouded, Herlands wrote Dewey that "the evidence demonstrates that Luciano's assistance and cooperation were secured by Naval Intelligence. . . . No practical purpose would be served by debating the technical scope of Luciano's aid to the war effort. . . . The crystal clear fact [is] that Luciano and his associates and contacts were responsible for a wide range of services."

Why was there so much secrecy? If the ONI had used criminals to stop sabotage and leaks of information on the East Coast docks, even if American criminals had made contact with their opposite numbers in Sicily in the interests of saving American lives during the invasion, how much public relations damage would this have done considering the universal public support for the war? It may be that something more discreditable took place.

The importation of narcotics into the United States has been one of the most profitable Mafia enterprises. Luciano was arrested on a narcotics charge in 1923. At that time he agreed, in exchange for a light sentence, to provide agents of the Federal Bureau of Narcotics with information enabling them to seize a large quantity of heroin stored in a Mulberry Street basement. Through the years Luciano continued, according to the chief of FBN, to feed the agency information about rival dope dealers.

The source of narcotics was overseas. Importation required a reliable network of smugglers—ships' captains, ordinary seamen, fishermen on small boats—to bring the raw product from North Africa and the Near East to the port cities of Italy and France for processing, and then into the United States. "Every one of them pipelines had been tied together by Vito," Luciano said, referring to Genovese's trip to Italy in the mid-1930s.

Genovese did not work alone. John Caputo, who had been deported from the United States in about 1942, was later known to be in charge of narcotics smuggling in the Paris-Marseilles area; Guiseppe Pici, who left the United States together with Luciano in 1946, was arrested in a narcotics raid in Milan in 1959; Pici's papers were found to contain lists naming hundreds of seamen, gangsters, and U.S. naval personnel, all of whom were part of the drug-smuggling operation. Nicolo Gentile, arrested in the United States in 1937 in connection with a worldwide drug-smuggling syndicate, and arrested again in 1940, fled to Italy to continue business from there.

The war caused some disruption of the established smuggling routes, but narcotics importation continued on a smaller scale, and profits remained high as scarcity drove the price up. Agent Follmer of the Narcotics Bureau, testifying before a Kefauver committee in Kansas City, said that in 1942, at the height of the war, Mafia groups in the United States "received smuggled drugs from Marseilles, France via Havana, Cuba."

According to Rear Adm. William Pye, during the war the navy found that it was deficient in basic intelligence, "especially in North Africa and Italy." To gather this basic intelligence, Lieutenants Titolo, Marsloe, and Alfieri first worked with the ONI-Mafia project in New York; they later joined the Italian invasion forces. Lieutenant Titolo, testifying before the Herlands Commission, said, "I had heard at the time that information was being received through small fishing vessels plying between North Africa, Sicily and the Italian mainland. I had heard that most of them were smugglers." According to Michele Pantaleone, during 1942 and 1943 serious acts of sabotage against Axis convoys took place along the western coast of Sicily; these could not have been carried out without the connivance of fishermen under Mafia control. On February 23, 1947, the *New York Times* quoted Murray Gurfein, who had made the first contact with Socks Lanza. Gurfein said that he knew that Luciano had been asked to use his contacts in the port cities and "from what I understand he did some good in creating the underworld counter-espionage system."

After his deportation to Italy, Luciano took a trip to Havana, where he joined Meyer Lansky, Vito Genovese, Joe Bonanno, and Mike Miranda. This group of old friends met, so they said, to holiday together and to hear Frank Sinatra sing at the Hotel Nacional. The Narcotics Bureau, however, was convinced that the agenda of the meeting was to turn Cuba into a center for narcotics smuggling. Harry Anslinger, Narcotics Bureau chief, threatened the Cuban government with a shutoff of medical supplies, and Batista reluctantly agreed to send Luciano back to Italy.

Luciano had hoped to settle in Cuba, but he made the best of things in Naples, where, with the help of a pharmaceutical company, he was able to divert hundreds of pounds of heroin destined for medical use to his own purposes.

Luciano always denied that he had anything to do with narcotics after his arrest in 1923: drug smuggling was Genovese's province. Or, Luciano might have said, was the province assigned to Genovese. According to drug enforcement officials, the war interfered with the normal supply routes for drugs, but as Agent Follmer testified and Ralph Salerno later confirmed, the routes opened up again as the Axis power waned. The business remained extremely profitable as scarcity drove prices up. Michele Pantaleone writes that Genovese was a friend of Sicilian Mafia chief Don Calogero; both men were involved in the black market in Allied goods. Pantaleone writes that after Luciano arrived in Italy he went into business with Don Calo in a candy factory in Palermo. The factory was shut down when newspaper stories intimated that workers were inserting drugs, rather than almonds, into candy. "From 1943 to 1946," Pantaleone writes, "the entire Sicilian Mafia dedicated itself to this black market traffic . . . and during the same years the foundations were laid for the drug traffic which . . . had one of its major distribution centers in Sicily."

With Genovese in Italy from 1936 all through the war years, and Luciano involved in a still-mysterious operation with the Office of Naval Intelligence, an argument can be made that, among other services, Luciano and his associates were able to offer the ONI an established network of men on small fishing boats and ships plying the coasts of North Africa, Italy, and France; organized originally for narcotics smuggling they were easily transformed for the purpose of conveying military intelligence.

The "technical" details of the Luciano project that the navy was anxious to keep secret may have been the existence of such a network—one that did not disband after the war but continued to smuggle drugs, perhaps even with some grant of immunity from authorities, while the use of narcotics became epidemic in the cities of the United States.

During the war, the *Martello* was smuggled into Italy. Information came back to Tresca by the same underground routes. Late in the 1930s he had known enough about Genovese's life in Italy to be able to cause some trouble for him. If, during 1942, Genovese had reason to fear that Italian authorities might learn he was engaged in espionage against the Fascist government, he had more than enough motive to eliminate the man who threatened such exposure. By late 1942 Mussolini was fighting for his life and unlikely to be concerned with an old personal enemy; a directly threatened gangster was another matter, and Vito Genovese's name has persistently been raised in connection with the Tresca assassination.

That there was a possibility of ONI knowledge of the murder must have reached the FBI. On September 8, 1943, an FBI agent asked Lt. Comdr. Rhea Whitley of the ONI "if the ONI had received any information concerning the killing of Carlos [*sic*] Tresca, to which he replied in the negative. It was pointed out to Commander Whitley that the Bureau was not interested in the murder as such but only in the groups and individuals involved."

Of course the ONI denied for many years that they had had any dealings with Luciano or the Mafia. If anything had existed on paper to confirm a connection between the Mafia project and Tresca's murder, it was destroyed with the rest of the files in 1944.

Chapter 29
Addendum

Yᴇᴀʀ after year, for more than a decade, Carlo Tresca's friends gathered on the anniversary of his death and scattered red carnations on the corner where he died.

Minna Harkavy sculpted a head of Carlo in bronze, which Margaret De Silver shipped to Sulmona. There, in 1945, with Ignazio Silone officiating, the bust was ceremonially placed in a public garden.

Roger Baldwin and Herbert Solow remained in touch with the district attorney's office. In 1945 Baldwin wrote to Dos Passos, "I share the conclusion . . . that the investigation is being blocked by powerful forces or political connections. I think they got the right man in Galante. . . . But Galante, a hired gunman, could not be made to talk even with the third degree! The trail through him would lead directly to Pope and he is, as you know, a powerful Tammany figure."

The Tresca Memorial Committee continued to press Governor Dewey and District Attorney Hogan to remove Louis Pagnucco from the case and to pursue an aggressive investigation. The investigation was proceeding, but without much energy. Some interesting items appear in the files. In 1946, for instance, a prisoner at Sing-Sing named Johnny Bester wrote to Governor Dewey saying he was "present on the night of January 10th, 1943 in a place called Nan's Tavern . . . in Brooklyn when this killing was planned for the next evening. I was there when the man who ordered Tresca's killing came and paid the man to do the job $6,000—I know who this man is and who the guys are who killed Tresca. The man behind the case is a millionnaire." The letter was sent on to Hogan, but there is no indication in the files that Bester was interviewed by anyone in the office. A 1953 memorandum in the district attorney's files states that Lepke Buchalter had provided information on the case.

Hogan wrote to Dewey in 1948, reporting on the status of the investigation. Hogan's office had left no stone unturned in considering "Tresca's anarchist activities, his anti-communist and anti-fascist crusades and propaganda, his attacks on the underworld . . . his possible use of that newspaper as an instrument of blackmail . . . and various aspects of his marital and extramarital and family life," yet, Hogan said, there was not a shred of evidence that could be used in court.

On May 12, 1953, CBS broadcast a half-hour television program called "Death of an Editor." Walter Cronkite introduced the show as "a part of history. . . . What you're going to see is—the truth." It was not exactly the truth. The editor is called Gino Corelli and his killer is called Salvatore Lucci. The story opens in Sicily. A Mafia messenger is sent to the United States, carrying instructions for the murder of Mussolini's old enemy Corelli. Lucci first reports to the police that his car has been stolen and then goes off, followed by a police officer, whom he knocks out with a blackjack before proceeding to kill Corelli.

The district attorney's office interviewed the scriptwriter about the source of his information. He told them his material had been supplied by the research department of CBS and consisted entirely of published accounts. He added that the program was presented as factual only because, according to the television code, fictional killers had to be punished for their crimes.

Jane Bobba came to New York in 1945 and stayed with her aunts Elizabeth and Kathie on East Twelfth Street. The older women reminisced a good deal about Carlo, talking about his favorite foods and Annie Gurley's fury at his black cigars. Kathie came home one night after attending a meeting where Earl Browder spoke: He was so boring! she said to Jane; I wish we had Carlo back again.

At some point in 1945 Margaret De Silver idly wished aloud that Carlo had had a son. She was acquainted with many people who knew Tresca did indeed have a son, but not until then was she told of Pete Martin's existence. Margaret set out to find him and located him in the army, on an island in the Pacific. In 1946 Pete came to New York, and Margaret greeted him with an open heart and purse. They later quarreled about Pete's second marriage, but when Margaret died in 1962 she left him ten thousand dollars in her will.

On one January 11, some ten years after his father's death, Pete went to the corner of Fifteenth Street and Fifth Avenue. Only a few people had braved the winter night that year to stand on the sidewalk spotted with red carnations. Pete found the occasion painful and touching, but he felt little connection to it. Carlo Tresca was a memory more than twenty years old; he might have dreamed him.

Elizabeth Gurley Flynn did not lead a celibate life after her return from Portland. She had a number of affairs with Party leaders and organizers, most of them men much younger than she. But her private writings tell of a profound loneliness: "Crowds which consume me but know me not. / I long for one, just one, who is my own, my very own!"

Elizabeth continued to live with her sister Kathie, the two of them the only survivors of the Flynn family. Elizabeth was elected to the Party's Political Bureau in 1941; she ran for the office of congressional representative in 1942; she wrote for the *Daily Worker* regularly.

In 1945 the famous letter from Jacques Duclos signaled Moscow's repudiation of Earl Browder's leadership of the Communist party in the United States. Flynn resisted the directive at first, expressing resentment at having policy "suddenly catapulted at us by a Communist Party from another country," but in the end she bowed. As a member of the National Board, she was interviewed to determine the extent of her "revisionist" errors as a follower of Browder's, and she said that she had been misled by Browder, and promised to study Marx and Lenin more closely.

Twelve top Communist leaders were indicted under the Smith Act in 1947, and Flynn took charge of the legal defense. In 1951, with a second group of leaders, Flynn was herself indicted. She spent almost a month on the witness stand, answering questions about her early life, trying to explain the theories and goals of the American Communists. She was at her best in such an arena. After watching her on the witness stand, I. F. Stone commented, "I could not help but admire the courage, the poise and the gentle firmness with which the elderly woman held her own before the jury and the judge."

Flynn was convicted along with twelve other Party leaders and in January 1955 was sent to Alderson Federal Penitentiary where she spent more than two years. She passed her sixty-fifth birthday in prison, lost seventy-five pounds, and learned the substance of Khrushchev's revelations to the Twentieth Congress.

"It's quite ghastly—hard to understand," she wrote Kathie. *"How could it happen and for so long a time?"* Next, she came to terms with the Soviet army's invasion of Hungary. Flynn emerged from prison in 1957, her faith unshaken. In 1961 she was elected national chairman of the Party, and in 1964 she went to Moscow.

By then she was quite ill. Pete Martin put her on the plane, "I mean *literally* put her on the plane; I had to help her up the lengthy stairs . . . and escorted E. to her seat, she looked so old and tired and frail."

Not long after her arrival in Moscow Flynn complained of stomach pains. On September 5 she died of acute gastroenteritis and a blood clot in her lung artery. Her body lay in state for a day in the Hall of Columns of the Soviet Trade Unions. According to her wishes, her body was cremated and her ashes flown to the United States for burial in Waldheim Cemetery near the graves of Bill Haywood, Emma Goldman, and the Haymarket martyrs.

Officially Vittorio Vidali remained in Mexico until 1947, although it is likely he was in Italy with the Communist partisans in 1943. In any case, by 1947 Vidali had returned to his native Trieste. When Tito broke with Stalin in 1948, Vidali led the anti-Tito forces and Radio Belgrade began to carry reports that Vidali would attempt to assassinate Tito.

In 1950 an American journalist who had attempted to interview Vidali a number of times met him in his office at Communist party headquarters in Trieste. Vidali referred to the Belgrade reports: "The Yugoslav people will handle [Tito] not Vidali," he said. "Yugoslavia cannot remain as a place from which an imperialist invasion can be launched against the Soviet Union." In answer to further questions he said: "Wherever I happen to be they always say I'm organizing agents to kill some anti-Soviet personality. . . . Tresca always had a wild imagination. I was in Mexico when he was killed. . . . I don't believe in killing opponents of the Soviet Union through my own actions. . . . Even in Spain Vidali was held to blame for every military or political leader who disappeared."

In February 1956 Vidali arrived in Moscow for the Twentieth Congress of the Russian Communist party. He felt some foreboding on the journey; something was in the air. When he arrived in Moscow he saw that no portraits of Stalin adorned the meeting hall, and he noticed repeated references to a "certain person" who had "fostered the cult of the individual." He could scarcely believe that Stalin himself was to be purged.

In Moscow Vidali met a number of his old comrades. Yelena Stasova, once Lenin's secretary, had long been a good friend to him and to Tina Modotti. In 1939 when Vidali was briefly in Paris after his escape from Spain, Stasova had sent a warning to him to get as far away as possible from the Soviet Union. Now, in 1956, Stasova recounted to him the fate of their old friends; the few who were still alive were "human wrecks" after all they had endured under Stalin; tens of thousands had suffered execution or prison or exile. Stasova believed that Stalin himself had arranged the assassination of Kirov in 1934 and then used the murder to justify the purges. That night, Vidali wrote, he was unable to sleep, was "speechless, horrified . . . all of this is fantastic, atrocious."

As the Congress continues Vidali meets with other old comrades. He learns of still others who were "shot as traitors for having plotted against the Soviet state." Many memories pass through his mind: He recalls the good old days in Moscow in the 1930s when he and his comrades spent evenings in talk and song and drink until they "went to bed filled to the brim with sentiments of international solidarity." Vidali's incredulity at so much bad news is odd, juxtaposed with his additional recollection that he himself had come under suspicion by Yagoda, the deputy head of the secret police, and had barely escaped the Soviet Union alive in 1934.

His claims to be speechless and horrified at the news in Moscow notwithstanding, Vidali had independent knowledge of many who perished: Willi Munzenberg, expelled as a Trotskyite, found dead in 1940; Bela Kun, Tukachevsky, Rykov, Bukharin, all designated "monsters" by Stalin: "I could still see their faces . . . all of them had been arrested and condemned, some to death, others . . . in prison or concentration camp."

Vidali grew morbid in Moscow in 1956. He counts the days until he can leave, wondering at the same time why he is "fed up and depressed" when he knows that the socialist system is going forward. "Was it really necessary to resort to death?" he wonders. "Couldn't they have acted as had been done in Lenin's day? Discuss." Could it be that Arthur Koestler was telling the truth?

But Vidali's doubts do not last long. Who *is* this Khrushchev anyway? he asks himself. "In fact it was Stalin who discovered [him] and guided him with a fatherly hand." Marx was right; doubt everything. "And begin by doubting the present critics of Stalin."

Before leaving for Trieste Vidali meets with Stasova again. He complains to her that not enough guidance has been given to the foreign delegates, who, after all, will be required to explain these matters at home: "We could explain everything with . . . dialectics," he points out; "we could justify many things by speaking about history, about revolutionary requirements, about the struggle of the new against the old, etc."

From 1958, Vidali served as a Communist deputy from Trieste, and from 1963 until 1968 as a senator. In 1970 he was attacked on the street and lost the sight of an eye. Until his health began to fail he made speeches throughout Italy condemning the terrorism of the Red Brigades.

During the last decade or so of his life Vidali poured out volume after volume of reminiscences. After all, as he said on his eightieth birthday, "During my life I have seen just about everything." He wrote about his years in the United States, about the Fifth Regiment, about his years in Mexico, about Tina Modotti. He recalled Sunday afternoon meetings with Carlo Tresca and others at Minna Harkavy's house, and he protested his innocence of Tresca's murder. Appended to his volume, *From Mexico to Murmansk*, is a reprint of a 1943 pamphlet by Ezio Taddei, who had worked with Tresca on *Il Martello*. Taddei places the blame for Tresca's murder on Frank Garofalo, Generoso Pope, and Carmine Galante. To this pamphlet Vidali added a letter written to him by Taddei in 1948, which restates the case. An additional page is appended on which Vidali notes that an agent of the Federal Bureau of Narcotics, John Cusak, also blamed Tresca's murder on Garofalo and Galante.

As he grew older, Vidali became obsessed with wiping the blot of "assassin" from his reputation. On his eightieth birthday he was honored in Trieste; children embraced him, a young girl gave him a bunch of flowers, and he made a long speech:

> Today, much has been said about my life. . . . During my lifetime I have seen just about everything. I was thinking about all that in these last few days: this is the fortieth anniversary of the assassination of Leon Trotsky. And after forty years, the international press continues to peddle the story of my participation in that murder. . . . I could tell you dozens of episodes and inventions which were used to create in world opinion the idea of a monster. . . .
>
> All of this has created a legend which only now, through my books, I am trying to put an end to: the questions of the murders of Tresca, of Nin, of Trotsky. And I will have to continue to write because, as you know—slander, slander—they will continue to slander, and some of it will be effective. I could continue to write, for sixty-three years of political activity constitute an enormous volume, and my life is an open book. . . . Naturally this book is badly written in some parts, incomprehensible in others, full of errors, erasures, notes; but it is the true book of my life, the book of a man of flesh and blood; of a living man who does not consider himself infallible . . . a man who thinks seriously when he can, and corrects his errors. . . .
>
> In these sixty-three years I believe I have always done my duty. . . . I was [a Stalinist] for thirty or forty years . . . and . . . I must still struggle against the remnants of Stalinism in myself. We were all enthusiastic Stalinists, but we have begun to understand and correct this. . . . Communism is the youth of the world, and we live with enthusiasm in us. When we open our eyes in the morning, the best thing of all is to be happy to live that day through and dedicate it to the struggle. . . . [It is] imposible for a man like me to retire to private life. This is not rhetoric but truth. I will always remember an article by Julio Antonio Mella who was murdered by Gerardo Machado, the Cuban tyrant: the day before his death he wrote: "Even after death we can be useful, even then we will be in the trenches."

Vidali died in the middle of November 1983; the last volume of his memoirs is entitled *Commandante Carlos*.

During the remainder of the 1940s the district attorney's office kept tabs on Frank Garofalo. His frequent meetings with Carmine Galante were noted. In 1950 a two-year investigation concluded that Galante was now the "head man of the Lower East Side mob and heads the alcohol, gambling, shy-locking and narcotics rackets in this community. He takes orders from no one but one Frank Garofalo."

In 1947 Garofalo applied for a renewal of his passport. In 1955 it was thought he had retired to Italy. But in 1956 a state trooper, on routine patrol near Binghamton, New York, stopped a speeding car in which the occupants, who gave false names, turned out to be Galante, Garofalo, and Joseph Di Palermo. Further investigation showed that the three had spent the previous night in a Binghamton hotel, meeting with Joe Bonanno and Joseph Barbera.

A year later, in October 1957, Garofalo, Galante, and Bonanno, among others, met at the Grand Hotel Des Pallmes in Palermo to discuss their mutual interests. A month later the discussion was continued at Joseph Barbera's house in Apalachin, New York, where Vito Genovese joined Galante and about sixty other criminals. Agents who raided the meeting and arrested those they could catch had no doubt that it had been called to discuss the importation of narcotics.

Garofalo did not attend the Apalachin meeting. He was in Sicily, in his home town of Castellammare Del Golfo, though scarcely in retirement. In 1965, Italian police organized a nationwide raid to crack down on drug smugglers; Garofalo was among those arrested. Also arrested during that raid was Vincenzo Martinez, onetime employee of Generoso Pope.

Generoso Pope died of a stroke in 1950. His obituary in the *New York Times* described him as a "colorful and sometimes controversial figure in New York business, political and philanthropic life . . . an outstanding example of an immigrant who made good in America." A number of distinguished public officials expressed their personal grief at his death.

After Pope's death his son Fortune continued the family friendship with Joe Bonanno. Fortune was a guest at the wedding of Bonanno's son Salvatore to Rosalie Profaci. In 1957, Fortune was Bonanno's traveling companion to Sicily, where in Palermo Bonanno had an important meeting with Carmine Galante and Frank Garofalo.

Pope's godson, Samuel DiFalco, who had briefly represented the Knickerbocker Trucking Company when Galante was employed there, became national chairman of the Italian-American League to Combat Defamation. In 1966, asserting ethnic defamation, he organized a protest against the publication of Joe Valachi's memoir of the life and structure of the Mafia—or the Cosa Nostra as Valachi called it. Shortly before he died in 1979, DiFalco, who had risen to surrogate court judge, was indicted for alleged corruption in the civil term of the New York Supreme Court.

Lucky Luciano died in Italy in 1962, shortly before he was about to be arrested by U.S. and Italian authorities for drug trafficking.

After Luciano's 1946 deportation from the United States, Vito Genovese made a bid to take control of his organization from Frank Costello. Costello, returning home to his apartment on Central Park West after dinner with friends, was shot, though not fatally, in the lobby of his apartment building. He seemed to have had objections to narcotics trafficking. Costello took the warning seriously and retired. Genovese became, according to Joseph Valachi, "the boss of all bosses under the table."

In 1958 Genovese was indicted on a narcotics conspiracy charge, along with thirty-five others in his organization, and was sentenced to fifteen years in federal prison, some of which he spent in the Atlanta Penitentiary in the company of Johnny Dio and Joseph Di Palermo. Genovese died of heart failure in prison in 1969.

By the early 1950s, Carmine Galante had risen from street hoodlum to a high position in the Bonanno organization. Bonanno sent him to Montreal in 1952, where, according to police sources, he was instrumental in forging the alliance between the New York Mafia and the French-Canadian gangs that came to be known as the French Connection. In addition to his recorded meetings with Garofalo and Bonanno in 1956 and 1957, he traveled to Miami and Cuba in 1958, according to narcotics agent Martin F. Pera, to meet with French, U.S., and Canadian drug traffickers. He was subpoenaed to testify before a federal grand jury in December 1957 but failed to appear. Early in January 1958, narcotics agent John Cusak testified before a legislative committee in Albany, identifying Galante as the "reputed" slayer of Carlo Tresca, acting on orders of Frank Garofalo. Cusak stated that at the present time Galante was engaged in a campaign to control the narcotics and gambling trades in Brooklyn.

Galante's name was included in the 1958 indictment that sent Genovese to prison, but he was in hiding at the time and remained in hiding until June 1959. In May 1960 he was indicted with twenty-nine others on a charge of narcotics conspiracy and was brought to trial. The trial ended in a mistrial when the foreman of the jury mysteriously fell down a flight of stairs in an abandoned building and broke his back.

In the 1962 retrial the defendants seemed again to hope for a mistrial. One defendant threw a heavy wooden chair at the prosecutor; others shouted and interrupted the proceedings in various ways. But of twenty-nine defendants, thirteen were found guilty of participating in an international narcotics conspiracy. Galante received a sentence of twenty years.

Galante served twelve years in prison. At Lewisburg Penitentiary he occupied a cell in G block, also known as Mafia Row. There, he and Jimmy Hoffa became friends; Galante was a model prisoner, helping guards to maintain order. He settled all disputes on his block, and he permitted no drinking. His authority was respected by his fellow inmates. He was known, according to one of them, as "a stone killer" who would not tolerate the smallest sign of disobedience.

Galante's life in prison was not unpleasant. He had the privilege of working in the hothouse, where he grew vegetables. He kept three cats and cooked meals for his friends. He also kept himself in top physical condition and not only retained his power in the Bonanno organization but increased it.

Bonanno disappeared for two years in 1964. In October 1964 an FBI wiretap picked up the voice of Raymond Patriarca talking about Bonanno's group. According to the FBI report of the telephone conversation, "Vito, the one in jail, was described as the muscle man for Lelow [Lilo]. It appeared to the informant that Lelow is the top guy of the Bonanno group in Canada."

When Galante was paroled in 1974, police kept him under surveillance. They noted that the acting boss of the Bonanno family, Philip Rastelli, seemed reluctant to give up control to Galante, but after Rastelli's son-in-law was shot to death on a Brooklyn street, Rastelli readily stepped aside.

A chauffeur drove Galante to his very modest place of business each day—the L&T Cleaners on Mulberry Street. People who passed him on the street in that neighborhood bowed slightly or touched him respectfully on the arm. He was reputed to be the inventor of the "black man test," an infallible test devised to determine the quality of heroin: a black heroin addict would be kidnapped and injected with a double bag; if he became comatose within a specified time, the narcotic was judged to be of the correct purity.

In 1977, Galante was charged with violating parole: as he had been in 1943, he was associating with Joseph Di Palermo, among other criminals. His lawyer this time was Roy Cohn, who denied that his client knew such people. Galante, Cohn asserted, spent his time on Long Island working in his daughter's garden.

Galante was returned to jail briefly. During 1978 he was in and out of jail as his lawyers fought to free him. In late 1978 there were indications that his rivals meant to kill him, and he was transferred, under a false name, to a prison in San Diego. But Galante was not afraid. He insisted on his release and was released on bail in March 1979.

On July 12, 1979, as he ate lunch on the patio of Joe and Mary's Restaurant in Brooklyn, several men wearing ski masks rushed into the backyard and shot him. As far as police ever determined, Galante's murder had something to do with gang rivalries over control of heroin.

Fifty-nine mourners attended the funeral, which was not a very elaborate one since Cardinal Cook denied celebration of the funeral liturgy. Helen Marulli, from whom Galante had long been separated, attended, along with Galante's favorite daughter, Nina, and his lawyer, Roy Cohn. At the gravesite the priest pronounced that he would leave "judgement to God."

At the site of Galante's murder another epitaph had been spoken. A man named Joe Bricolli spat on the van that was taking Galante's body to the morgue. A reporter present asked him why he had done so. "It was during the war and I was working very hard against the fascist Mussolini with my friend, my hero, Carlo Tresca. Galante was the man who killed Tresca. . . . Garbage," said Bricolli of Galante. "He killed a hero and he sold heroin to children."

If by now there is no doubt that Galante was the de facto murderer, the identity of the person on whose order he acted is still not clear. My own conviction is that the simplest explanation is the correct one in this case, and that Frank Garofalo fills the role of instigator.

The circumstances that provide Garofalo's motives have already been discussed: his initial attempt in 1934, as Generoso Pope's agent, to silence Tresca; the public confrontations between Garofalo and Tresca in 1942, once again involving Garofalo's association with Pope and, in addition, his relationship with Dolores Facconte; the continuing tension between Tresca and Pope, to Pope's disadvantage and, thus, to Garofalo's discredit as the enforcer of Pope's will. We can assume that, just as anyone would, Garofalo wished to prevail over Tresca and redress his grievances. But Garofalo was unlike anyone else in that he inhabited a world of crime and violence and Galante was very near to hand.

Recently an unexpected source has elaborated on Garofalo's motives. He is Ambrogio Donini, whom we have met in New York in the late 1930s, a refugee working as an editor on *L'Unita del Popolo*. After the war Donini returned to Italy and became a Communist senator and an ambassador to Poland. In 1982 Donini was interviewed by an Italian journalist who was interested in the Tresca murder. Donini spoke of a crucial role played by Ezio Taddei.

We have also met Taddei before. He, too, was a refugee who arrived in the United States in the late 1930s. Taddei was a writer, he identified himself as an anarchist, and Tresca gave him a job on the *Martello*. Few people have had a good word to say for Taddei. Even Vidali, who made use of Taddei's exoneration of him, has called him a "sneaky man." But certain facts about Taddei's behavior can be established.

On January 12, the day after Tresca's murder, Taddei made a statement to the police. He said: "My conviction is that the Communist Party killed Carlo Tresca. . . . The Communists are trying to get control of the Mazzini Society. . . . Carlo told me last month he had a big dangerous job and the Communists were going to push them out and that we should prepare. . . . I am convinced that the murder was politically inspired, nothing personal. He was a woman's man but he was getting old. With money he was liberal."

While this statement of Taddei's does not offer specific knowledge of the murder, it demonstrates a bias consistent with Taddei's history. In 1941 and again in 1942, Taddei's disputes with the Communists had spilled over into physical fights. The last altercation occurred in November 1942 when Taddei stormed into *L'Unita's* offices with the intention of beating up Donini; unable to locate Donini he beat up an accountant and broke some lamps and windows.

On these occasions, as he had in the past, Tresca befriended Taddei. When Taddei arrived in the United States Tresca had raised money for his maintenance. He gave him a job. When legal difficulties arose from Taddei's head-on confrontations with the Communists, Tresca raised money for his defense. Two weeks before his death, however, Tresca told a number of people that he had quarreled with Taddei. He did not see Taddei again.

By the end of January, despite his earlier violent differences with and accusations against the Communists, Taddei was working at *L'Unita*. He now accused Generoso Pope and Frank Garofalo of the murder. And on February 14 Taddei made a speech at a Rand School memorial meeting for Tresca, placing full blame for Tresca's murder on Pope and Garofalo.

Taddei remained loyal to this version. In March *L'Unita* reported, presumably on information provided by Taddei, that an attempt had been made to kidnap or kill Taddei shortly before his Rand School speech, implying that the motive was to silence him. Taddei also now said that the District Attorney's office, Louis Pagnucco in particular, was pressuring him not to make any further charges against Pope and Garofalo.

Taddei wrote to Vidali in 1948. In this letter he vindicated the Communists of all responsibility for Tresca's death and restated charges he had previously made against Luigi Antonini and Vanni Montana—that they and their allies had conspired to charge the Communists with the murder. "Carlo Tresca was my friend," Taddei wrote to Vidali, "and he had full trust in me." Making no mention of their quarrel, Taddei added that he had telephoned Tresca at the *Martello* office at 8:30 on the night of January 11 and had had an amiable chat with him.

Taddei may have spoken to Tresca that night but, as he well knew, Tresca had been alone in his office at that time and there would be no one to confirm or contradict his claim of a friendly telephone call. As for Taddei's charges against Antonini and Montana, Antonini certainly villified Taddei after Taddei turned against Pope; and no doubt he and Montana did simply decide, for ideological reasons, to blame the Communists, just as August Bellanca, who had different sympathies, decided to blame Fascists. It would appear that very few people told the truth in this case except when it served a particular political or personal agenda.

When Donini spoke about these matters forty years later, he said that as he understood the sequence of events, the following had occurred: a few weeks before the murder, Pope had made a final attempt to come to terms with Tresca. To bring about a conciliation he sent Garofalo to Taddei with a peace offering for Taddei to transmit to Tresca. Taddei carried the message; perhaps he urged Tresca to accept the offer. An infuriated Tresca then ordered Taddei out of his office.

If this is a plausible explanation for the quarrel between Tresca and Taddei, why did Taddei fail to report the incident to police? Donini believes that Taddei hoped to parlay his knowledge into some advantage with Pope. When he did not succeed, and was perhaps threatened by Garofalo, he sought protection in publicity and made his accusations in *L'Unita* and at the Rand School. The Communists did not quibble when a former adversary turned into a political asset.

Assuming that Donini is right, then three weeks or so before the murder, Generoso Pope would have known that Garofalo's mission was unsuccessful and that Tresca would persist in his efforts to keep Pope out of the Italian-American Victory Council. We know that Pope was very eager to suppress opposition. This has been shown most clearly in the 1942 report by Casimir Palmer, which told of Pope's attempt to bribe Mazzini members, and his particular interest in Tresca's activities. Palmer stressed Pope's interest in Tresca several years later when he related the events of his report to the Tresca Memorial Committee.

There were, of course, other antifascists opposed to Pope who did not suffer Tresca's fate. Gaetano Salvemini was the most prominent among them and he was at least as outspoken as Tresca. But neither Salvemini, nor any of the others, had also incurred Garofalo's wrath.

Salvemini returned to Italy after the war, as Tresca had hoped to do. There he denounced both the United States and the Soviet Union for cooperating in policies that, he said, were designed to keep Italians "obedient" to the many "stupidities" of their past. People complained that Salvemini did not understand Italy any longer, that he had been too long in exile, that he expected too much. To these criticisms he replied, "My only rule is to behave so that I won't have to spit at myself when I shave in the morning."

As the postwar years wore into the cold war years, and many of Tresca's old friends made a sharp turn to the right in the political journey they had begun as rebels, it is easy to imagine Tresca claiming Salvemini's rule for his own.

Abbreviations

CT   Carlo Tresca's unfinished autobiography, a copy of which is deposited in the Manuscript Division of the New York Public Library.

DA   The investigatory file compiled by the New York district attorney's office.

EGF   Elizabeth Gurley Flynn's memoir, *I Speak My Own Piece: Autobiography of The Rebel Girl* (New York: Masses and Mainstream, 1955).

FBI   Tresca's FBI file obtained under the Freedom of Information Act.

NA   National Archives, Washington, D.C.

Nomad   An unpublished biography by Max Nomad, "Carlo Tresca: Rebel without Uniform," deposited at the Center for Migration Studies, Staten Island, New York.

NYPL   New York Public Library.

Omagio A book of tributes, *Omagio alla memoria imperitura di Carlo Tresca,* among the Tresca Memorial Committee papers at the New York Public Library.

OWI   Office of War Information.

PD   The investigatory file compiled by the New York Police Department after Tresca's murder.

Tam   Tamiment Institute Library at New York University.

TMC   Tresca Memorial Committee papers, Manuscript Division, NYPL.

WKCT   "Who Killed Carlo Tresca?" is a 1945 publication by the Tresca Memorial Committee.

WS   Archives of Labor History and Urban Affairs, Wayne State University, Detroit, Michigan.

Notes

PREFACE

Omagio alla memoria imperitura di Carlo Tresca, a substantial source of information about Tresca's life, was published by the *Il Martello* group in March 1943. TMC.

Arturo Giovannitti on Tresca's anarchism is in WKCT.

Max Eastman's quotes in the *New Leader,* January 16, 1943.

Alexander Herzen from *My Past and Thoughts,* vol. 3 (London, 1968).

The final epitaph was spoken by Tresca's old anarchist friend Aldino Felicani, in his oral history at Columbia University's Oral History Archives.

PROLOGUE

The details of Tresca's murder are contained in the files of the New York Police Department and the New York district attorney's office. Accounts of the murder also appear in a booklet issued by the Tresca Memorial Committee titled "Who Killed Carlo Tresca?" published originally in 1945. This edition is among the papers of the TMC in the Manuscript Division at the NYPL. It has been reprinted, with an introduction by Warren Hope (Harrisburg, Pa., 1983). The *New York Times* is an additional source; reports appear beginning January 12, through January 27, 1943.

The policies of the OWI will be discussed in a later chapter. See, for instance, John P. Diggins, *Mussolini and Fascism: The View from America* (Princeton, N.J., 1972), and James E. Miller, "A Question of Loyalty: American Liberals, Propaganda and the Italian-American Community, 1939–1943," *Maryland Historian* 9 (Spring 1978).

Dr. Umberto Gualtieri is quoted in the *New York Times,* January 12, 1943. John Dos Passos wrote about his lunch with Tresca in *The Theme Is Freedom* (New York, 1956). Reports of the lunch also appeared in the *World Telegram* (Jan. 12) and *PM* (Jan. 13).

The office building at 96 Fifth Avenue also carried the address 2 West Fifteenth Street (which is the address that appears on *Il Martello* letterhead). The painter Esteban Vincente had a studio in the building and described the building to me. Jerre Mangione wrote of visiting Tresca's office, in *An Ethnic at Large* (New York, 1978). Descriptions of the office also appear in WKCT.

Events occurring in the *Martello* office on January 11 are taken from statements made by participants to PD and DA.

On the anarchist movement see, for instance, Paul Avrich, *The Haymarket Tradgedy* (Princeton, N.J., 1984); James Joll, *The Anarchists* (New York, 1964), in which Proudhon's quote is cited; Daniel Guérin, *Anarchism: A History of Libertarian Ideas and Movements* (New York, 1962). See also Rudolph J. Vecoli, ed., "Italian American Radicalism: Old World Origins and New World Developments" (New York, n.d.).

Sidney Solomon discussed his conversation with Tresca with me in New York in October 1978.

Guiseppe Calabi interviews in PD and DA.

Tresca's daughter, Beatrice Rapport, kindly gave me copies of letters written by her father to her and her family.

I interviewed James T. Farrell in New York in September 1979.

CHAPTER 1. MY NATIVE PLACE

The basic sources for Tresca's life are his never-finished autobiography (CT); Max Nomad's biography (Nomad) also unpublished, rather dry and pedantic, but using Tresca's newspapers; the *Omagio* compiled by his comrades in the *Martello* group in 1943 and containing a good deal of information. Also important is Max Eastman's "Troublemaker," a two-part profile published in the *New Yorker*, September 15 and September 22, 1934.

Tresca's four newspapers are central to his life. *Il Proletario*, which he edited under the auspices of the Italian Socialist Federation, 1904–1906; *La Plebe*, the first of his independent papers, 1906–1909; *L'Avvenire*, 1909–1917; and *Il Martello*, 1917–1943. Some microfilm copies are at the Immigration History Research Center in Minneapolis. For the newspapers I have depended heavily on Tresca's FBI files, which contain numerous excerpts made by the Post Office Department which kept close watch on the foreign-language radical press, and on Nomad.

Another important source are the files kept by the Political Police in Rome, cited in chapter 13.

Material on the Tresca family was supplied by Tresca's daughter, Beatrice Tresca Rapport, in interviews in Arlington, Massachusetts, in the fall of 1978, and by Peter Martin, Tresca's son, in interviews in New York in the fall and winter of 1978.

Descriptions of Sulmona approximately contemporaneous with Tresca's life are from Baedeker's *Southern Italy* (New York, 1908); more recent descriptions can be found in Gilbert Highet, *Poets in a Landscape* (New York, 1957); and Ignazio Silone, *The Story of a Humble Christian* (London, 1970).

For political and economic conditions in Italy at the turn of the century see Dennis Mack Smith, *Italy: A Modern History* (Ann Arbor, 1959); on Mussolini see idem, *Mussolini: A Biography* (New York, 1982); Angelica Balabanoff, *My Life as a Rebel* (New York, 1938). CT cites the meeting with Mussolini.

On the padrone system see, for instance, Oscar Handlin, *The Uprooted* (New York, 1951) and CT.

The Rev. Falconi's accusation and the Italian ambassador's letter are in FBI.

CHAPTER 2. FAMILY LIFE

Material on Helga Guerra Tresca from Beatrice Tresca Rapport.

The 1908 rape charge documents are in the Court of Quarter Sessions, February Session, 1908, Commonwealth of Pennsylvania. The brief by J. Joseph Murphy is attached.

The immigration inspector's call on Helga Tresca in FBI.

For Palizzolo, see the *New York Times,* June 9, 1908. Also, Arrigo Petacco, *Joe Petrosino* (New York, 1974). For more on Petrosino see the *New York Times,* March 14, 15, 19, 1908, and Francis A. J. Ianni, *A Family Business: Kinship and Social Control in Organized Crime* (New York, 1972).

Accounts of the 1909 knife attack are in CT and in Max Eastman's *New Yorker* profile.

CHAPTER 3. THE BULL OF LAWRENCE

Tresca's activities in 1910 and his trial for libel are cited in CT and in *L'Avvenire,* August–November 1910.

Errico Malatesta is quoted in Joll, *The Anarchists.*

Of the many studies of the IWW, the most valuable is Melvyn Dubofsky, *We Shall Be All* (New York, 1969). See also Joyce Kornbluh, ed., *Rebel Voices: An IWW Anthology* (Ann Arbor, 1965); Philip S. Foner, *The Industrial Workers of the World, 1905–1917* (New York, 1965); Paul F. Brissenden, *The I.W.W.: A Study of American Syndicalism* (New York, 1919 and 1957).

Reports of the Commission on Industrial Relations on the Lawrence strike (and also of the Paterson strike of 1913) are in the National Archives, Department of Labor, R.G. 174.

Specifically, see Elizabeth Gurley Flynn, *I Speak My Own Piece: Autobiography of the Rebel Girl* (New York, 1955); reprinted in 1973 as *The Rebel Girl.* This is the first and only volume of what was a projected two-volume autobiography. It covers Flynn's life through 1926, which includes her years with Tresca. She is reticent about their personal relationship (although not as reticent as is Tresca, who barely mentions her in his autobiography), but her book is of great value as a personal testament of a lifelong radical, though her views of the IWW years are colored by her later commitment to the Communist party.

See also Mary Heaton Vorse's memoir, *A Footnote to Folly* (New York, 1935). The Vorse papers, documenting her long friendship and correspondence with Flynn, are at the Archives of Labor History and Urban Affairs, Wayne State University, Detroit.

William D. Haywood's *The Autobiography of Big Bill Haywood* (New York, 1929) is also of great interest, although it suffers from being written (even ghostwritten) while Haywood was gravely ill in Moscow.

The events of the Lawrence strike were extensively covered in the *New York Times* for 1912.

The quotations from Tresca and Flynn are from their memoirs.

The Flynn papers are now at Tamiment Institute Library located in the Bobst Library at New York University. *The Maidens of the Rocks* and the underlined copy of *Sonnets from the Portuguese* are among them.

Beatrice Tresca Rapport told me about life in the Tresca household after Lawrence; the details of the divorce suit and custody battle are in FBI.

CHAPTER 4. ELIZABETH GURLEY FLYNN

Flynn's memoir and her papers remain the best sources of her life. There is not yet a full-scale biography, but Rosalyn Fraad Baxandall has recently published a collection of Flynn's writings and letters, *Words on Fire* (New Brunswick, N.J., 1988), with a long introductory essay.

Other sources I have used for Flynn's life are Helen Camp's Ph.D. dissertation, "Gurley: A Biography of Elizabeth Gurley Flynn," Columbia University, 1980; Margaret Gerteis, "Coming of Age with the Industrial Workers of the World: The Early Career of Elizabeth Gurley Flynn," master's thesis, Tufts University, 1975; Joe Doyle, "Make Way for Elizabeth Gurley Flynn," *AIS-Eiri: The Magazine of Irish America*, vols. 2, 3, and 4.

Theodore Dreiser, "An East Side Joan of Arc," *Broadway Magazine*, September 1906.

For Flynn at the free speech fight in Montana, see George Venn, *Montana: The Magazine of Western History*, October 1971.

CHAPTER 5. CARLO AND ELIZABETH

Max Eastman first met Tresca in 1913 and they remained friends. Eastman's memoirs, *Enjoyment of Living* (New York, 1948) and *Love and Revolution* (New York, 1964), are excellent sources for the atmosphere of the prewar Greenwich Village, *Masses* period of radicalism. Also see Daniel Aaron, *Writers on the Left* (New York, 1961) for the involvement of the literati with the radicals. Lillian Symes' quote is from Lillian Symes and Travers Clement, *Rebel America* (Boston, 1972).

For the hotel workers' strike, CT and EFG. Also the *New York Times*, January 14 and 25–28, 1913.

Paterson strikers recalling the strike are quoted from Deborah Shaffer and Stewart Bird's film, *The Wobblies*. Shaffer and Bird interviewed surviving Paterson strike participants; I am grateful to Shaffer for allowing me to see the transcript.

On the Socialist party and the IWW see Dubofsky, *We Shall Be All;* also Milton Cantor, *The Divided Left: American Radicalism, 1900—1975* (New York, 1978); David Shannon, *The Socialist Party of America* (New York, 1955). Stow Persons and Donald Egbert, eds., *Socialism and American Life* (Princeton, 1952) is a valuable overview.

Tresca appears in Mabel Dodge Luhan's *Movers and Shakers*, vol. 3 (New York, 1936). Granville Hicks's biography, *John Reed: The Making of a Revolutionary* (New York, 1936) places Reed and Tresca in the Paterson jail, as does CT. Flynn's letter recalling Dodge was written to Agnes Inglis (1950) and is in the Labadie Archives at the University of Michigan, Ann Arbor. John Reed's piece appeared in the *Masses*, June 1913. Flynn and Haywood are quoted in Joyce L. Kornbluh, ed., *Rebel Voices* (Ann Arbor, 1965).

The Paterson pageant was described in detail in the *Herald Tribune*, June 8, 1913. Also see Linda Nochlin, "The Paterson Strike Pageant of 1913," *Art in America*, May–June 1974.

A copy of the Paterson pageant financial statement is reprinted in Luhan, *Movers and Shakers*.

Flynn's speech was made before the New York Civic Club Forum on January 31, 1914. A manuscript copy is in the Labadie Collection.

Dominic Mignone is quoted in the film *The Wobblies*.

CHAPTER 6. BEFORE THE WAR

Vorse, *Footnote to Folly*, describes in detail the organization of the unemployed demonstrations of the winter of 1913–1914. Also see Emma Goldman, *Living My Life*, vol. 2 (New York, 1970). Ben Gitlow, *I Confess* (New York, 1940), later a Communist party leader, and later still a bitter and not always reliable witness, recalls Flynn at the meetings. CT and FBI also contain material.

The accounts of the Ludlow events from CT and FBI. John D. Rockefeller testimony cited in *New York World*, April 7, 1914.

Flynn's letters to Vorse in Vorse collection, WS.

The confrontation between Tresca and Haywood appears in CT. I can find no specific corroboration for it, but in *Living My Life*, Goldman confirms that Haywood opposed the Caron funeral demonstration and warned Berkman against it; Goldman also confirms Flynn's descriptions of the violent harangues given at the demonstration.

The events of 1915 are in FBI. Flynn's speaking tour of 1915 is in the IWW file, WS.

Tresca's attendance at Goldman's Red Revel cited in Richard Drinnon's biography of Goldman, *Rebel in Paradise* (Chicago, 1961).

FBI files report the Philadelphia incidents and expulsions from Paterson and Bayonne.

For Flynn and Joe Hill, see EGF, and Philip S. Foner, *The Case of Joe Hill* (New York, 1965).

CHAPTER 7. MESABI

For Flynn's speaking tour in 1915, see EGF.

Her description of the Mesabi Range is from a letter to Vorse, September 1939, WS.

For the Mesabi Range strike, see Dubofsky, *We Shall Be All*, and other IWW studies.

George Andreytchin's quotations are from the IWW Chicago trial transcript, July 24, 1918. Copy in IWW files, WS.

Tresca's "eye for an eye, blood for blood" is a phrase he used often, reported in Paterson by Max Eastman and at Mesabi by local newspaper reporters, and incorporated in FBI. The account of his trip to Grand Rapids in CT.

Flynn's letters to Vorse in WS, as are letters from Tresca to Vorse. In *Footnote to Folly* Vorse describes her 1916 trip to the Range.

Flynn's poems to Tresca were first called to my attention by Rosalyn Baxandall, and also by Helen Camp, both of whom gave me copies. I later saw the poems when Flynn's papers were at Communist party headquarters in New York and at the American Institute of Marxist Studies (AIMS) in New York. The AIMS office has since been closed; the CP was a poor guardian of the papers (restricting access and claiming loss). Both holdings are now at Tamiment. The poem quoted here, "Mesaba Thoughts to Carlo," was written in 1939.

The photo mounting that contained Tresca's photograph is at Tam.

James Gilday's statement is among Frank Walsh papers, Manuscript Division of NYPL, a good source for the Mesabi Range strike.

In his authoritative study of the IWW, *We Shall Be All,* Dubofsky argues that there is no evidence of Haywood's indifference to the prisoners and that Flynn, Tresca, and Ettor were jealous of Haywood's growing prominence. He points out that the IWW general executive board made a sufficient five thousand dollars available to the defense campaign, that Haywood's autobiographical account was ghostwritten, and that the accuracy of Flynn's memoirs is questionable. But although federal officials destroyed the IWW files in 1923, enough evidence remains to counter Dubofsky's claim that the quarrel was "entirely personal." The financial report of the strike committee, published on January 22, 1917 (IWW file, WS), shows total expenses for the defense to be $31,469. In *The Nation,* February 17, 1926, Vorse recalls that Flynn had to leave the Range to find money for the defense. Letters from Flynn to sympathetic friends soliciting money for the defense are in the Rose Pastor Stokes papers, Tam, and the John Nicholas Beffel papers, WS. This, combined with references to early disagreements with Haywood in CT, seems enough to infer disagreements on matters of substance.

Flynn's speech at the Virginia Opera House in *Solidarity,* December 16, 1916.

Alfred Jaques's letter in files of Department of Justice, National Archives, Mesabi 182749.

While there is no published evidence that, as Flynn wrote in EGF, Haywood "blasted us publicly," her account, Haywood's, and Tresca's all agree substantively on Haywood's feelings toward Flynn and Tresca.

CHAPTER 8. WAR AND REPRESSION

On government raids and IWW trial, see Dubofsky, *We Shall Be All,* and other IWW studies cited in Chapter 3. Frank Little's lynching is in Dubofsky, EGF, and others. Also see Ralph Chaplin, *Wobbly: The Rough and Tumble Story of a Radical* (Chicago, 1949). See Philip Taft, "The Federal Trials of the IWW," *Labor History,* Winter 1962, for among other things the statement of Sen. Henry Ashurst.

The full version of Arturo Giovannitti's poem "When the Cock Crows: To the Memory of Frank Little, Hanged at Midnight" appeared in *Solidarity,* September 22, 1917, and is reprinted in Kornbluh, *Rebel Voices.*

Tresca's letter to Vorse in Vorse Collection, WS.

Informants' reports on Tresca's activities, and the letter from Ralph Easley, in Department of Justice file 188937-62, February 16, 1918, NA. Also FBI.

The letter from Tresca to Ralph Schiavini, September 25, 1917, in FBI.

On the arrest of Flynn and Tresca, Military Intelligence Files 10110-219 and 10110-308, NA.

For IWW legal strategies see EGF; Dubofsky, *We Shall Be All;* Taft, "Federal Trials of IWW."

A copy of the circulated letter to "Friends and Sympathizers" is in Rose Pastor Stokes's papers, Tam.

Documents cited in the severance case are in Department of Justice, R.G. 188032, NA, including Flynn's letter to Wilson. A copy of her "Sabotage" pamphlet is in the IWW papers, WS.

Haywood's letter to John Reed cited by Robert A. Rosenstone, *Romantic Revolutionary: A Biography of John Reed* (New York, 1981).

For Haywood and Emma Goldman in Moscow, see Emma Goldman papers, NYPL, Box 1. Also Emma Goldman, *My Disillusionment in Russia* and *My Further Disillusionment in Russia* (New York, 1923 and 1924). Also see Theodore Draper, *The Roots of American Communism* (New York, 1957).

CHAPTER 9. ALL OF THEM ANARCHISTS

Alexander Berkman's diary cited in Drinnon, *Rebel In Paradise*. The bibliography for the Red Scare and the Sacco-Vanzetti case is vast; I cite only a fraction. On the Red Scare, Robert K. Murray, *Red Scare* (Minneapolis, 1955); William Preston, Jr., *Aliens and Dissenters* (Cambridge, Mass., 1963); also Julian Jaffe, "The Anti-Radical Crusade in New York, 1914–1924," Ph.D. dissertation, New York University, 1971.

On Sacco and Vanzetti, this initial listing is without regard to the authors' sympathies in the case. Francis Russell, *Tragedy in Dedham: The Story of the Sacco-Vanzetti Case* (New York, 1972); Louis Jouglin and Edward Morgan, *The Legacy of Sacco and Vanzetti* (New York, 1948); Eugene Lyons, *The Life and Death of Sacco and Vanzetti* (New York, 1927); Felix Frankfurter, *The Case of Sacco and Vanzetti* (Boston, 1927); Herbert B. Ehrmann, *The Untried Case: The Sacco-Vanzetti Case and the Morelli Gang* (New York, 1960); Ehrmann, *The Case That Will Not Die: Commonwealth vs. Sacco and Vanzetti* (Boston, 1969); David Felix, *Protest: Sacco-Vanzetti and the Intellectuals* (Bloomington, Ind., 1965).

The controversy about the case has blossomed again recently. Francis Russell, *Sacco and Vanzetti: The Case Resolved* (New York, 1986). Russell, who took Tresca's statement made in the late 1930s as a clear indication of Sacco's guilt, has written this second book which he claims ends all ambiguity. In contrast, see William Young and David E. Kaiser, *Postmortem: New Evidence in the Case of Sacco and Vanzetti* (Amherst, Mass., 1985).

In addition to these volumes, I have consulted the transcripts of reminiscences of Aldino Felicani and Roger Baldwin in the Oral History Archives at Columbia University.

For a brief, interesting discussion of Sacco and Vanzetti's political views, see Eric Foner, "Sacco and Vanzetti," *The Nation*, August 20, 1977. Of particular value is Nunzio Pernicone, "Carlo Tresca and the Sacco-Vanzetti Case," *Journal of American History* 66 (December 1979). With wide and deep scholarship in the Italian-American anarchist movement, Pernicone has closely analyzed the anarchist dimension of the Sacco-Vanzetti case and Tresca's position in the anarchist movement and role in the case. I have relied on his analysis.

Peter Kropotkin's statement is quoted in Joll, *The Anarchists*. See Joll also for a concise history of the anarchist movement. Also George Woodcock, *Anar-*

chism: A History of Libertarian Ideas and Movements (New York, 1962). See also Vecoli, "Italian American Radicalism," particularly Nunzio Pernicone.

On the quarrel between Tresca and the Galleanisti, see Pernicone, "Tresca and the Sacco-Vanzetti Case."

Quotations from Sam Dolgoff and Jack Frager are from interviews during 1979.

For the June 2, 1919, bombings see Murray, *Red Scare*, and Jaffe, "Anti-Radical Crusade." Report of the Washington bombing in files of the War Department 10110-1279, NA, along with a copy of "Plain Words."

For Eugenio Vico Raverini, see *Il Martello*, December 1, 1920. A statement by Tresca on Frederick Blossom and Raverini is in Margaret Sanger papers, Sophia Smith Collection, Smith College. The article by Tresca is in the *New York Call*, June 14, 1920.

On Elia and Salsedo: editorial in the *New York American*, May 5, 1920; the press release from the Workers Defense Union by John Nicholas Beffel, dated January 1921, in Vorse Collection, WS. See also the *New York Call*, June 10 and June 12, 1920, for Salsedo's arrest and death.

Vanzetti's letter to Tresca in FBI.

In response to a query for information about Tresca placed by me in the *New York Times*, I received a note from Mary Hunter and interviewed her in New York in February 1979. She was in her eighties and in poor health, but very lucid. Her memories of Tresca and Flynn, Fred Moore and the Sacco-Vanzetti case were clear and full of detail. Although she knew little about events she did not witness (she said she had little interest in politics), the events of which she spoke are tangentially supported by other sources. So, although Mary Hunter is nowhere cited in the literature on the Sacco-Vanzetti case, there is every reason to accept her statements about her role in it, and also her recollections of Tresca and Flynn over the next few years.

Lola Darroch's letter to Fred Moore and Moore's letter on "Pew" are cited in Felix, *Protest*.

For a full discussion of Tresca's position in the Sacco-Vanzetti case and his knowledge, or lack of it, of Sacco's guilt, see Pernicone, "Tresca and the Sacco-Vanzetti Case."

Tresca's letter to the Boston defense committee in FBI.

A copy of the telegram from Tresca and Giovannitti to Haywood in IWW files, WS, as is Haywood's reply to Baldwin.

The attacks in *Il Proletario*, the reply in the *Martello*, and accusations by the Socialists are cited in Nomad.

Sam Dolgoff and Jack Frager discussed with me Tresca's political position in the 1920s and the intra-anarchist feuds. Of Galleani, Dolgoff said: "I couldn't look at the man. He was like a priest."

William Thompson's interview with Vanzetti cited in Russell, *Tragedy in Dedham*.

Roger Baldwin, Sidney Hook, and James T. Farrell all repeated to me that sometime during the late 1930s Tresca did say that Sacco was guilty. Francis Russell has continued, with increasing certainty but weak evidence, to assert Sacco's guilt. See his *Sacco and Vanzetti: The Case Resolved*. For a challenge to his view, see the exchange of letters, *New York Review of Books*, May 29, 1986; Paul

Avrich, *New Republic,* April 7, 1986; Dorothy Gallagher, *The Nation,* August 2 – 9, 1986.

Emma Goldman's letter, Emma Goldman papers, NYPL.

CHAPTER 10. SICK AT HEART

Flynn's work with the Workers Defense Union can be followed in the Flynn papers at the Wisconsin State Historical Society. See also EGF, and Baxandall, *Words on Fire.*

Vorse's quote from her tribute to Flynn in *The Nation,* February 17, 1926.

Roger Baldwin's statements are from my interview with him. Baxandall, *Words on Fire,* says that Baldwin was one of Flynn's lovers, but gives no dates or details of the affair.

James Cannon, in *The First Ten Years of American Communism* (New York, 1962), recalled his and Vincent St. John's visit to Staten Island.

Mary Hunter supplied information about her meetings with Tresca and Flynn.

The sources for Bina Flynn are interviews with her children Peter Martin and Jane Bobba, conducted during 1979 and 1980. Len Giovannitti and Roma Reiger, the children of Arturo Giovannitti, both recalled visits of Tresca and Flynn, in interviews in spring 1979.

CHAPTER 11. THE UNITED STATES AND ITALY
VERSUS CARLO TRESCA

See Dennis Mack Smith, *Italy* and *Mussolini.* Also Diggins, *Mussolini and Fascism;* F. L. Carsten, *The Rise of Fascism* (Berkeley, Calif., 1969).

Lenin's speech appeared in *Il Martello,* January 29, 1921; Tresca's *Martello* article in April 1919.

For Lenin's directive see Balabanoff, *My Life as a Rebel.*

The Malatesta quote cited in Guérin, *Anarchism.*

W. J. Burns's memo in FBI.

Tresca's letter to a friend was to Federico Arcos; a copy was sent to me by Arcos.

Tresca's speech in Cleveland in FBI; Ambassador Caetani's letter in State Department files and in FBI.

The banquet for Judge Elbert was reported in the *Baltimore Sun,* January 12, 1925. For the case against Tresca, see the American Civil Liberties Union publication "Foreign Dictators of American Rights: The Tresca and Karolyi Cases," 1925. Copy in TMC.

An account of the trial appeared in *Il Martello,* December 22, 1923.

The government's role in gathering evidence and bringing the case to trial can be followed in Department of Justice files (Carlo Tresca) 61-1335.

CHAPTER 12. WOMEN AND CHILDREN

Peter Martin and Jane Bobba have supplied much of the material about their mother and their Aunt Elizabeth in this chapter. An additional source for

Bina Flynn is Susan Jenkins Brown, *Robber Rocks: Letters and Memories of Hart Crane, 1923–1932* (Middletown, Conn., 1969). Brown knew Bina and Romolo Bobba during that period in New York and Connecticut and is good on the atmosphere of the time.

Pete Martin's story "The Germans" appeared in *City Lights*, October 1952. Tresca's letter to Beatrice, a copy given to me by her.

I saw Flynn's journal at Communist party headquarters in New York. At that time, according to an inventory made for the Library of Congress, two filing cabinets of papers were missing, and I was told they had been misplaced. I understand all Flynn's papers have now been found and moved to Tamiment Institute Library, as have the Flynn papers that were at the American Institute of Marxist Studies. Unless otherwise noted, Flynn material in this chapter can now be found in her papers at Tamiment.

On the Passaic strike, see Theodore Draper, *American Communism and Soviet Russia* (New York, 1986); Gitlow, *I Confess;* Vera Weisbord, *A Radical Life* (Bloomington, Ind., 1975); and telephone interviews with Vera Weisbord, April 1979.

Flynn's affair with Albert Weisbord is cited in Baxandall, *Words on Fire.*

Joe Ettor's letter to Flynn in Flynn papers at AIMS (probably now at Tamiment).

Romolo Bobba testified about his life during the IWW Chicago trial, August 6, 1918. Copy of transcript in IWW papers, WS.

The twentieth anniversary dinner for Flynn in her papers, Tam. Also see Gitlow, *I Confess.*

Flynn's illness in EGF. Her letters to Vorse are at WS. Tresca's telegram to Equi, the doctor's reports and dental X ray, Equi's letter to Flynn's friends are all in Flynn papers, Tam.

On Tresca's relationship with Minna Harkavy, Beatrice Tresca Rapport and Bernard Harkavy, a nephew of Minna Harkavy, supplied material (interviews in New York, December 1979). See also Ben Gitlow, *The Whole of Their Lives* (New York, 1948).

For Moissaye Olgin's career see Draper, *American Communism and Soviet Russia* and *Roots of American Communism.* See also Irving Howe, *World of Our Fathers* (New York, 1976).

Irving Ignatin wrote to me about his encounter with Tresca at Harkavy's house; letter dated January 27, 1979.

The telegram signed "Carlo and Louis" in FBI.

Flynn's letter to Vorse, in Vorse collection, WS; her letter to Agnes Inglis is in Labadie Collection, University of Michigan. Flynn wrote to Inglis a number of times in the 1930s. In July 1934 Flynn said she had visited Bina and Romolo and their three children in Miami, Arizona, the previous summer, "a hot, arid district and my sister pines for the EAST."

CHAPTER 13. FASCISTS HOME AND ABROAD

Otto Kahn quote on Mussolini is cited by Diggins, *Mussolini and Fascism.*

The ACLU petitioned for commutation of Tresca's sentence on January 22, 1925; Assistant Attorney General William Donovan replied to Roger Baldwin that a pardon was under consideration. FBI.

The anecdote about the hard-boiled eggs was told me by Lester Coleman, who was Tresca's physician in 1942. (I fail to understand the plumbing.) Tresca described conditions in Atlanta Penitentiary in an article in the *World*, April 14, 1929.

For the clashes between fascists and antifascists in this period see Diggins, *Mussolini and Fascism.*

Tresca to Max Eastman, from Eastman's *New Yorker* profile.

Alberto Cupelli's article on Tresca was published in *Il Mondo*, January 1943, as a memorial piece. Copy in Department of Justice files 146-7-51-1092.

The *World*, March 16, 1926, reports Rome proceedings to deprive Tresca of his Italian citizenship. Additional material in FBI and Tresca's file in Immigration and Naturalization Service.

The letter from Ambassador De Martino cited by Alberto Cupelli in *Il Mondo.*

For the Greco-Carillo case see "Next Please," a pamphlet published by the International Labor Defense, copy in TMC. Also see Diggins, *Mussolini and Fascism;* Robert Morse Lovett, *All Our Years* (New York, 1948); *Omagio alla memoria imperitura di Carlo Tresca. The Lantern,* a Boston magazine, contains excerpts of summation speeches by Hays and Darrow in the January and February 1928 issues.

A very important source for Tresca remains in Rome, in the files of the Ministero dell-Interno, Direzione Generale di Pubblica Sicurezza, Casellario Politico Centrale Busta 5208: Carlo Tresca, at the Archivo Centrale dello Stato, Roma. These reports on Tresca's activities are not in any archive in the United States.

Tresca's letter appealing for funds was sent to me by Federico Arcos.

CHAPTER 14. VITTORIO VIDALI

Vittorio Vidali was known as Enea Sormenti in the United States and as Carlos Contreras in Spain and in Mexico. Later chapters follow Vidali's life after his deportation. In his old age Vidali published a number of volumes of memoirs; one of these, *Diary of the Twentieth Congress of the Communist Party of the Soviet Union* (Westport, Conn., 1984), is available in English. His memoirs present Vidali in heroic mold; his view of his life and of history might easily be called revisionist.

Additional sources for Vidali are Mildred Constantine, *Tina Modotti: A Fragile Life* (New York, 1975); Maria Caronia, *Tina Modotti: Photographs,* with an introduction by Vittorio Vidali and an essay by Caronia (Milan, 1979). Also see Robert D'Attilio, "Glittering Traces of Tina Modotti," *Views,* Summer 1985.

On the antifascist movement in the 1920s see Diggins, *Mussolini and Fascism,* and Draper, *American Communism and Soviet Russia.*

Tresca's New York Police Department file contains material on Vidali's 1926 arrest and deportation.

On Ignazio Silone in Moscow in 1927 see, for example, Robert Conquest, *The Great Terror* (New York, 1968).

Vidali's letter to "Nino" is in the Immigration History Research Center, Minneapolis.

CHAPTER 15. WHEELS WITHIN WHEELS
On the Maranzano killing see, for instance, Alan Block, *East Side West Side: Organizing Crime in New York, 1930–1950* (Cardiff, England, 1980). Versions of this Mafia war are cited in almost every book dealing with the Mafia in the United States. It was a pivotal event for organized crime, resulting in the ascension of Lucky Luciano and the establishment of a coordinating body. See also Dennis Eisenberg, Uri Dan, and Eli Landau, *Meyer Lansky: Mogul of the Mob* (New York, 1979).

Tresca's statements on the blackmail of illegal aliens are part of a biographical article in the *Baltimore Post*, December 7, 1933.

The anecdote about the bootlegger was told by Max Eastman in his *New Yorker* profile and again in the *Herald Tribune*, January 12, 1943.

On the Staten Island demonstrations see Diggins, *Mussolini and Fascism*. A detailed and essential source for Italian-American fascism is Gaetano Salvemini, *Italian Fascist Activities in the United States* (Staten Island, N.Y., 1977), with an important introduction by Philip Cannistraro.

For the Terzani case, see Diggins, *Mussolini and Fascism*. The case is also cited in Max Nomad's biography of Tresca, and in *Omagio* and TMC.

For Cerbini see also the *New York Times*, August 12, 1932; for Cerbini and Caradossi, see Salvemini, *Italian Fascist Activities in the United States*.

CHAPTER 16. CARLO AT FIFTY
An account of the banquet in Tresca's honor is reported in the *Herald Tribune*, May 25, 1931.

The report from the Italian consul general is in the files of the Ministero dell-Interno, in Rome.

Margaret De Silver's sons, Harrison and Burnham De Silver, provided recollections of their mother and Tresca in interviews in New York during the winter and spring of 1979. Beatrice Tresca Rapport, Roger Baldwin, and Peter Colt Josephs also contributed recollections. Max Eastman, who spent the summer of 1934 in Chilmark as a neighbor of Tresca and Margaret De Silver, published his anecdotal profile of Tresca that September.

Edmund Wilson mentions Margaret De Silver in *The Thirties* (New York, 1982). James T. Farrell spoke of the confidences made to his wife.

CHAPTER 17. VIDALI GOES TO SPAIN
Since I have not discussed the Spanish Civil War except insofar as Vidali's role as a Soviet functionary is concerned, and since the literature is so vast and publications continue, as does heated correspondence in various journals, I do not offer a general bibliography, which in any case is readily available. Vidali is cited in Hugh Thomas, *The Spanish Civil War* (New York, 1961); Burnett Bolloten, *The Grand Camouflage: The Communist Conspiracy in the Spanish Civil War* (New York, 1961); and other general histories. Specific citations are below.

For an assessment of the scholarship on the war from a perspective sympathetic to anarchism, see Noam Chomsky, "Objectivity and Liberal Scholarship," in his collection, *American Power and the New Mandarins* (New York, 1967). George Orwell, *Homage to Catalonia* (New York, 1952) is of course the classic personal testament, as well as an indictment of Soviet conduct of the war. The counterargument is best made by E. J. Hobsbawm, "The Spanish Background," in Hobsbawm's collection, *Revolutionaries* (New York, 1975). Hobsbawm is critical of "the irrelevant vendettas of Stalin's secret police" and of the "discouraging" of the revolution. "But the basic point is that [the Communists] fought to win the war and that without victory the revolution was dead anyway," thus criticisms of Soviet policy "alas, remain academic." Chomsky disagrees with even the technical argument of superior Communist military efficiency, writing that Communist policy was bound to fail "because it was predicated on the assumption that the Western democracies would join the antifascist effort if only Spain could be preserved as, in effect, a Western colony. Once the Communist leaders saw the futility of this hope, they abandoned the struggle which was not in their eyes an effort to win the Civil War, but only to serve the interests of Russian foreign policy."

For other anarchist views of the Spanish conflict, see Joll, *The Anarchists,* and Guérin, *Anarchism.* For an unfortunately rare collection of Emma Goldman's writings on the war and the revolution see David Porter, *Vision on Fire* (New Paltz, N.Y., 1983).

Vidali's return to the Soviet Union with Modotti is cited in Constantine, *Tina Modotti;* Caronia, *Tina Modotti: Photographs;* and D'Attilio, "Glittering Traces." D'Attilio interviewed Vidali in Trieste and Rome, primarily about his life in the United States. Shortly before Vidali's death I wrote to him in Trieste asking, among other questions, when he first went to Spain. Sylvia Thompson reported his answer: 1931, although his stay was not a long one at that time.

Walter Duranty, Moscow correspondent for the *New York Times,* was well known for his sympathy with the Soviet government. His reports appeared on May 17 and 18, 1931, and are cited by Anita Brenner, "Class War in Republican Spain," *Modern Monthly,* September 1937.

Emma Goldman's quote is among Goldman papers, NYPL.

Jesus Hernandez, *La grande trahison* (Paris, 1953). See also Julian Gorkin, "Spain: First Test of a People's Democracy," in Jeanne Kirkpatrick, ed., *The Strategy of Deception* (New York, 1963).

Response to the CNT declaration of "proletarian revolution" is cited by Brenner "Class War in Republican Spain." See also Walter Krivitsky, *In Stalin's Secret Service* (New York, 1939); and Hugo Dewar, *Assassins At Large* (London, 1951).

Claud Cockburn, the British *Daily Worker* correspondent in Spain, wrote of his meeting with Vidali in *A Discord of Trumpets* (New York, 1956). Anna Louise Strong's interview with Vidali cited in Bolloten, *Grand Camouflage.*

Copy of Vidali's eightieth birthday speech was brought to me from Vidali by Sylvia Thompson in fall 1983. Also see Thomas, *Spanish Civil War,* for battle of Guadalajara.

Herbert Matthews, in *Half of Spain Died* (New York, 1973), reports Hemingway on Vidali. D'Attilio, in "Glittering Traces," notes that in Norman Fuentes, *Hemingway in Cuba* (Havana, 1984), papers found after Hemingway's death indicate that in the last days of the war Hemingway joined Vidali in shooting some unarmed prisoners suspected of fascist sympathies.

The charges against the POUM made by *Trebala,* an organ of the PSUC (combined Socialist and Communist parties in Catalonia).

On Camillo Berneri, see Emma Goldman papers at NYPL and Tam, and Porter, *Vision on Fire.*

On Andrés Nin and the suppression of the POUM see Orwell, *Homage to Catalonia;* Dewar, *Assassins at Large;* Bolloten, *Grand Camouflage;* Thomas, *Spanish Civil War;* Gorkin, "Spain"; Conquest, *The Great Terror.* Miquel Valdes is cited in Dewar.

Emma Goldman's letter to Roger Baldwin, September 12, 1937, in her papers at the NYPL; her article on the POUM trial in her papers at Tam.

For the left-liberal atmosphere in New York and Ralph Bates's talk, see Alfred Kazin, *Starting Out in the Thirties* (New York, 1980).

Hugo Oehler and Liston Oak are cited by Brenner in "Class War in Republican Spain." See also Harvey Klehr, *The Heyday of American Communism: The Depression Decade* (New York, 1984).

Liston Oak testified before HUAC during the first session of the 80th Congress, in 1947. George Mink is a murky figure in the story of the CPUSA and the GPU. The best source for Mink is Jan Valtin, *Out of the Night* (New York, 1941). Valtin, whose real name was Richard Krebs, worked with Mink in Europe where both were Soviet agents. Mink was apparently born in Russia; he claimed relation to S. Lozovsky, head of the Profintern. He apparently began his career giving industrial information to AMTORG, the Soviet trade agency in the United States. He was instrumental in the formation of the Marine Workers Industrial Union and was arrested in Copenhagen in 1935 as a Soviet spy. Except that his name was brought up during the investigation of Tresca's murder, Mink seems to have vanished in the late 1930s. See David Dallin, *Soviet Espionage* (New Haven, Conn., 1955), and Gitlow, *I Confess.* Gitlow, however, must be read cautiously. Also see Liston Oak in the *New Leader,* March 15, 1947.

Dos Passos, *The Theme Is Freedom,* recounts his conversations with Tresca and experiences in Spain. Also see Aaron, *Writers on the Left.*

Tresca on Mink in *Il Martello,* March 7, 1938.

The letter from Walter Starrett to John Nicholas Beffel, in Beffel papers at Tam.

The Antonini memo is in the ILGWU Archives, Antonini Collection. Tresca's letter to Dubinsky, ILGWU Archives, Dubinsky Collection.

The pamphlet by Pietro Allegra, "The Moral Suicide of Carlo Tresca," is in TMC.

John Dewey's letter to Emma Goldman, February 21, 1939, in Emma Goldman papers at Tam.

For Vidali's and Modotti's last days in Spain and their escape to Paris, see Constantine, *Tina Modotti,* and Caronia, *Tina Modotti: Photographs.* According to Caronia, Vidali arrived in New York a month before Modotti and waited for her there.

In a 1950 interview with Vidali, Seymour Freidin writes that Vidali was on Constantine Oumansky's staff: *This Week* Magazine, New York *Herald Tribune,* February 5, 1950.

CHAPTER 18. HOME AGAIN

Flynn to Agnes Inglis in the Labadie Collection. She added, "The immediate reason that brought me home is that my dear good brother, Tom, died suddenly in January." Tom Flynn's death was a suicide. When I first interviewed Flynn's friends and family members, a number of people told me that Flynn's son, Fred, had died a suicide. This is not so and was no doubt a confusion with Tom Flynn's death.

Flynn's presence at Norman Thomas's birthday is in W. A. Swanberg, *Norman Thomas: The Last Idealist* (New York, 1976).

LaGuardia's offer to Flynn to enter Democratic party politics was related by Jane Bobba. She also told me the story of her father's brief Party membership. Peter Martin recalled Bina's reaction to her sister's decision to join the Party.

Rose Cannon's remark is recorded in Flynn's journal.

A clipping from the *Daily Worker* (n.d.) reports Flynn's Paterson appearance.

Flynn's letters to Vorse, Vorse collection, WS.

Flynn's love affair was related to Helen Camp by Frances Onipede, Kathie Flynn's daughter. The poems are among Flynn's papers at Tam.

CHAPTER 19. TROTSKYISM AND POYNTZISM

On the occasion of Tresca's indictment on federal charges, the *New York Times*, September 11, 1923, referred to the story in the United Mine Workers newspaper of May 1922, citing Tresca's participation in the coal strike.

Tresca's 1928 speech in Philadelphia cited by Warren Hope in WKCT.

John Ballato, owner of Ballato's Restaurant, told me about Tresca's dinners with Trotsky in an interview in New York, May 1979. James T. Farrell recalled Tresca's remarks about Trotsky.

Max Eastman tells the story of Tresca's warning to him in *Love and Revolution*.

For the Dewey commission see Isaac Deutscher, *The Prophet Outcast* (Oxford, 1963); *Not Guilty: Report of the Commission of Inquiry into Charges Made against Leon Trotsky in the Moscow Trials* (New York, 1938); Victor Serge with Natalya Sedova, *The Life and Death of Leon Trotsky* (New York, 1975).

Stalin's speech to the Central Committee cited in Max Eastman, *Love and Revolution.*

A particularly intriguing book on the Trotsky assassination is by Gen. Leandro Sanchez Salazar and Julian Gorkin, *Murder in Mexico* (London, 1950). Salazar was former chief of the secret service of the Mexican police; Trotsky's letter to Mexican officials, written a week after the May 23 attack, is cited here. Gorkin was an ally of Trotsky's in Moscow; in Spain, Gorkin published Trotsky in the POUM organ, *Batalla*, but became estranged from him when Trotsky directed "a violent polemic" against the POUM. See also Serge and Sedova, *Life and Death of Leon Trotsky;* Deutscher, *The Prophet Outcast;* Isaac Don Levine, *The Mind of An Assassin* (New York, 1959); Conquest, *The Great Terror.*

On July 25, 1947, Louis Budenz, a former Communist party official, testified before a New York grand jury on the 1938 disappearance of Juliet Stuart Poyntz. Budenz was also questioned about the Trotsky assassination and proved knowledgeable about the arrangements made for the successful attack. Copy of his testimony is in Tresca's DA file.

A confidential report in the files of Military Intelligence Department,

R.G. 165, Folder 20, NA, issued November 20, 1940, reads, "It is assumed that the fascist organizations maintain some connection with the Nazi and Communist parties in the United States through the pacts set up in Europe." In July 1942 the Examiner of the Mails wrote a memo to the FBI naming Vidali as one of "German and Russian agents" acting in concert. FBI. There are a number of reports on this collaboration during the period of the Nazi-Soviet Pact. Whittaker Chambers, in *Witness* (New York: 1952), reported that he was concerned about such collaboration when he went to see Assistant Secretary of State Adolph Berle in September 1939; Allen Weinstein, in *Perjury* (New York, 1978), quotes from Berle's diary of his meeting with Chambers: "A good deal of the Russian espionage was carried out by Jews; we know now that they are exchanging information with Berlin; and the Jewish units are furious to find they are, in substance, working with the Gestapo." Salvemini, *Italian Fascist Activities in the United States,* writes that when war broke out in Europe in September, 1939, Italian Fascists "made common cause with the German Nazis, the Coughlinite anti-Semitic Catholics, the Communists and their fellow travellers."

Valentin Gonzales, *Life and Death in the U.S.S.R.* (Paris, 1951).

Interview with Vidali by Freidin in *This Week.*

For the early careers of Juliet Poyntz and Ludwig Lore see Draper, *The Roots of American Communism,* and *American Communism and Soviet Russia.* Also Gitlow, *I Confess* and *The Whole of Their Lives;* Irwing Howe and Lewis Coser, *The American Communist Party: A Critical History, 1919–1957* (Boston, 1957); Cannon, *First Ten Years of American Communism.*

Tresca wrote about Poyntz and Epstein in *Modern Monthly,* March 1938. Herbert Solow's article is in the *New Leader,* June 20, 1939, and additional material in Solow papers at Hoover Institution Library, including a manuscript, "The Communist Lady Vanishes." See also the *New York Times,* February 8 and 9, 1938, for reports of Tresca's charges on the Poyntz disappearance and his federal grand jury testimony. Also see Felix Morrow in the *Militant,* January 16, 1943.

For Lore and Poyntz in 1936, see Guenther Reinhardt, *Crime without Punishment* (New York, 1952). This book lacks documentation and is presented as direct experience of the author's work for the FBI. It is impossible to judge its accuracy, though some details are supported by other sources.

Also see Weinstein, *Perjury,* for Chambers' relationship with Lore in this period. *PM,* December 20, 1944, published a biographical article on Poyntz when she was declared legally dead; it describes the state of her apartment when detectives saw it six months after her disappearance.

Diggins, *Mussolini and Fascism,* cites the statement in *L'Unita Operaia.*

Emma Goldman's letter to Tresca in her papers at the NYPL.

For the Robinson-Rubens case: Tresca's article in *Modern Monthly;* Herbert Solow, "Stalin's American Passport Mill," *American Mercury,* July 1939; Krivitsky, *In Stalin's Secret Service;* Chambers, *Witness;* Weinstein, *Perjury; PM,* December 20, 1944; *Militant,* February 14, 1938.

Louis Budenz testified (DA) that he had been told by Clarence Hathaway, editor of the *Daily Worker,* not to mention either the Robinson-Rubens or Poyntz case in the paper; Budenz was then managing editor. When he asked

Hathaway why the paper did not defend itself against Tresca's charges, Hathaway told him that Party secrets might be involved.

See also reports in the *New York Times,* December 10–17 and 28–31, 1937, and January 25, February 6 and 11, 1938.

CHAPTER 20. THE BULL OF LAWRENCE NO MORE

Edmund Wilson, in *The Thirties,* recorded the anecdote of Tresca and Dawn Powell, which occurred at a going away party for John Dos Passos.

Interviews with Anna Walling Hamburger in New York in the fall of 1979, and with James T. Farrell.

Trotsky's telegram to Tresca, dated April 19, 1939, is in a scrapbook in TMC.

All letters to and from Luigi Antonini are in Antonini papers at the ILGWU Archives. Many of Tresca's letters are undated.

The anecdote about August Bellanca was told to me by John Ballato.

The announcement of *Il Martello*'s bankruptcy was reported in the *New York Times,* July 2, 1938.

For Cape Cod in the 1930s, interviews with Harrison De Silver, correspondence with David Chavchavadze; also Wilson, *Thirties;* Kazin, *Starting Out in the Thirties.*

Emma Goldman and Eleanor Fitzgerald's letters are in the Goldman papers at Tam. A copy of Tresca's reply was sent to me by Federico Arcos; another copy is in the Labadie Collection.

The quotations from the *Martello* are cited in Nomad; Flynn's *Daily Worker* article is among her papers.

CHAPTER 21. 1942

A photograph of Tresca, nose wrapped in bandages, at Polyclinic Hospital appeared in the *New York Post,* February 26, 1941. He is quoted: "I don't theenk I die. I must be strong to fight. Mussolini is on his last leg."

Fred Flynn died of a chest tumor, apparently malignant. Flynn's quotes are from her papers, as is the book Tresca gave to Fred. Agnes Inglis wrote Ralph Chaplin, July 10, 1945 (Labadie Collection), about Fred's college years at Ann Arbor, where, at his mother's request, she had made inquiries about him, "as she was all in the dark about him. I found he was an 'A' scholar in engineering for three years and then just stopped going to classes, but did not tell his mother. He spent his time at the Union playing checkers and chess . . . the doctors laid his action in stopping [to] a breakdown. . . . I wrote his mother and said I guessed she would just have to let him go his own way. All there was that could be said was he played checkers and chess."

A record of the Flynn-ACLU proceedings is in Corliss Lamont, ed., *The Trial of Elizabeth Gurley Flynn and the ACLU* (New York, 1968). Margaret De Silver was no longer on the ACLU board at that time but apparently encouraged Flynn's expulsion. Roger Baldwin later deeply regretted the incident.

On the Mazzini Society see Diggins, *Mussolini and Fascism,* and Salvemini, *Italian Fascist Activities in the United States,* particularly the introduction by Philip Cannistraro.

Tina Modotti's death was sudden; she left a dinner party in Mexico City and died in the taxi on her way home apparently of a heart attack. Vidali's enemies charged him with involvement in Modotti's death.

WKCT is a concise source for many 1942 events leading up to the murder.

For Pacciardi, see Thomas, *Spanish Civil War.* Pacciardi's activities in 1942 documented in OSS papers, R.G. 226, Box 127; Foreign Nationalities Bureau of OSS, Entry 86, NA. See also Girolamo Valenti papers in Tam, and Diggins, *Mussolini and Fascism.* The letter from Vidali to *L'Unita del Popolo* and the exchange between Tresca and Pacciardi cited in WKCT. The letter from Pietro Allegra to Francesco Frola in FBI.

For Generoso Pope, State Department papers 800.011811, NA, contain a confidential biographical memo on Domenico Trombetta (one of the few Italian-American fascists imprisoned during the war). Pope and Jack Ingenieros were all associated, and were all known to be profascist. Also see Diggins, *Mussolini and Fascism,* on Pope.

The *Martello* article on Pope (October 28, 1934) denounced him in both English and Italian. Girolomo Valenti, editor of *La Stampa Libera* and a friend of Tresca's, later told investigators that Tresca had named Garofalo to him. Garofalo's name seldom appears in the literature on the Mafia. An exception is Joe Bonanno's autobiography, *A Man of Honor* (New York, 1984), in which Bonanno calls Garofalo "my right-hand man." FBI documents identify Garofalo as an associate of both Bonanno and Pope.

Pope's activities on Mussolini's behalf are carefully detailed by Salvemini and Diggins. *La Parola* (May 1941) cites Pope's editorials in *Il Progresso* for November 17, 1935; Pope's speech at the Central Opera House was May 19, 1935; reproduction of the check given by Pope to the Italian government in Girolomo Valenti papers, Tam. Also see Miller, "A Question of Loyalty"; *Il Mondo,* the organ of the Mazzini Society, June, August, October, November 1940, examined the contents of Pope's newspapers. Salvemini, *Italian Fascist Activities in the United States,* notes that after the New York election of 1933, Pope, Ferdinand Pecora, Edward Corsi, and Charles Poletti controlled the Italian vote in New York. Pope's 1936 conference in Washington and the 1937 Columbus Day celebration cited by Diggins, *Mussolini and Fascism.* A copy of Pope's editorial on Italian anti-Semitism is in the Herbert Lehman papers, Columbia University. A draft of a letter from Franklin Roosevelt to Pope (n.d., but 1940), in the Charles Poletti papers, Columbia University, thanks Pope for his professions of support. *Il Mondo* of November 1940 published the result of its examination of *Il Progresso's* contents.

Harold Ickes recorded visits from Count Carlo Sforza in September 1940 and April 1941. Ickes spoke to Roosevelt about Pope in early April: *The Secret Diary of Harold L. Ickes,* vol. 3 (New York, 1954).

Pope's statement critical of Mussolini reported in *Time,* September 22, 1941. *Il Mondo* then challenged him to make the denunciation in the Italian-language section of *Il Progresso,* which Pope did a few days later.

The letter from Casimir Palmer in papers of Department of State, 740 EW.00119 Control (Italy portion), Diplomatic Branch #865-20211 Mazzini Society, NA; Palmer's letter to the memorial committee in TMC.

For Pope during the war years, see Diggins, *Mussolini and Fascism,* and Miller, "Question of Loyalty." Correspondence between Pope, Governor Lehman, and Charles Poletti in Lehman and Poletti papers.

Philip Cannistraro, who is researching a biography of Pope, told me of this 1934 incident between Antonini and Pope.

Salvemini's letter to Antonini in Antonini papers, ILGWU.

The account of the September 10 dinner, and its aftermath, is cited in a number of sources: PD and DA, FBI. Also in WKCT and "The Tresca Case," a pamphlet by Ezio Taddei, 1943, in TMC.

For war events in Italy see Dennis Mack Smith, *Italy and Mussolini.* Beatrice Tresca Rapport told me that the Tresca family in Italy—Tresca's brother Leilo and Arnaldo and their children—were harassed and interrogated when copies of *Il Martello* appeared in Italy.

Letter from Garibaldi Alliance in Mexico to *L'Unita del Popolo* is in FBI. All letters cited to and from Mexico are included in FBI.

The relationship between the Office of Naval Intelligence and the Mafia is the subject of a later chapter.

The dual banquets of November 14 are discussed by Ezio Taddei in "The Tresca Case," which was first given as a speech by Taddei on February 14, 1943.

Minutes of the meetings of the Foreign Language Division of the Office of War Information in OWI papers, FLD, Entry 86. The OWI was then still known as the Office of Facts and Figures (OFF); the FLD was frequently represented by Alan Cranston.

Meeting of December 6 in FBI.

Purchase of the car on December 23 and 24, in PD and DA.

Antonini recorded his conversation with Tresca about Vidali's presence in New York in the March 1943 issue of *Giustizia* and repeated it insistently for years. If Vidali was in the vicinity, no one claimed an actual encounter with him; the story always comes back to Tresca's reported statement via Antonini.

A report of the late night December 24 telephone call and expedition is in PD.

The Mazzini Society meeting of December 30 is reported in WCKT and in Giuseppe Calabi's statement to police.

In the February 1950 issue of *Giustizia,* Antonini wrote again of Tresca's sighting of Vidali, reinforcing it this time by Parenti's statement.

The New Year's Eve dinner at Giamboni's is noted in PD. A draft of a letter from John Beffel to Muriel Rukeyser, April 10, 1945: "Likely you have heard that Carlo was often given to outspoken comments at restaurant dinner tables on men he regarded as enemies . . . speaking about 'criminal records' and 'official archives'" (Beffel papers, WS).

Vanni Montana's statement about his telephone call to Tresca in PD.

Joseph Genco, retired FBI agent (interviewed in Rockville Center, New York, fall 1980), said that he met Tresca in 1942. He said he considered Tresca "a man of principle," a source of information rather than an informant, as "he never would have sold out. You would never offer him money for information." FBI documents show that Guiseppe Lupis, editor of the

Mazzini organ *Il Mondo,* was also a source of information to the FBI on fascist activities.

PD and DA memos trace Tresca's movements in the days before the murder. The letter of invitation to the meeting of January 11 is in PD.

The dinner of January 9 is in PD and reported in *PM* on January 13, 1943. Tony Ribarich told the PD the automobile incident.

Galante's movements on January 11 in DA and PD.

Max Eastman's quote on Tresca's death is in the *Omagio.*

Accounts of the police findings and autopsy report are in PD and DA. Funeral accounts are in the *New York Times* and the *Daily News,* January 17, 1943; *Time,* January 25, 1943; and DA and PD. The *New York Journal American* for January 18 reported that films were taken at the funeral and screened, in slow motion, by police.

CHAPTER 23. THE MAN WHO KILLED CARLO TRESCA

The material on Carmine Galante is in PD and DA. Parole officer Fred Berson told his story in *After the Big House* (New York, 1952), but changed the names of all participants. He also gave an interview to the *Brooklyn Eagle,* December 29, 1949. Berson was fired from his job in May 1944 and insisted that it was because he knew too much about the case, but it is unclear that he knew anything apart from following Galante to the car.

Galante's criminal record is in PD and DA and was published in the *New York Sun* on January 13, 1943, and the *Daily News* and the *Herald Tribune* on January 14.

Eleazar Lipsky was the assistant district attorney who worked on the case from the first night; I interviewed him in New York in 1979 and 1980. Louis Pagnucco, the assistant district attorney who supervised the investigation under District Attorney Frank Hogan, did not answer my letters requesting an interview or respond to requests relayed to him through others.

The Funicello statement is in DA, dated July 29, 1943. It is nine single-spaced, legal-sized pages long. Jacob Grumet, who was head of the homicide bureau in 1943, said in a telephone interview in the winter of 1979 that although Funicello may well have been telling the truth, the courts would call him a "polluted source."

CHAPTER 24. FOR ALL KNOW

On Mafia penetration of the clothing unions see, for instance, John Hutchinson, *The Imperfect Union: A History of Corruption in American Trade Unions* (New York, 1970); Harry Anslinger, *The Murderers* (New York, 1961); David Dubinsky and A. H. Raskin, *A Life with Labor* (New York, 1977); Daniel Bell, *The End of Ideology* (New York, 1960); Bonanno, *A Man of Honor;* Peter Maas, *The Valachi Papers* (New York, 1968); Block, *East Side West Side;* Burton B. Turkus and Sid Feder, *Murder Inc.* (New York, 1951); Howe, *World of Our Fathers;* Matthew Josephson, *Sidney Hillman: Statesman of American Labor* (New York, 1952).

For Hillman and Orlofsky, see Block, *East Side West Side,* and Turkus and Feder, *Murder Inc.*

Writing in the *New York Post* on December 21 and 23, 1943, labor columnist Victor Riesel denied that Hillman had in any way consorted with Lepke; Riesel accused Thomas E. Dewey, who was then running for the presidency, of planting the story to weaken labor support of FDR.

A letterhead of the American Labor party, Second Assembly District, carrying Frank Citrano's name, is among the Vito Marcantonio papers at the NYPL. For a history of the ALP see Kenneth Waltzer, "The American Labor Party: Third Party Politics in New Deal–Cold War New York, 1936–1954," Ph.D. dissertation, Harvard University, 1977. Also see idem, "The FBI, Vito Marcantonio and the American Labor Party," in Athan Theoharis, ed., *Beyond the Hiss Case* (Philadelphia, 1982).

After the signing of the Nazi-Soviet Nonaggression Pact of 1939, the initial unity between Communists, Socialists, and Social Democrats in the ALP broke down. The Marcantonio papers (NYPL) indicate that after a quarrel with Antonini in 1941, Marcantonio began an investigation of Antonini "to bring to the public and the authorities the truth" about labor racketeering in Local 89. In February 1941, Marcantonio wrote that he was going to give the result of his investigation to the district attorney. In this connection a previously mysterious item in Tresca's FBI file assumes significance: in 1941 when Francesco Cerbini related the story of the 1934 attempt to kidnap Tresca and send him to Italy, Cerbini added that Antonini now needed a similar lesson because of what he had been saying about Marcantonio. The remark is consistent with military intelligence reports about cooperation between Communist and Fascist agents during the period of the Nazi-Soviet pact: Cerbini, a known Fascist agent, was, idly or not, speaking on behalf of Marcantonio, a known Communist sympathizer. No inference should be drawn that Marcantonio had any knowledge of Cerbini or his activities.

All other material in this chapter is drawn from DA, PD, and FBI.

CHAPTER 25. MUSSOLINI TOLD VITO

The partial list of books below are general sources for Vito Genovese and his associates who are discussed in following chapters. Few of these volumes are equipped with a scholarly apparatus, but many are based on investigatory agency sources. Although those that rely on material supplied by mafiosi themselves must be used carefully, in the absence of a public archive of Mafia documents, they are essential reading for students of the subject.

Humbert S. Nelli, *The Business of Crime* (New York, 1976); Dom Frasca, *King of Crime* (New York, 1959); Maas, *Valachi Papers;* Ed Reid, *Mafia* (New York, 1952); Ralph Salerno and John Tompkins, *The Crime Confederation* (New York, 1965); Charles Siragusa, *The Trail of the Poppy* (Englewood Cliffs, N.J., 1966); Michele Pantaleone, *The Mafia and Politics* (New York, 1966); Fred J. Cook, *Mafia!* (New York, 1973); Guiseppe Selvaggi, *The Rise of the Mafia in New York from 1896 through World War II* (New York, 1978); Martin A. Gosch and Richard Hammer, *The Last Testament of Lucky Luciano* (New York, 1981); Fred-eric Sondern, Jr., *Brotherhood of Evil* (New York, 1959); Virgil W. Peterson, *The Mob: 200 Years of Organized Crime in New York* (Ottawa, Ill., 1983); Eisenberg, Dan, and Landau, *Meyer Lansky.*

The Boccia murder is discussed by Reid, *Mafia;* Maas, *Valachi Papers;* Frasca, *King of Crime;* Gosch and Hammer, *Last Testament of Luciano.* Testimony about the murder was given by John F. Shanley of the New York Police Department to the Senate Committee on Organized Crime and Illicit Traffic in Narcotics. Also in statements by Ernest "The Hawk" Rupolo to Louis Pagnucco, March 21, 1946, in DA.

Nino Mirabini interview with Pagnucco, March 26, 1946, in DA.

Luciano discusses Genovese's 1936 trip to Italy in Gosch and Hammer, *Last Testament of Luciano.* Also see Maas, *Valachi Papers.* Luciano, who denies that he himself was involved in narcotics, says he had a falling-out with his "underboss," Genovese, and claims that only Genovese trafficked in drugs; after Genovese's departure from the United States, Luciano heard of his activities through "Lisbon and other places because we had plenty of pipelines in and out of Europe. We heard Vito had gone big into junk." Luciano adds that Italian pilots brought narcotics in and out of Italy even during the North African war and that he was shown a letter from Genovese regarding new routes when the Allied armies took over in North Africa. Luciano's claim that he had nothing to do with narcotics trafficking is untrue; Genovese's involvement is substantiated by the Federal Narcotics Bureau in a later chapter.

The most authoritative account of Genovese's black market activities is given in Reid, *Mafia,* which contains in the chapter "A Man Named Vito and the AMG" the transcript of O. C. Dickey's interview with Brooklyn district attorney George Beldock, September 1, 1945.

Correspondence between the New York Police Department and the Department of State on Genovese's extradition in Department of State, R.G. 59, September 12 and October 2, 1944. NA.

The death of Pete La Tempa in Reid, *Mafia;* Gosch and Hammer, *Last Testament of Luciano;* and Block, *Organizing Crime.* Block cites Judge Liebowitz's courtroom speech. The memorandum by General Clarke is cited by Alan Block and Marcia Block in "Fascism, Organized Crime and Foreign Policy: An Inquiry Based on the Assassination of Carlo Tresca," a paper given at the conference of the American Society of Criminology, San Francisco, 1980.

Ernest Rupolo's interview with Vincent Dermody in DA.

The Genovese affair had consequences for Charles Poletti. Agent O. C. Dickey, in his statement to George Beldock, reported that Poletti, once lieutenant governor of New York and, in Dickey's time, with the Allied Military Government in Rome, obstructed Dickey's efforts to extradite Genovese. Luciano referred to Poletti as a "good friend," in Gosch and Hammer, *Last Testament of Luciano.* Poletti contemplated a lawsuit against the publisher of Reid's *Mafia* in which Dickey's testimony appears, but did not pursue it: Poletti papers, Columbia University.

The Genovese-Tresca story was repeated to me in May 1985 by a man who works for the Teamsters Union as, he says, "a consultant." He asked not to be named. He said he had grown up with Galante, who was his special mentor, and that Galante had told him Genovese was doing a favor for Mussolini and that the contract was given to Galante by Chick Wilson (Frank Citrano).

CHAPTER 26. GHOULISH RED-BAITING

Flynn's article in the *Daily Worker* was dated November 18, 1945. Her poem titled "To C.T., February 22, 1945, En Route to Chicago" is with Flynn papers.

George Kennan's letter from Moscow is cited in Gabriel Kolko, *The Politics of War* (New York, 1968). For Stalin's letter, see *Stalin's Correspondence with Roosevelt and Truman* (New York, 1965). For internal political events in Italy and Allied responses from 1943, see Dennis Mack Smith, *Italy;* Kolko, *Politics of War;* S. J. Woolf, *The Rebirth of Italy* (London, 1972); Frank Rosengarten, *The Italian Anti-Fascist Press, 1919–1945* (Cleveland, 1968); Bradley F. Smith, *The Shadow Warriors: OSS and the Origins of the CIA* (New York, 1983); Richard Harris Smith, *OSS* (Berkeley, Calif., 1972); C. R. S. Harris, *Allied Military Administration of Italy, 1943–1945* (London, 1957); Julius Braunthal, *History of the International: World Socialism, 1943–1968* (Boulder, Colo., 1980); Francis Lowenheim, Harold Langley, and Manfred Jonas, *Roosevelt and Churchill: Their Secret Wartime Correspondence* (New York, 1975).

H. G. Nicholas, ed., *Washington Despatches, 1941–45* (Chicago, 1981) is a collection of reports written primarily by Isaiah Berlin while in the Special Survey Section of the British embassy in Washington; the reports were intended to interpret U.S. political events to Britain. Berlin told me that he met Tresca probably in 1941, before U.S. entry into the war, and that Tresca was concerned with organizing aid for Britain.

Margaret De Silver's letter appeared in the *Militant* on July 26, 1943. She wrote it originally for the *New Leader* but it was refused by them, probably because of its indictment of Roosevelt's Italian policy. TMC.

For the OWI see Diggins, *Mussolini and Fascism;* Miller, "A Question of Loyalty"; John M. Blum, *V Was for Victory* (New York, 1976).

The Special War Policies Unit, War Division of the Department of Justice, monitored the Italian press and issued reports summarizing the response of various newspapers to government policies. For instance, the unit reported that the Mazzini Society organ *Nazioni Unite* on December 17, 1942, criticized the effort to unite former fascists with antifascists, while *L'Unita del Popolo* (December 16, 1942) praised the "fervent" antifascist activities by all political denominations in the Chicago branch of the IAVC. NA.

Joseph R. Starobin in *American Communism in Crisis, 1943–1957* (Los Angeles, 1975) describes the International Workers Order as "an important [Party] adjunct, serving as a reservoir of . . . Party funds [which] served to enlarge the Party's contact with trade unions and Democratic Party politics."

The controversy about Tresca was played out in the New York newspapers, beginning with the *New York Post* on January 18, 1943. In addition to the major dailies, the issue was reported in the *New Leader,* January 23; the *Militant,* January 30; *Nazione Unite,* January 28; *The Call,* January 29.

The correspondence between Antonini and Bellanca is in the OWI Records of the Director, R.G. 28, Entry 221, Box 1070, NA. Additional correspondence is in Antonini file at ILGWU and August Bellanca papers, Amalgamated Clothing Workers of America Collection, Cornell University.

Requests for an interview with Sen. Alan Cranston received no reply.

For the further shattering of the Italian organizations, see Diggins, *Mussolini and Fascism*. The Department of Justice Special War Policies Unit and OWI files, R.G. 208, document the disarray. See also Gaetano Salvamini, "Italian Fascist Activities in the U.S.," pamphlet published by the American Council on Public Affairs, Washington, D.C., 1940.

For the Communist response to the controversy, see the *Daily Worker*, January 20 and 23; the *Worker*, January 24 and 31, 1943.

Letters between Mexico and the United States and William Stokes's telegram to *Time* are in FBI. The incident was also reported in the *New York Times*, April 4; the *New Leader*, April 17, reported Gorkin's accusation of Vidali.

Alexander Orlov quote cited by Dallin, *Soviet Espionage*.

CHAPTER 27. TWO THOUSAND MILES AWAY

The letter from Antonini to Norman Thomas is in TMC (n.d.).

The FBI's interview with Pagnucco and Lipsky, January 18, 1944, is in FBI. Unless specifically noted otherwise, all references in this chapter to the FBI and the district attorney's office are from their respective files.

All the correspondence between Mexico and the United States was intercepted by U.S. Postal Censorship and included in Tresca's FBI file. These letters are almost always paraphrased by the agency except for occasional material in quotation marks.

On the ALP, see Michael Waltzer, "American Labor Party"; also Alan Schaffer, *Vito Marcantonio: Radical in Congress* (Syracuse, 1966); Josephson, *Sidney Hillman;* Kenneth Waltzer, "FBI, Marcantonio and the American Labor Party."

For the Marine Workers Industrial Union see Valtin, *Out of the Night*. Norman Thomas wrote to the FBI on August 14, 1950, calling attention to a report by Victor Reisel that Mink was in the San Francisco area. FBI.

For Liston Oak testimony see notes in chapter 17. For Mink, also see Harvey Klehr, *The Heyday of American Communism: The Depression Decade* (New York, 1984). For Ernest Ramsey see Jack B. Tenney, *Red Fascism* (Los Angeles, 1947).

Military Intelligence Department (MID) memo on the NMU dated November 20, 1940, R.G. 165, Folder 20, NA. Blackie Myers's speech of December 9, 1940, cited in Eugene Lyons, *Red Decade* (New York, 1941). See also Klehr, *Heyday of American Communism*.

"Memorandum on the Assassination of Carlo Tresca and the Italian Situation" (n.d. but written in the week following the assassination) in the Records of the Director, OWI, R.G. 208, NA.

"Political Aspects of the Tresca Murder" in Records of the OSS, R.G. 208, NA, dated January 19, 1943.

The denunciation of Iganzio Silone by the Communists is cited in "secret" OSS report, "The Communists and the Italian Crisis," R.G. 226, NA.

Margaret De Silver's visit to Washington and her letter to Silone in FBI. Also see Gustav Regler, *The Owl of Minerva* (London, 1959). Regler writes of seeing a caricature of himself in a Mexican Communist newspaper: a snake dotted with swastikas writhing in the "tree of treachery" that grows from the skull of Trotsky.

CHAPTER 28. THE PROJECT

At least twice during his lifetime Lucky Luciano told a journalist that he knew something about the Tresca murder. The first time was in the early 1950s when Luciano told Michael Stern that, while still in prison, he had offered the names of Tresca's killers to Governor Dewey in exchange for a pardon but Dewey had refused to make a deal. Stern published the interview in *No Innocence Abroad* (New York, 1953) and gave the information to the Tresca Memorial Committee, which read his statement at a memorial meeting in 1954. Again in the early 1960s, Luciano told his biographers (Gosch and Hammer, *Last Testament of Luciano*) that Vito Genovese had been instrumental in the Tresca murder. Since Luciano was in prison when the Tresca murder occurred, it was possible that he was only boasting to show he still had inside knowledge. But a close look at this period of Luciano's career shows him actively engaged with his associates.

The narrative of this chapter is construed in part from many secondary sources. For a partial listing see those in chapter 25. In addition see Guiseppe Selvaggi, *The Rise of the Mafia in New York* (New York, 1978); Estes Kefauver, *Crime in America* (New York, 1968); R. Harris Smith, *OSS;* Norman Lewis, *The Honored Society* (New York, 1964); Richard N. Smith, *Thomas E. Dewey and His Times* (New York, 1982); Kermit Roosevelt, *The Overseas Targets: War Report of the OSS*, vol. 2 (New York, 1976); Ianni, *A Family Business.*

Two books are especially useful: Rodney Campbell, *The Luciano Project* (New York, 1977); and Pantaleone, *Mafia and Politics.* Campbell's book is based on the files of the Herlands Commission, created by Governor Dewey in 1954 to vindicate himself of charges of accepting a large sum of money from Luciano in return for the pardon. The commission investigated the wartime collaboration between the Office of Naval Intelligence and the Mafia. The final report was kept among Dewey's papers and not released until after his death in 1971.

Michele Pantaleone, a Sicilian, born in Villalba (also the native town of Don Calogero Vizzini, until his death leader of the Sicilian Mafia), served as a Socialist deputy in Palermo. In the introduction to the book Carlo Levi writes that Pantaleone "has been conditioned by and concerned with, this fundamental problem of the Mafia."

George H. White testified about his meeting with Del Grazio at the Kefauver committee Hearings on Organized Crime in 1950–1951, part 7.

Gurfein's meeting with Lanza is cited in Richard N. Smith's *Thomas E. Dewey.*

The list of Luciano's visitors at Great Meadow cited by Campbell, *Luciano Project.*

Destruction of the ONI-Mafia project files in Campbell: testimony by Commander MacDowell to Herlands Commission.

Wiretaps on Lanza's phone in 1942 were placed by District Attorney Hogan and revealed discussions of ONI-Mafia business. In December 1942, Harry Bridges of the West Coast ILWU was threatening an East Coast strike. Comdr. Charles Haffenden of the ONI consulted with Luciano's lawyer, Moses Polakoff (Campbell, *Luciano Project*). Meyer Lansky (Eisenberg, Dan, and Landau, *Meyer Lansky*) said that he and Luciano helped Haffenden stop the waterfront strike and get information to the ONI on the terrain of Sicily; the navy, in return, gave the Mafia a free hand on the docks.

Richard Harris Smith, in *OSS*, writes that OSS responsibility for Italian espionage was "preempted by the Office of Naval Intelligence." Pantaleone, in *Mafia and Politics*, writes that if Allied troops had not been assured of cooperation for a Sicilian landing, they would have run less risk by landing in Tuscany or Sardinia. Also see Lewis, *Honored Society*, and Ianni, *Family Business*.

According to Eisenberg, Dan, and Landau, in *Meyer Lansky*, and Campbell, in *Luciano Project*, Lt. Joachim Titolo was involved in the ONI-Mafia project in New York. Campbell reports Titolo's testimony before Herlands. Titolo received the Legion of Merit for his wartime work. Coincidentally, after the war Titolo worked for the New York district attorney's office for a time and was involved with the Tresca investigation.

Pantaleone, in *Mafia and Politics,* writes, "From 1943 to 1946 the entire Sicilian Mafia dedicated itself to this black market traffic which made large fortunes for its chiefs."

Polakoff's 1943 motion for reduction of Luciano's sentence cited in Campbell, *Luciano Project,* and Richard N. Smith, *Dewey.*

Journalist Michael Stern reported to the Tresca Memorial Committee that it was Luciano who brought up Tresca's name in their interview. He told Stern only that the killers were professionals, that the order had come from Italy, and that three men were involved. Dewey denied through his lawyer that Luciano ever offered up the names of Tresca's killers. TMC.

Comdr. Charles Haffenden's letter in support of Luciano's clemency plea and Murray Gurfein's affidavit both cited in Campbell, *Luciano Project*. Dewey's statement on the commutation cited in Richard N. Smith, *Dewey;* Gosch and Hammer, *Last Testament of Luciano;* and Campbell, *Luciano Project*.

Pagnucco testified about his visit to Luciano before Herlands, cited in Campbell, *Luciano Project*.

Gen. William Donovan's statement about Luciano cited in Stern, *No Innocence Abroad*.

Rear Admiral Espe cited in Campbell, *Luciano Project*.

Material on Luciano's narcotics career can be found in Anslinger, *The Murderers*. Anslinger was head of the Narcotics Bureau. Also see Eisenberg, Dan, and Landau, *Meyer Lansky*. Estes Kefauver, in *Crime in America,* discusses drug smuggling. Joe Valachi connected Genovese with a Corsican drug smuggler in Marseilles. Guiseppe Pici and Nicolo Gentile cited by Pantaleone, *Mafia and Politics,* and Anslinger, *The Murderers*. John Caputo cited in Reid, *Mafia*.

Agent Follmer's testimony cited by Kefauver, *Crime in America*.

Rear Adm. William Pye cited in Campbell, *Luciano Project*.

The Cuban meeting of Luciano and his friends is cited by Anslinger, *The Murderers,* and Eisenberg, Dan, and Landau, *Meyer Lansky,* among other citations.

Charles Siragusa, chief of the U.S. Narcotics Bureau in Rome, investigated Luciano's diversion of heroin supplies. One of Luciano's associates, Carlo Miglidori, head of the pharmaceutical company, pled guilty; cited in Anslinger, *The Murderers.* Also see Salerno and Tomkins, *Crime Confederation,* for a discussion of wartime drug trafficking.

The suggestion that Luciano provided the ONI with a ready-made espionage apparatus of Mafia drug traffickers appears in a throwaway sentence in Selvaggi, *Rise of the Mafia in New York.* Selvaggi's undocumented book is based on interviews with criminals deported from the United States to Italy. I attempted to get in touch with Selvaggi in Rome, and left messages with his agent in New York, but was unable to reach him. Although Selvaggi builds no case for his assertion, I found that it fit too many of the facts to be disregarded. Chapter 29 shows involvement in narcotics trafficking by Garofalo, Galante, Luciano, and Genovese. We also now know that our intelligence agencies have no scruples about alliances with members of organized crime, most recently with drug smugglers in Central America in connection with U.S. policy in that region. See Leslie Cockburn, *Out of Control* (New York, 1987).

Pietro Russo, professor of history at the University of Florence, discussed the Italian-American antifascist press at a conference at Columbia University, October 13, 1983, sponsored by the Center for Migration Studies; he characterized the anarchist press as a point of reference for Italians under Fascism.

CHAPTER 29. ADDENDUM

Interview with Roger Baldwin. His letter to Dos Passos, June 20, 1945, is in Beffel papers at WS.

District Attorney Hogan's letter to Governor Dewey cited in William Keating, *The Man Who Knew Too Much* (New York, 1956). Keating's book is an account of his experiences in the New York district attorney's office.

The CBS television script is in TMC.

Hannah Green, a friend of Margaret De Silver and of the novelist Dawn Powell, wrote to me about Peter Martin and Margaret De Silver, in addition to material supplied by Peter Martin.

For Flynn's numerous affairs see Baxandall, *Words on Fire.*

Flynn's response to the Duclos letter is cited in Isserman, *Which Side Were You On?* and Bella V. Dodd, *School of Darkness* (New York, 1954).

Flynn's letter to Kathie cited by Helen Camp in "Gurley," as is her illness in Moscow.

Richard Harris Smith, in *OSS,* writes that the OSS used former Spanish Civil War veterans, including Americans from the Lincoln Battalion, to work with the Italian resistance; Bradley F. Smith, *Shadow Warriors,* also discusses British and U.S. shortages of links with the Italian resistance and writes that the British Special Operation Executive used their Moscow contacts to parachute NKVD operatives into Italy. In his interview with Vidali in 1950,

Seymour Freidin said that Vidali was working with the Italian resistance in northern Italy in 1943. Freidin also reported that Vidali was on the staff of the Soviet ambassador, Constantine Oumansky, in Mexico, "the NKVD boss for North and South America." When I spoke to Freidin on the telephone (August 1987), he could no longer remember the source of his information but suspected that he was told about Vidali by government sources in Washington.

For Vidali in Moscow in 1956, see Vidali, *Diary of the Twentieth Congress of the Soviet Union*. Yelena Stasova's warning to Vidali is cited in Caronia, *Tina Modotti*.

Sylvia Thompson, widow of American Communist party leader Robert Thompson, knew Vidali well and saw him in Trieste shortly before his death. She brought me his answers to some questions I had written him and gave me a copy of his eightieth birthday speech.

Except as noted, material on Garofalo is from PD and DA.

Garofalo's arrest with Galante and Di Palermo in October 1956 cited by Sondern, *Brotherhood of Evil*. Martin F. Pera, Narcotics Bureau agent, testified to the 1957 meeting in Palermo before the Congressional Select Committee on Improper Activities in the Labor and Management Field (part 32). Garofalo's arrest in 1965 was reported in the *New York Times*, August 3–5, 1965. Of the ten men arrested, seven had lived in the United States. The FBI, which conducted an investigation into Facconte and Garofalo in 1942, released the report to me under the Freedom of Information Act. However, it is so heavily deleted that nothing can be gleaned from it. Appeals to the Department of Justice for the full report were unavailing.

Generoso Pope's obituary appeared in the *New York Times*, April 29, 1950. Fortune Pope's relationship with Joe Bonanno is cited by Bonanno in his autobiography, *A Man of Honor*.

DiFalco's role in protesting the publication of Valachi's memoir is cited by Maas, *Valachi Papers*. DiFalco's indictment for corruption and his death reported in the *New York Times*, March 8, 1979.

Luciano's pending arrest for drug trafficking in Italy reported in the *New York Times*, January 27, 1962.

On Genovese, John Shanley, N.Y.C. Intelligence Unit officer, testified before the Senate Investigating Committee on Organized Crime and Illicit Traffic in Narcotics, 1963. See also Frasca, *King of Crime*, and Maas, *Valachi Papers*.

Martin F. Pera's testimony cited above.

John Cusak's testimony reported in the *New York Times*, January 10, 1958. Details of Galante's 1960 and 1962 trials reported in the *New York Times*, May 18, 1960; June 5, 1962; July 10, 1962; July 26, 1962. On Galante in prison see Vincent Teresa, *My Life in the Mafia* (New York, 1973).

In August 1979, after Galante had been murdered, I interviewed Lt. Remo Franceschini (head of the Organized Crime Intelligence Section of the New York Police Department) who said that Luciano, Genovese, and Galante had set up the Sicily heroin trade. Of Galante he said: "He was a vicious guy. A cold, cold fish. Very perceptive. Pure steel. He paid his dues. You don't get many people who spent as much time in jail as Galante did and still retain and build power. We knew he had connections with Santos Trafficante and Carlos Marcello; these people have sat down and talked."

Roy Cohn quoted in the *New York Times*, March 4, 1978. The bribing of Galante's parole officer reported in the *New York Post*, June 9, 1978.

For reports on Galante's murder and funeral, see *New York Times*, July 13, 1979; the *Daily News*, July 13, 1979. Especially see Michael Daly, "Death of a Godfather," *Rolling Stone*, August 23, 1979.

Furio Morroni, an Italian journalist who worked in New York for several years, became interested in the Tresca murder. He conducted interviews with Donini and with Vidali and generously discussed them with me.

Taddei's statement to police is in PD.

Gaetano Salvemini's experiences on his return to Italy are cited in Alfred Kazin, *New York Jew* (New York, 1978).

Index